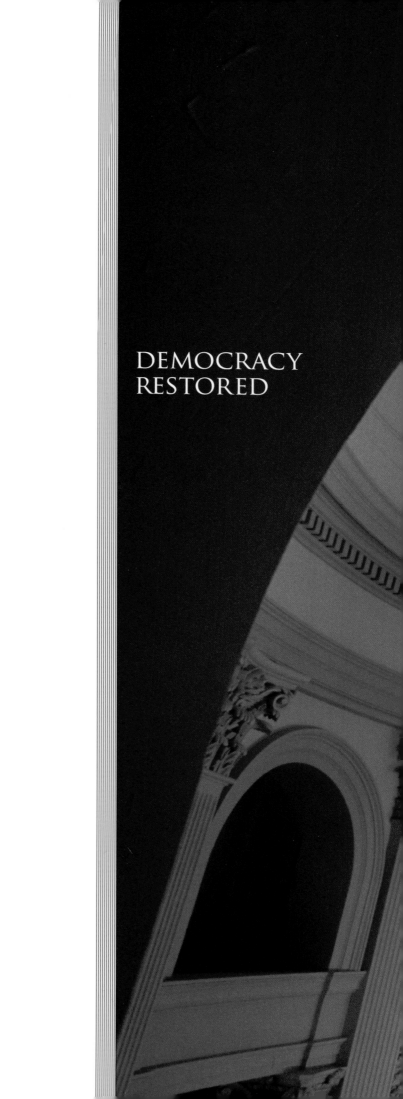

DEMOCRACY
RESTORED

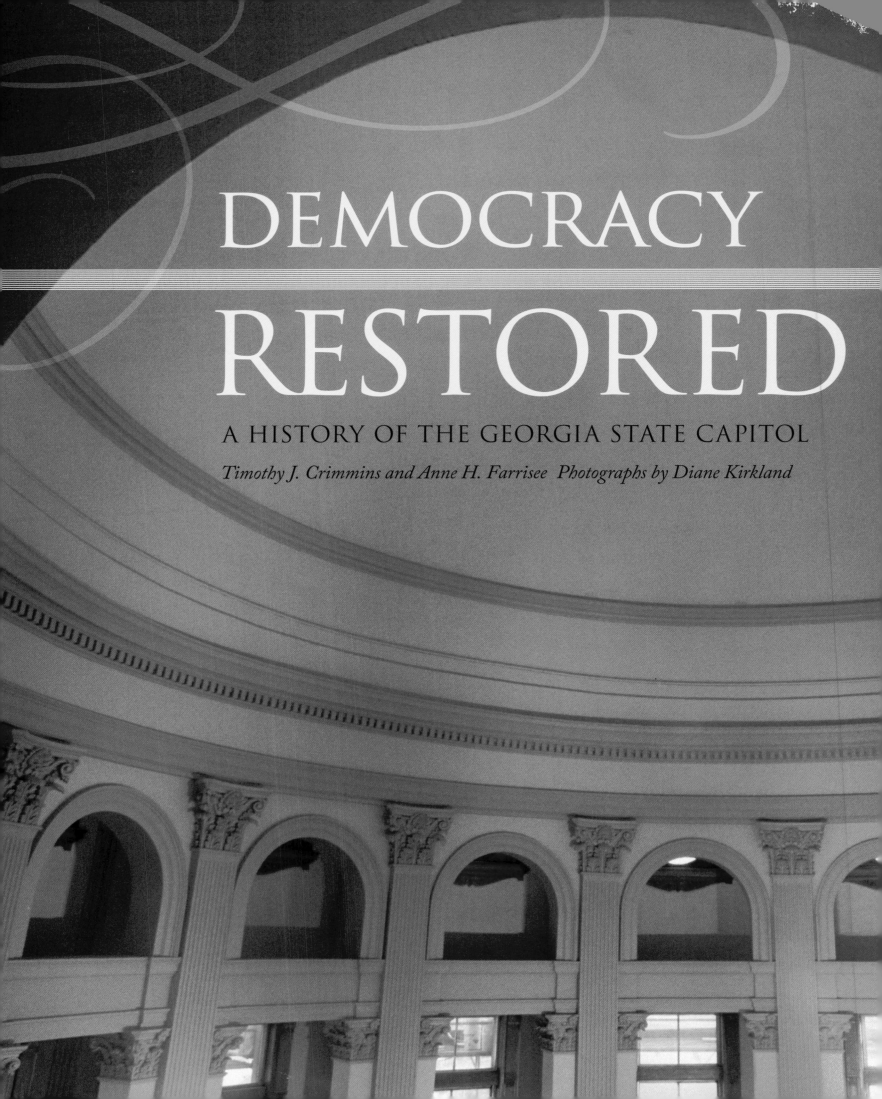

DEMOCRACY
RESTORED

A HISTORY OF THE GEORGIA STATE CAPITOL

Timothy J. Crimmins and Anne H. Farrisee   Photographs by Diane Kirkland

Published in
association with the
Georgia Humanities Council

The University of Georgia Press
Athens and London

FRONT ENDSHEET: *West façade elevation*, 1883, Edbrooke and Burnham (Courtesy of the Georgia Archives)

BACK ENDSHEET: *West façade elevation*, 1994, and dome cross section, 1996, Lord, Aeck & Sargent Architecture (Courtesy of Lord, Aeck & Sargent Architecture)

© 2007 by the University of Georgia Press

Athens, Georgia 30602

Designed by Mindy Basinger Hill

Set in 11/16 pt Adobe Caslon

Printed and bound by Four Colour Imports

The paper in this book meets the guidelines for permanence and durability of the Committee on Production Guidelines for Book Longevity of the Council on Library Resources.

Printed in China

11 10 09 08 07 C 5 4 3 2 1

Library of Congress Cataloging-in-Publication Data

Crimmins, Timothy.

Democracy restored : a history of the Georgia State Capitol / Timothy J. Crimmins and Anne H. Farrisee ; photographs by Diane Kirkland.

Published in association with the Georgia Humanities Council.

     p. cm.

Includes bibliographical references and index.

ISBN-13: 978-0-8203-2911-6 (hardcover : alk. paper)

ISBN-10: 0-8203-2911-8 (hardcover : alk. paper)

1. Georgia State Capitol (Atlanta, Ga.)—History. 2. Georgia State Capitol (Atlanta, Ga.)—Pictorial works. 3. Atlanta (Ga.)—Buildings, structures, etc. 4. Political culture—Georgia—History. 5. Georgia—Politics and government. I. Farrisee, Anne H., 1961– II. Georgia Humanities Council. III. Title.

F294.A88G463 2007

975.8'231—dc22   2006023754

British Library Cataloging-in-Publication Data available

CONTENTS

PREFACE

Capitol histories, as a rule, focus on the architectural qualities of monumental governmental edifices. In the United States, fifty-one working capitols provide space where elected state (and in one case, national) representatives gather to pass laws and approve budgets. In many states, earlier capitols, such as Georgia's old statehouse in Milledgeville, have been retired and put to new use. The architectural form of each of these statehouses was chosen consciously to symbolize the higher purposes of democratic governance. Most employ a blend of Greek and Roman architectural elements, selected because of their associations with what is popularly acclaimed as an idyllic age of early democracy. Consequently, statehouse historians like to call their subjects "Temples of Democracy," and the histories they produce are typically large, handsome volumes, heavily illustrated with lavish photographs that find resonant symbolism in the statehouse architecture.[1]

Besides serving as cultural icons, capitols are places of history, where legislative debates raged, governors proclaimed, and courts ruled. As a whole, these events recount the complex and varied tale of a state's past. Many capitol histories tend to the celebratory, rarely revealing the more insalubrious stories of the past. In some cases, a seminal historical event or events can freeze the past of a capitol in a particular time, where it remains, functioning as a history lesson rather than as a working statehouse. Some statehouses are literally capitol museums, where past events are recounted by uniformed guides or reenacted by costumed actors for visitors who seek a slice of history.

The former State House of Pennsylvania in Philadelphia is such a place. Its brief service as a meeting place for our national government, where the Declaration of Independence and the U.S. Constitution were signed, is now enshrined in our national memory by its current identity as Independence Hall. However, this was not always the case. Almost demolished in 1816 and then extensively remodeled into office space, the building went unlauded until 1824, when the Marquis de Lafayette, one of the last living legends from the

American Revolution, visited Philadelphia. During a public ceremony in the meeting hall, Lafayette spoke movingly of the "sacred walls" wherein "was boldly declared the independence of these United States." His sentiments took hold in the city and, ultimately, the nation. Henceforth, the old State House was known as Independence Hall, its cracked, unusable bell was dubbed the Liberty Bell, and both were elevated to icon status. Thus the building and an episode in its past were linked and implanted together in American historical memory.[2]

This account of the Georgia Capitol is also a conscious effort in historical memory making. From the laying of the Capitol cornerstone on September 2, 1885, to the legislative procession into the newly restored legislative chambers on January 10, 2000, successive generations of Georgians have created a history distinctive to our state. Citizens and their elected representatives have delivered orations, erected memorials, marched in demonstrations, and staged pageants that have intentionally and unintentionally imbued the Capitol with particular significances. It is our intention to give voice to the building by telling some of these stories while giving an account of the Georgia State Capitol itself. This is the story of a statehouse that has suffered neglect for much of its history, but which has undergone an extraordinary renovation in the last decade. With its magnificent restoration, however, the Georgia Capitol is not encased in amber. It remains a working center of state government, and its history continues. This volume traces the first 120 years of the Capitol in narrative and pictorial forms. The pictures—both historic and contemporary—reveal the power of the Capitol's architecture, the changing symbolism of its monuments and memorials, and the beauty of its restoration.

The work of this volume included the efforts of numerous individuals involved at various stages of the Capitol's restoration effort. The documentation of the Capitol history began in 1994 with research undertaken by the Commission on the Preservation of the Georgia Capitol. Research has been supported with grants from the National Park Service's Historic American Building Survey and the Georgia Building Authority. The authority's executive director, Luther Lewis, was especially instrumental in advancing the project.

We owe many thanks to Richard Funderburke, whose voluntary research unearthed many historical details from the Capitol's past. For the better part of two years, Richard combed archives, scoured newspapers, and scanned arcane tomes to ferret out facts for our Capitol history. He also contributed his own research into the struggle for women's suffrage and served as a sounding board as we developed our organizing themes.

Equally important to our endeavor has been Diane Kirkland, who produced the contemporary photographs that grace this book. Diane also contributed many of the prerestoration photographs that document the previous treatments of the legislative chambers and corridors. Diane did much of her work when she was senior photographer for the Georgia Department of Economic

Development. We are deeply indebted to the department for this contribution to our history.

We thank Senator George Hooks, who not only championed funding for the Capitol restoration but also garnered legislative support for the publication of this book. To Jamil Zainaldin, president of the Georgia Humanities Council, we are indebted for the support of his organization in conceiving this project; in building collaborations with the Georgia Department of Economic Development and the *Atlanta Journal Constitution*; and in carrying out the work of dissemination after its publication.

Susan Turner, Scott Thompson, and other members of the architectural firm of Lord, Aeck & Sargent (LAS) helped us to understand the original design and construction of the Capitol as well as the remaining physical clues that reveal pieces of its past. Many of the line drawings of the Capitol included in this volume were produced by LAS.

Numerous others aided us along the way. In the Office of the Secretary of State, Dorothy Olson, Travis Hutchins, and Timothy Frilingos opened their files, both electronic and paper, to us. Graduate research assistants Jennifer Evans, Gisela Collazo, and especially Laura Drummond, who also assisted with getting photographic permissions, spent many hours sifting through documentary sources. At the Georgia Archives, Gail DeLoach shepherded us through photographic research. The library and archives staff members at the Atlanta History Center and the University Library of Georgia State University provided patient guidance to both of us and to our assistants.

At the University of Georgia Press, editor-in-chief Nancy Grayson has been an enthusiastic supporter of this project and a sage counselor guiding us through the necessary manuscript revisions. We are grateful to assistant managing editor Jon Davies for his careful reading of our text.

Finally, we each have been supported by people of great patience and understanding. For this, Crimmins is grateful to Jill Auerbach, and Farrisee thanks her husband Bill and two children, Colleen and Declan.

Having spent a dozen years peeling away the layers of the Capitol's past, we are pleased to be able to share with a larger audience some of what we have learned. Former speaker of the House Tom Murphy said that if the Capitol walls had ears and a mouth, they could impart many an interesting tale. This volume attempts to tell some of those stories.

A DEDICATED CAPITOL

1

At midmorning, on July 3, 1889, the members of the Georgia House and Senate awaited word from Governor John B. Gordon. They were assembled in the legislative chambers that had served them for the past twenty years, the Opera House Capitol located on Marietta Street in the heart of downtown Atlanta. At 10:00 a.m. the official notice came: the new State Capitol, located on Washington Street six blocks to the southeast, was ready for their occupancy. To honor the occasion, the House and the Senate passed joint resolutions to convene as a single body and parade from their old quarters to the new. Three and a half years earlier, the members of the General Assembly had marched along the same route to witness and memorialize the laying of the cornerstone as the walls of the new Capitol were just rising from the ground. Now they assembled to journey to the completed structure where the governor and the state government offices had recently relocated. The legislative processions were designed to bring public attention and add symbolic meanings to the majestic building that would henceforth serve as the center of Georgia government.

In front of the old Capitol, the legislators formed a line that proceeded two by two, heading east on Marietta Street. Senate President Fleming duBignon led the senators, followed by Speaker Pro Tempore Marvin B. Calvin and the members of the House of Representatives. The line of over two hundred marchers, described as a "kind of go-as-you-please" affair by a reporter from the *Macon Telegraph*, eventually stretched nearly two city blocks as the assembly moved along the streets of Marietta, Broad, and Hunter (now Martin Luther King Jr. Drive).

The parade was a high art in nineteenth-century America. Torchlight political parades had become a staple in American cities early in the century. Almost thirty years earlier, military marches in cities had helped to recruit soldiers to fight in the Civil War. Since then, periodic memorial parades had commemorated those who had fallen in battle. When civic organizations such as the Masonic Order convened in towns and cities, they often marked the occasions with Main Street marches, some of which were organized behind marching bands, while others tended toward a less-structured movement similar to that of the Georgia General Assembly that morning. Regardless of the participants' marching form, ceremonial parades were intended to add significance to the occasions they marked. A reporter from the *Atlanta Constitution* captured the symbolic purpose of the legislators' pageant when he noted: the "body walked deliberately and quietly, unattended by any flourish of trumpets. It was democratic simplicity personified in the representatives of the people."[1]

The destination of the march was a place of assembly meant to symbolize in stone the democratic ideals of American representative government. By the time Georgians voted to make Atlanta the permanent capital of the state in 1877, state capitols had evolved into a recognizable style and form of American architecture that mimicked elements of ancient Greek and Roman design as a way to symbolize the democratic institutions housed within. Statehouses were also to be monumental in size, situated in prominent locations in their cities, divided to accommodate all the functions of state government, and open to public views, public gatherings, and public voices. Georgia's new Capitol, designed using this popular vocabulary, was intended to serve as a temple of democracy for the state.[2]

As the members of the Georgia General Assembly walked toward their new workplace, they observed firsthand all the elements of nineteenth-century statehouse design. Their first view of the new Capitol, as they crossed

Marietta Street in front of the old Capitol, 1875. Marietta Street was the widest boulevard in downtown Atlanta in the late nineteenth century. At the corner of Marietta and Forsyth streets stood the Kimball Opera House, which served as Georgia's Capitol from 1869 to 1889. The statehouse, seen here in the right foreground, was the starting point for many grand political pageants. (Courtesy of the Georgia Archives, Vanishing Georgia Collection, ful1070-93)

Inaugural parade for Governor Alexander Stephens, 1882. A formal parade honoring the inauguration of Governor Alexander Stephens formed on Marietta Street on October 26, 1882. The Opera House Capitol appears with its clock tower in the upper right center of the photo. Similar crowds gathered to view the two legislative parades from the old Capitol to the new, first for the cornerstone ceremony on September 2, 1885, and nearly four years later for the dedication on July 3, 1889. (Courtesy of the Lane Brothers Collection, Special Collections Department, Georgia State University Library)

over the railroad tracks on the Broad Street bridge, allowed them to appreciate the prominence of their new place of assembly. In a city where the tallest structures were narrow church spires and four-story commercial buildings, the new Capitol was an impressive edifice. Its nearest rival, a few blocks to the northwest, was the massive Kimball House hotel. Its red brick facade towered above the nearby three- and four-story storefronts along Decatur Street, but its busy Victorian design could not compete with the statehouse's classical grandeur and monumentality. When completed in 1889, the Capitol was Atlanta's largest landmark, with a mass and height that defined and dominated the capital city.

State capitol sites generally were selected for any of three topographical advantages: elevation; an open, parklike setting; and proximity to the open vistas provided by a river or a bay. Atlanta's Capitol was distant from any water features, but its elevation and parklike setting emphasized the grandeur of the edifice and provided good views of the structure from vistas near and far. The hill on which the Capitol was built was fifty feet higher than the surrounding streets, allowing the ground itself to serve as a pedestal for the building.[3]

The members of the July 1889 procession had their first close-up view of their new workplace after they climbed the hill, passing by the Shrine of the Immaculate Conception and the Central Presbyterian Church, and turned onto Washington Street. Included among the marchers was a lone African American, seventy-three-year-old Samuel A. McIver, a House representative from Liberty County, along the Georgia coast. In a state where 45 percent of the population was African American and 61 of 139 counties had black majorities, a government truly representative of the state's demographics would have included significant numbers of black elected officials at all levels. Although the U.S. Congress had sustained the right of African American men to hold elective office earlier in the century, in the South, legislative restrictions and white intimidation had all but eliminated black participation in the political process.

Representative McIver proceeded with his colleagues up the hill to the newly completed Capitol, and as he turned onto

View of the Capitol from the northwest, 1889.
The new statehouse towered over downtown
Atlanta because of its elevated location,
open setting, and sheer size. Built on a hill,
its four stories, central dome, cupola, and
statue combined to reach a height of 272 feet,
the equivalent of a fourteen-story building.
(Courtesy of the Kenan Research Center at the
Atlanta History Center)

Washington Street, he beheld the imposing new statehouse. Waiting at the new
Capitol to greet the members of the General Assembly was John B. Gordon, the
governor who had summoned the legislators to the new temple of democracy
but who was also one of the political leaders most responsible for restricting
African American participation in the political affairs of the state.

Gordon had been a distinguished Civil War general, visible badges of which
were his wounds from the Battle of Bloody Lane—a bullet scar on his left
cheek and a useless left arm. His brilliant military leadership had endeared
him to many white Georgians and propelled him into the U.S. Senate in 1873,
where he remained until 1880. In the unsettled aftermath of the war, Gordon
had also served as the leader of Georgia's Ku Klux Klan. The KKK targeted
African Americans, using violence to prevent them from voting and holding
elective office. By the time Gordon was elected governor in 1886, the results
of these efforts to curtail black voting were clear, as McIver's lone presence in

the General Assembly attested. While Representative Mc-Iver and his fellow African Americans saw injustice in this skewed political representation, most white elected officials regarded their domination of politics as the natural order of things in the South and saw no disjuncture between the democratic ideal and the reality of its practice in Georgia. For them, the new Georgia Capitol was, indeed, a temple of democracy.

John B. Gordon, 1894. John B. Gordon, the governor of Georgia who presided over the dedication ceremonies of the new Capitol in 1889, parlayed his status as a popular Confederate general into a political career. In the aftermath of the Civil War, he was the titular head of the state's Ku Klux Klan, helping Democrats to regain political control. He served as United States senator from 1873 to 1880 and was elected governor in 1886. (Courtesy of the Georgia Capitol Museum)

As they approached the main (west) entrance of the new Capitol, the legislators encountered a building in the middle of a mostly empty four-and-a-half-acre lot. The open space around the structure allowed those who approached to notice its monumentality and view its classical detailing from several vantage points. These grounds would eventually provide a parklike setting for the edifice, but since the funds for the first phase of this task had been approved only six months earlier, the stone walkways, tree and shrub plantings, and lawns had yet to be completed. In time, the green of lawn and foliage would soften the hard impression of the stone exterior.

Senator duBignon led his colleagues south down Washington Street until he arrived at the center of the Capitol Square block. The new Capitol's elevation required all who approached to move upward, an important feature—common to temple design—that signaled the movement from ordinary activities of daily life to the extraordinary duties of civic endeavor. To gain entrance, they would have to ascend twice. DuBignon turned the procession and began the short climb up seven steps to the west plaza, which rose gently upward to the stairs of

Capitol and grounds, c. 1890. This view from the corner of Hunter Street (now Martin Luther King Jr. Drive) and Washington Street reveals a building without the parklike setting seen today. The lawns, sidewalks, newly planted trees (dwarfed by electrical poles), and walkways that surround the building were installed in early 1891. (Courtesy of the Kenan Research Center at the Atlanta History Center)

West facade, temple front, 1994. The familiar temple front of the American statehouse, with its origins in Egyptian, Greek, and Roman architecture, is intended to convey a message of majesty and tradition. Its stairs require those who enter to process upward, symbolizing the rise above the ordinary activities of daily life. (Courtesy of the Library of Congress)

the main entrance. The stone plaza, signaling the openness of government, was intended to be an elevated gathering place for official events and citizen assemblies, a forum for the exchange of ideas between the government and the people. The legislators themselves were establishing the precedent for such pageantry with their stately procession. Looking up, the legislators could view the temple front of the Capitol's main entrance.

The temple front extended out from the main axis of the building, crowned with a pediment above the two-story chambers of the House of Representatives. Supporting the chambers were massive stone columns, with stairs leading up to and through them. Charles Goodsell describes the temple front of American statehouse architecture as "a splendid front porch, or portico," which can be found in the design of two-thirds of the nation's state capitols. This form was developed by the Egyptians, the Greeks, and the Romans for their temples and palaces and was then refined during the Renaissance for a variety of state and ecclesiastical uses. The nineteenth-century Classical Revival styles brought back the temple front, and it became a staple of American architecture in the design of

West facade elevation, 1994. The Georgia State Capitol faces four directions, with four asymmetrical facades that are four stories high. The entrances are ordered in size by their function and orientation to the center of the city. The west main entrance is the grandest, as marked by the relief design carved into its pediment and the wide expanse of steps leading up to five columned openings. (Courtesy of Lord, Aeck & Sargent Architecture)

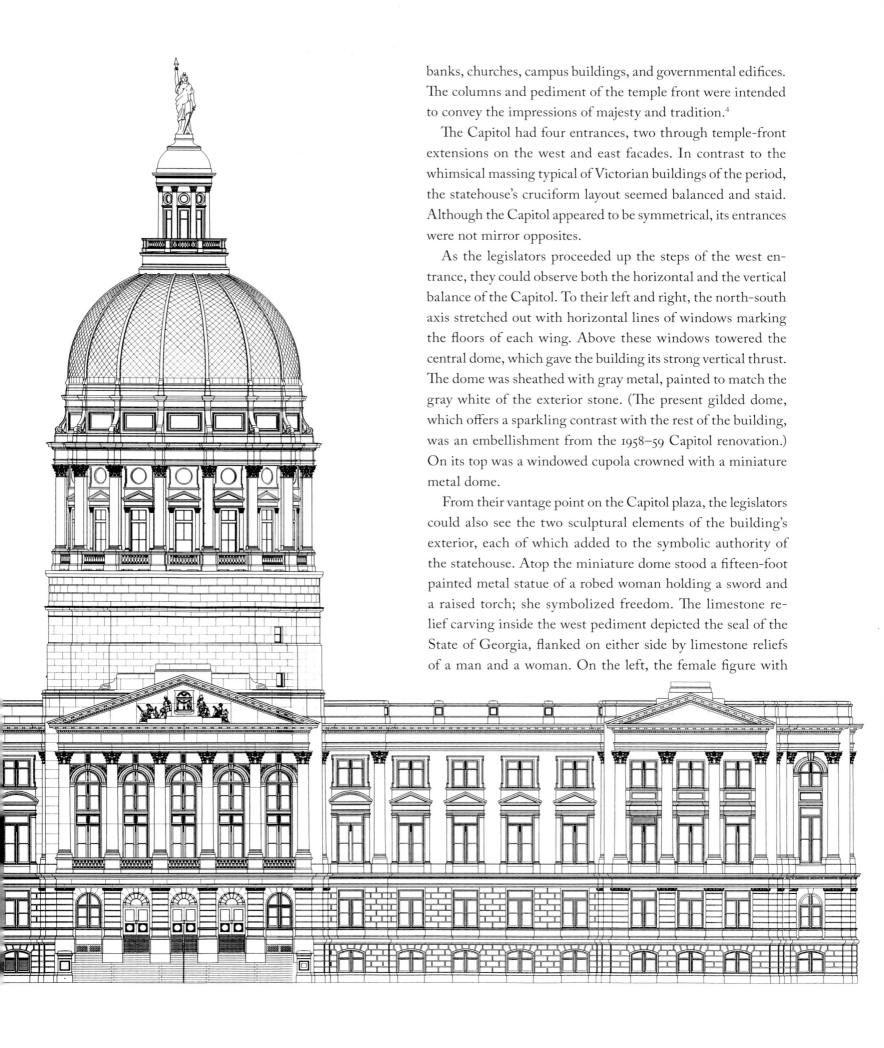

banks, churches, campus buildings, and governmental edifices. The columns and pediment of the temple front were intended to convey the impressions of majesty and tradition.[4]

The Capitol had four entrances, two through temple-front extensions on the west and east facades. In contrast to the whimsical massing typical of Victorian buildings of the period, the statehouse's cruciform layout seemed balanced and staid. Although the Capitol appeared to be symmetrical, its entrances were not mirror opposites.

As the legislators proceeded up the steps of the west entrance, they could observe both the horizontal and the vertical balance of the Capitol. To their left and right, the north-south axis stretched out with horizontal lines of windows marking the floors of each wing. Above these windows towered the central dome, which gave the building its strong vertical thrust. The dome was sheathed with gray metal, painted to match the gray white of the exterior stone. (The present gilded dome, which offers a sparkling contrast with the rest of the building, was an embellishment from the 1958–59 Capitol renovation.) On its top was a windowed cupola crowned with a miniature metal dome.

From their vantage point on the Capitol plaza, the legislators could also see the two sculptural elements of the building's exterior, each of which added to the symbolic authority of the statehouse. Atop the miniature dome stood a fifteen-foot painted metal statue of a robed woman holding a sword and a raised torch; she symbolized freedom. The limestone relief carving inside the west pediment depicted the seal of the State of Georgia, flanked on either side by limestone reliefs of a man and a woman. On the left, the female figure with

a Mercury emblem in hand and an anchor at her feet, symbolized shipping and commerce. Next to her a male figure wielding a hammer suggested labor and industry. On the right side, the male figure, helmeted and holding a sword, represented the armed force necessary to protect liberty and establish justice. The accompanying female figure held a horn of plenty, symbolizing the fruits of the soil and the prosperity of peace. The participants in the all-male legislature who passed underneath these figures may have grasped their symbolism, but few appreciated the irony inherent in the choice of females to represent liberty, business enterprise, and prosperity. In 1889, by constitutional restriction, no women could vote or be voted for in the United States. Furthermore, because they did not have an elective voice, women had little power to change legislation passed by an all-male legislature, and a number of Georgia laws reflected this bias. When the legislature marched up the Capitol steps in 1889, the movement for women's suffrage was marshaling in Georgia, but it would take thirty-three years of political activity before two women would walk up these same steps as elected members of the General Assembly.

At the top of the steps under the grand front porch of the Capitol, heavy wooden doors opened to admit Senate President duBignon and his fellow legislators. A one-story, dimly lit entrance hall served as a passageway to the central rotunda, which dramatically opened upward and outward to bright and soaring public spaces. The ceiling of the rotunda rose seventy-five feet, drawing the eyes of the leg-

Capitol west front. The west front of the Capitol features sculptural elements that underscore the building's symbolism. The allegorical figures in the pediment represent commerce, industry, justice, and prosperity; the crowning statue on the cupola symbolizes freedom. (Courtesy of Diane Kirkland and the Georgia Department of Economic Development)

islators upward to the shafts of light shining in from the windows surrounding the dome drum. Archways facing in four directions admitted light from two floors above. Beneath the legislators' feet, a soft brightness emanated from translucent glass blocks that let in light from the first floor below. To their

OPPOSITE PAGE, BOTTOM *Floor of the rotunda.* The centrality of the rotunda to the Capitol made it a natural gathering place for small assemblies from the day of its dedication. Press conferences, announcements, and small ceremonies occur here almost daily. (Courtesy of Diane Kirkland and the Georgia Department of Economic Development)

TOP LEFT *West pediment, 1884.* In Edbrooke and Burnham's original plan, the sculptural elements in the west pediment featured the state seal with a background of Georgia landscapes. Rising above the pediment was a statue of a woman holding up a tablet, suggesting that laws would be enacted and upheld in the Capitol. (Courtesy of the Georgia Archives, RG 1-8-30)

TOP RIGHT *West pediment.* George Crouch, the sculptor who executed all the ornamental stonework on the Capitol, replaced the Georgia landscape in the Edbrooke and Burnham drawing of the west pediment with allegorical figures. Here a worker with hammer and apron represents industry. (Courtesy of Diane Kirkland and the Georgia Department of Economic Development)

OPPOSITE PAGE *Rotunda dome.* The height of the rotunda and its lighted dome draw the eyes of visitors upward to one of the building's most striking architectural features. (Courtesy of Diane Kirkland and the Georgia Department of Economic Development)

ABOVE *View through the rotunda.* An opening in the rotunda wall frames a view of the distant south atrium and its fourth-story doorway. (Courtesy of Diane Kirkland and the Georgia Department of Economic Development)

right and left as they moved into the rotunda, they could see archways opening into the north and south atria.

Although contemporary accounts did not report where the House members split off from the senators as they marched to their respective chambers, the rotunda would have been the logical place. From this central point in the building, the line could have split as the senators moved toward one staircase and the representatives toward the other. From the rounded, relatively contained space of the rotunda, with its circular walls and domed ceiling, the legislators passed into the rectangular atria, where straight lines and right angles marked the limits of the spacious, galleried halls. The processions moved across the atria to the two stately staircases—one in the north hall and one in the south—that led up to the third floor, where their legislative chambers were located.

As the members of the House and the Senate processed up these stairs, they again enacted a ritual upward movement, symbolizing the higher purpose of their legislative duties. From the landings of the staircases, the legislators could view the splendor and majesty of the three-story halls, where Corinthian columns supported overlooking balconies. The light from the windows of clerestories shone in from above, whitewashing the subtle colors of the atria. The pale peach walls and soft green columns and trim produced an impression of lightness and openness that was not characteristic of Victorian taste. Whereas the main corridors in most state capitols of the period employed a riot of patterns in a wide range of hues, the halls of the Georgia Capitol were quite chaste. This restraint was not accidental but budgetary, reflecting the relative poverty of a state whose agricultural economy lagged behind the growing and diversifying economies of states in other regions of the nation. The limited funds available for decorative painting had

ABOVE *Senate chamber.* After its 1998–2000 renovation, the Senate now appears much as it did in 1889. However, today's legislators enjoy modern conveniences such as amplified sound, higher light level, air conditioning, and a network linking their laptop computers. (Courtesy of Diane Kirkland and the Georgia Department of Economic Development)

OPPOSITE PAGE *House chamber.* When legislators marched into their hall on July 3, 1889, there was a great hubbub caused by the lottery that determined seat assignments. The House has almost three times as many members as the Senate, and its sessions are often livelier and louder than those of its counterpart across the building. (Courtesy of Diane Kirkland and the Georgia Department of Economic Development)

been parceled out to the legislative and judicial chambers, the state library, and the offices of constitutional officials.

The atria's expanse, their grand staircases, and the wide hallways created an arena that allowed the public to view the legislative procession that morning, but more significantly, these open spaces were also intended to make public the business of government. Representatives would move to and from the legislative chambers in public view, giving constituents the opportunity to approach them to discuss matters before the legislature. The open stairs and corridors of the Capitol made it difficult for those who conduct the people's business to arrive and depart secretly, and the public procession of legislators into their chambers on July 3, 1889, set the precedent.

As the senators reached the top of the stairways and marched east to their chambers, they approached the wide-open doors

with anticipation. Here they discovered a brilliant contrast to the simple two-toned walls in the public areas. In every direction their eyes met extravagant color treatments, typical of the age, adorning plaster walls and molded plaster columns. A coved ceiling was stenciled with stars and introduced a golden motif, thought to be in keeping with the white oak finish of the wooden window surrounds, wainscoting, gallery railings, desks, and the presiding officer's podium. Other warm colors, including metallic copper, competed among the medley for the legislators' attention. Beneath their feet, a flower-patterned carpet exploded with even more color. A brilliant fifty-four-light chandelier hung in the center of the chambers. At the rear of the chamber, above the main floor, a gallery set off with wooden balustrades was crowded with spectators eager to witness the opening session in the new Capitol. Senate President

duBignon moved to the oak podium on the dais of the chamber to call the Senate to order.

On the opposite side of the Capitol, the members of the House were still filing into their equally lavishly decorated chamber, which was larger than the Senate hall to accommodate their greater numbers. Similarly elaborate appointments greeted them: coved ceiling, ninety-light chandelier, wooden dais, podium and desks of cherry wood, two-story windows, ballustraded gallery, and flowered carpet. "Delicate shades of yellow, gold, and buff in graceful designs" giving the impression of a "mass of stars and spangles" paralleled the decorative

paint treatments in the Senate. Wooden beams painted in "rich, darker colors" divided the brightly decorated ceiling, creating panels "painted antique blue and ornamented with silver figures." The frieze and capitals were decorated "in colors varying from a rich dark red to gilt old gold and buff with a delicate tracery of antique blue." The dull red walls of the chamber matched the cherry finish of the wooden wainscoting, railings, and furniture.[5]

The members of the Senate and the House went about their duties of organizing themselves quite differently, with the House using a populist method and the Senate one that was more hierarchical. President Fleming duBignon had predetermined the seating for the Senate, so its members filed in orderly fashion down the aisles that led to their desks. In contrast, the 144 members of the House arrived in chambers without assigned seats. Under the direction of Speaker Pro Tempore Marvin Calvin, each member filed past a box from

Third-floor plan. The cruciform floor plan of the Capitol makes the building appear balanced even though it is not entirely symmetrical. Each end of the building housed a different component of state government—the state library to the north, the Senate to the east, the state supreme court to the south, and the House of Representatives to the west. One floor below, the executive offices of the governor were located on the northeast corner. (Courtesy of Lord, Aeck & Sargent Architecture)

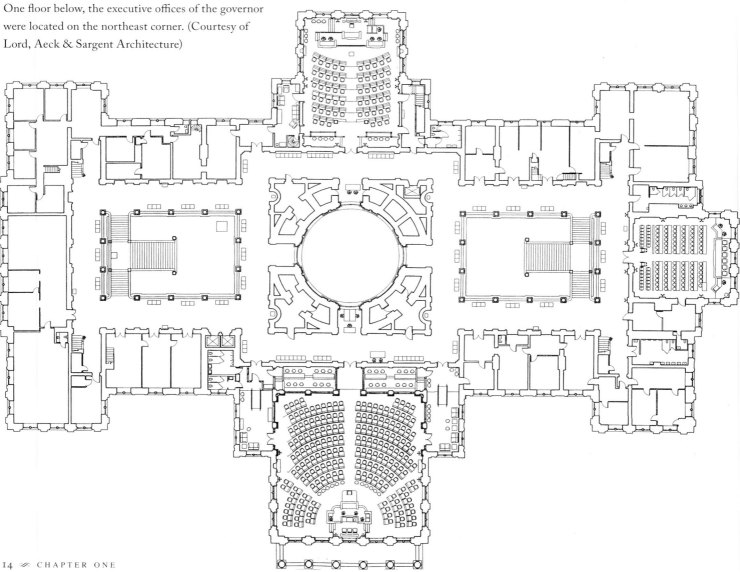

which he drew a paper indicating the chamber desk that would be his for the session. Apparently the only one exempted from the lottery was Samuel McIver, who was assigned a seat in the extreme corner of the hall to the right of the Speaker.[6]

The public galleries of each chamber, which had separate entrances on the fourth floor, were full to overflowing with those who had come to witness the inaugural sessions in the new building. Galleries were critical to the democratic intention of American statehouse design. Elected representatives were to carry out the work of the people in chambers where the public could witness their actions. Designed as part of the legislative chambers, the galleries were fitted with the same decorative details, including light fixtures, paint treatments, wood balustrades, and trim. Those who came to witness legislative action shared the chambers with their representatives, but not necessarily the vote. Women—many of whom were the wives or daughters of legislators—predominated in the galleries. The stripes and patterns of the women's dresses were a counterpoint to the black suits (many of which were new for the occasion), dark ties, and white shirts of the men on the floor below.

Having processed into their new chambers and organized themselves for their legislative duties, the members of the House and the Senate adjourned until the following day. Meanwhile, Governor Gordon was busy welcoming one and all to the new building. An *Atlanta Constitution* reporter noted that the "good right arm of the Governor was taxed severely all day."[7]

At the formal dedication ceremonies the following day, July 4, 1889, Governor Gordon used the occasion to sound familiar political themes. At noon the governor presided over a joint session of the General Assembly to celebrate the completion of the new Capitol. The governor's speech attempted to capture the splendor of the new building, which he formally accepted from Evan P. Howell, chairman of the Capitol Commission, on behalf of the state. "I accept from your hands Georgia's new and superb Capitol. In the fashion of its architecture, in the symmetry of its proportions, in the solidity of its structure, in the beauty of its elaboration, and the completeness of its arrangements, it is worthy of the dignity and character of this great commonwealth."[8]

The governor emphasized that the new Capitol had been built under budget and was unscathed by the taint of corruption, a point intended to evoke memories of the previous Republican administration. Invoking applause from his audience,

he proclaimed, "From granite base to iron dome, every chiseled block and molded brick, every metallic plate and marble slab is as free from official corruption as when they lay untouched by mortal hand in the original purity in the bosom of mother earth." Gordon was renowned for his oratorical prowess and his tongue did not fail him that day. "Built on the crowning hill of her capital city, whose transformation from desolation and ashes to life, thrift and beauty so aptly symbolize the state's resurrection, this proud structure will stand through the coming centuries a fit memorial of the indomitable will and recuperative energies of this great people and the unswerving fidelity and incorruptible integrity of their chosen representatives." Gordon then figuratively engraved the cornerstone with a list of what he called "our ancestral canons," which included "a perpetual union of co-equal states" and "the support of the state governments in all their rights as the surest bulwarks against anti-republican tendencies."[9]

Governor Gordon's vision of a New South "democracy" was echoed in the *Atlanta Constitution* the next day. There an article proclaimed a new "era of liberty" by contrasting the previous day's session in the new Capitol with the opening of the legislature on July 4, 1868, in the "old rookery" of the City Hall / County Courthouse Capitol. The maligned multipurpose facility had once stood on the site of the current statehouse, where it had served as the meeting place for the first legislative session in Atlanta, a postwar gathering that had included thirty-two elected African American representatives. "The new capitol, rising in all the grandeur of its imposing and massive proportions from its solid foundations, does not contrast more strongly with the old rookery it has supplanted than our imperial commonwealth does with the wrecked and shattered military district of twenty-one years ago. . . . But reconstruction, bayonet rule and poverty belong to the past. The men who assembled in the Capitol yesterday live in an era of liberty, prosperity and progress."[10]

After the formal speeches, the joint session adjourned. Fourth of July celebrations awaited elsewhere in Atlanta. Two blocks from the Capitol, thrill seekers boarded streetcars pulled by a minilocomotive called a steam dummy. They traveled to Grant Park just a mile and a half to the east, where special events included a hot air balloon rising, a baseball game, and a hanging trapeze act. Steam dummies signaled the dramatic changes that technological innovation had brought to everyday urban life by 1889. Horse-drawn trolleys, in use in Ameri-

Capitol lighted at night. In 1889, the lights from the Capitol shone like lone beacons on the Atlanta skyline. Today floodlights on the exterior help the Capitol to compete for attention with taller and brighter skyscrapers. (Courtesy of Diane Kirkland and the Georgia Department of Economic Development)

can cities for a half a century, had permitted the middle class and elite to escape from the crowded core of nineteenth-century cities into landscaped and picturesque parks built on the urban fringe. In the late 1880s, horses were being replaced with new power sources for trolleys: steam and electricity. In turn, electricity was also replacing gas as a source of urban lighting, and electrically illuminated evening events were the rage.

Capitol at night. This undated postcard view of the Capitol suggests how it appeared the night of its first evening reception on July 4, 1889. Atlanta newspapers described the building as "ablaze with light." On its elevated site, the interior lights of the Capitol could be seen shining from miles away. (Courtesy of the Georgia Capitol Museum)

That night Atlantans could choose between two lighted events. Grant Park was strung with electric lights for the holiday, and the Capitol was to be completely lit with its fancy new gas fixtures. Those who attended the Grant Park festivities strolled under lights strung among the trees. A mile and a half to the west they could see the majestic Capitol, light streaming out of the two-story windows of the Senate chambers, the round windows of the dome drum, and clerestory windows of the cupola.

For the occasion, the new Capitol was not just lit up; it was opened up to one and all. Any citizen who wanted to visit the building could come to shake hands with Governor Gordon and rub shoulders with members of the General Assembly. Although the governor's suite included a reception room, for this occasion Governor Gordon and his wife went to the state library, which occupied the third and fourth floors of the north end, to receive visitors. They stood in the two-story central room, forty-six feet high and seventy feet long, which served as a reading and reception room. The walls had decorative pilasters and elaborate stenciling, two fireplaces with a mirrored mantle and elaborately carved pediment, and two sixteen-light chandeliers. At either end, columned and arched openings led to two one-story rooms forty-five feet in length, where wooden stacks held the library's books. A reporter for the *Savannah Morning News* characterized the state library as "by far the handsomest section in the building."[11]

At the evening ceremonies in the new temple of democracy, the white press noted the break from the usual etiquette of race relations by pointing out that "the color line was not drawn" at the governor's reception and that "many prominent colored citizens with their families were to be seen in the crowd." However, the color line in the statehouse was redrawn immediately after the dedication. African Americans who came to the statehouse were directed to separate seating in the House and Senate galleries, sent to separate lavatories, and excluded from eating facilities that served other visitors. In the ensuing decades, a formal color line created by Jim Crow laws passed and signed in the Capitol itself would bring more rigid segregation.[12]

The dedication ceremonies brought state officials and citizens into three of the four great public rooms in the Capitol: the House and Senate chambers and the state library. Missing from the ceremonies was the judicial branch of government, whose physical presence in the Capitol could be seen in the well-appointed courtroom at the top of the south atrium staircase. (Since the relocation of the court's activities from the Capitol in 1956, the room has been converted for meeting use by the House and Senate Appropriations Committees.) The executive and legislative branches of government had worked together to plan the public opening of the Capitol. The following day, the *Savannah Morning News* noted that for "some unexplained reason the supreme court was conspicuously absent. It is understood that they were overlooked, unintentionally of course, by the [planning] committee."[13]

OPPOSITE PAGE *State library, 1890.* The site of Governor John Gordon's reception the night of the Capitol dedication, the state library was used for gatherings as well as a law library. This once grand space is now subdivided into three levels of legislative offices. (Courtesy of the Kenan Research Center at the Atlanta History Center)

Supreme court chamber (now the Appropriations Committee Room). After the departure of the judicial branch in 1956, the courtroom was reconfigured and renovated as a meeting space for legislative budget committees. In the late 1990s, the room was restored with its original finishes and lighting while maintaining its modern function. (Courtesy of Diane Kirkland and the Georgia Department of Economic Development)

Although the supreme court justices did not formally mark the occasion with speeches and a reception, their courtroom was one of the grand public spaces of the new Capitol. The Supreme Court Room had a twenty-two-foot-high ceiling and was "finished in white oak and frescoed in a style of quiet magnificence somewhat similar to the senate chamber." Its adjoining library had a balcony supported by wrought-iron scroll brackets, a spiral staircase, and two eight-light chandeliers above six oak tables. Along the west hallway, the judges had offices that were "large and elegantly frescoed."[14]

The crowd of citizens who moved about the new Capitol on the evening of July 4, 1889, demonstrated the logic of the open plan of this noble governmental building. They gathered in the atria and rotunda on the second floor and viewed the offices

Rotunda. Barely visible windows high in the rotunda and arched openings along its walls allow exterior light to illuminate the narrow cylindrical space. (Courtesy of Diane Kirkland and the Georgia Department of Economic Development)

of the governor, the secretary of state, and the superintendent of education. They had access to the corridors of power on the third floor leading to the great rooms of the Capitol: the House and Senate chambers, the state library, and the Supreme Court Room. In 1889 one building was more than large enough for Georgia's governmental functions, but not for long. Although there was room to build out offices on its first floor, the building was full by 1910, and employees were soon moving into rented space nearby. Today, the Capitol is the center of a governmental campus of state buildings. It retains the offices of the governor and the secretary of state, and it houses the legislative chambers and offices for the legislative leadership. The judicial branch of government has left the Capitol altogether, while many executive and legislative offices and departments are located in buildings that ring the Capitol. Computerization has allowed other departments to move further away and around the state, but the Capitol remains the actual as well as the symbolic center of Georgia's government.

West plaza and entrance. The legislative session, held each January through March, is the busiest time on the Capitol plaza. Interest groups offer promotions to capture the attention of legislators and fellow citizens. The front steps are also a popular location for press conferences and demonstrations. (Courtesy of Diane Kirkland and the Georgia Department of Economic Development)

While thousands of histories can be told of the Georgia statehouse, what follows will weave three interlocking tales. One story traces the building itself: its predecessors, its design and construction, the physical changes that have modified its appearance over the years, and the restoration of many of its original finishes in the last decade. Another account addresses the symbolic accretions of statutes, flags, portraits, and civic rituals that, like its dedicatory ceremonies, added new layers of meaning to an already symbolic structure. A third narrative follows the legislative and judicial battles, within and without its walls, that sought to limit or extend the democratic freedoms of many of Georgia's citizens. The first story starts long before the 1889 dedication, with the attempts of a new state to establish a permanent capital. The other two tales begin several generations later, after the Civil War, when Georgians struggled to fashion a new government and a new statehouse in a new capital city.

2

A RENTED CAPITOL

Twenty years before the 1889 Capitol dedication, state leaders staged another festive Capitol event in Atlanta. On the evening of January 12, 1869, Georgia's prominent white civic leaders knew exactly where they needed to be, joining the crowd at the corner of Forsyth and Marietta streets, where a new state Capitol stood ablaze with gas lights. Still called the Kimball Opera House by many, it had been fitted out handsomely for its new governmental purposes. The largest building in post–Civil War Atlanta, the five-story brick structure dominated its block and sported a mansard roof topped by a clock tower. Georgia's most powerful men and their wives climbed a marble and granite staircase and followed the sounds of music up another flight to the main legislative floor. A steady stream of four thousand guests filled the building beyond capacity, packing some areas so tightly that people could move only in unison.[1]

Many in the crowd were Atlantans celebrating more than the opening of a statehouse. This splendid new Capitol represented the ascendance of their city as the political capital of Georgia. Atlanta had become the hub of a growing network of rail lines that crisscrossed the state and linked Georgia to its neighbors and the nation. The city's growth rate far exceeded that of any other Georgia city, but it badly needed a postwar infusion of investment funds. Becoming the state capital, a badge of urban significance for any municipality, would bring capital. Atlanta was also becoming a nexus for urbanizing African Americans, who were absent from the dedication ceremonies that evening.

Approaching the hub of conversation and band music, visitors entered the dazzling seventy-five-foot-square House chamber. The colorful patterns of the frescoed walls and ceiling captured their attention, but all eyes were drawn to the magnificent lighting fixture that hung down almost forty feet from the large ceiling dome. A huge circle of gas jets, each surrounded by a fluted mirror, threw the flames' reflections to the far corners of the room. A balcony ran around three sides of the chamber, providing enough space to seat five hundred spectators. Tonight it was packed with guests admiring the view and one another, while on the walls portraits of Georgia's heroes, transported from the previous Capitol in Milledgeville, returned their glances with steady gazes. At the other end of the second floor, the guests entered the Senate chamber, an equally opulent but smaller version of the House chamber.

Kimball Opera House, c. 1878. Rising from the rubble of postwar Atlanta, the Kimball Opera House was the biggest building in town when the City of Atlanta leased most of it for the state's use as a capitol. By the day of its dedication, January 12, 1869, civic boosters had been working for more than twenty years to relocate the capital in Atlanta. (Courtesy of the Georgia Archives, Small Print Collection, ful0648)

Having seen the showiest spaces, most visitors made their way back to the second main floor, where guests greeted acquaintances and perhaps congratulated their hosts, Hannibal and Edwin Kimball, who owned the building. As they left, visitors passed through the first floor, where five empty spaces awaited retail clients. From the street, the more curious guests climbed the outside entrance to view the fifth floor, which consisted of residential apartments whose dormer windows punctuated the Second Empire roofline. Continuing their climb up to the turret, they could marvel at the view of the growing city as evidenced by soft gaslights visible along the streets for miles around. The reception ended at 10:00 p.m., when the band played "Dixie" and the crowd responded with the enthusiastic applause that usually greeted the popular tune. Originally composed for use in a Northern minstrel show, "Dixie" had become the Confederacy's unofficial national anthem after it was played at Jefferson Davis's 1861 inauguration. Now it symbolized the return of white Democratic control of statehouse politics.

The cheering, smiling attendees had varying reasons to feel jubilant that evening in 1869. Republicans had brokered the deal for the Kimball Opera House to be transformed into a statehouse. Their Second Empire–style building would serve as Georgia's state Capitol for twenty tumultuous years. The Democrats felt even more celebratory, for during the previous legislative session, they had banished the General Assembly's black legislators and dealt the Republicans a crushing defeat. The luster of the splendid new Capitol would soon fade as Democrats used it to symbolize the failure of Georgia's Republican Party and its attempt at biracial Reconstruction government.

Throughout the evening, guests could hear muttering among the compliments, congratulations, and applause. The Opera House was rented for only five years, although Atlanta had promised suitable space for up to ten years. The project's developer, Hannibal I. Kimball, was a newly arrived northerner and friend of the controversial Republican governor, Rufus Bullock. He had used his contacts to secure state funding to complete the construction of the building and convert its middle floors to state use. Kimball retained control of the rest of the building, which he turned into residential and commercial spaces. The splendid decorative finishes, furniture, lighting, and even the heating and plumbing systems had all been paid for with state funds. The empty half of the bottom floor was advertised for commercial establishments and the top floor for residential apartments. As the Democrat-aligned *Atlanta Constitution* reported the next day, "the idea of making a cheap lodging house out of the top of so elegant a building seem[ed] really absurd."[2]

The real concern about a statehouse, however, lay ahead. Only four years out

Kimball Opera House advertisement, c. 1870. Despite the Kimball Opera House's glamour, some Georgians resented having their state capitol in rented quarters. Owner Hannibal Kimball did not hesitate to capitalize on the capitol's presence when marketing the other rental spaces in the building. (Courtesy of the Kenan Research Center at the Atlanta History Center)

Louisville, c. 1900. The state government moved to Louisville, an east Georgia town located halfway between Savannah and Atlanta, in 1796. When Milledgeville became the state capital ten years later, Louisville remained a small town, as seen in this photograph taken almost one hundred years later. Its dominant feature, the eighteenth-century slave market seen in the center of this photograph, still stands today. (Courtesy of the Georgia Archives, Small Print Collection, spc13-021c)

of a devastating war, the state was cash poor. Atlanta would donate land, but other states had spent millions to build their capitols. Relocation seemed ludicrous to legislators from Baldwin County and other areas near Milledgeville, where the former Capitol stood empty, but capital relocation was nothing new to Georgia. The General Assembly had moved the seat of state government many times since 1776, and four cities had served as official capitals before Atlanta. The colonial and first state capital was Savannah, until the British captured the city in December 1778. The rebel capital relocated to Augusta until May 1780, when the British captured that city and the legislature fled to Heard's Fort, eight miles from present-day Washington, Georgia. In August 1781, the legislature returned to Augusta until the following May. The legislature then alternated between Augusta and Savannah until the General Assembly named Augusta as the official capital in 1785.[3]

These first two Georgia capitals did not have custom-built capitols; neither city constructed a building to serve the specific needs of a statehouse. Early state legislatures in Savannah assembled in several buildings, including Christ Church, and may have met for several years in the Filature, a silk-production structure converted to public meeting space in the 1770s. In Augusta, the legislature met first in a residence and then rented a larger building downtown.[4]

These buildings were capitols only by virtue of their function; the concept of a state capitol barely existed at the time. True statehouses did not appear until the 1780s, in South Carolina, Virginia, and Delaware. Some states created new interior cities for their capitals to spur growth and to be more centrally located as settlers moved westward, as did Georgia in 1786 when the General Assembly created the town of Louisville as the new capital site. This planned capital was located on the Ogeechee River about thirty miles southwest of Augusta. Land-lot sales funded the construction of the statehouse and other public buildings, but financial and construction problems delayed the project ten years.[5]

Georgia's first planned Capitol was a two-story brick rectangle measuring about forty by sixty feet. Completed in 1796, the building had few of the characteristics common in later state capitols except for its elevated site up the hill from the river. Each floor contained a lobby and three rooms, one of which served as a legislative chamber and was probably larger than the other two. The ground floor contained the House of Representatives chamber, a land office, and a secretary's office. Above it were the Senate chamber, governor's office, and state treasury. The awkward room arrangement was outdated before the building was complete. Other capitols, such as the statehouse of Delaware, placed their legislative chambers on the same floor. The Louisville capitol was probably of Georgian or Federal design, both popular styles in 1796. The Greek Revival craze was still twenty years away, though Thomas Jefferson had already designed a state capitol for Virginia in the form of a Roman temple.[6]

Neither the Capitol nor the capital was destined for success.

As Georgia's population shifted north and west as new territories became available for settlement, Louisville was no longer centrally located. Rather than invest more state resources in a low-lying town that showed little potential for growth, in May 1803 the General Assembly appointed a commission to select another "permanent" capital site more centrally located at the fall line of the Oconee River. By late 1804 the town of Milledgeville was platted and approved by the legislature. Four twenty-acre squares were reserved for public use, and the surrounding smaller land lots were sold to fund the new statehouse. Construction began in 1805 and continued after the legislature convened there in 1807. The eighty-thousand-dollar building served as Georgia's Capitol for over sixty years, with a brief exception in 1865, when the General Assembly met in Macon for several months.

Built only ten years after the Louisville capitol, the Milledgeville Capitol came much closer to the emerging concept of an American statehouse. Its large lot was atop the town's highest hill, ensuring visibility from all sides. The two main streets, Washington and Jefferson, intersected at Statehouse Square. Both the elevated site and the street arrangement allowed dramatic vistas of the stately public building. Three stories tall and 53 by 160 feet, the Capitol was an imposing structure for the young town. Each brick facade featured a pediment

Georgia State Capitol at Milledgeville, c. 1830. Standing in the center of a twenty-acre lot at the highest point in town, the statehouse dominated the capital city of Milledgeville. Constructed in 1807 as a simple rectangular brick structure, the building was remodeled drastically twenty years later when a two-phase renovation added north and south wings, and heightened, stuccoed, and crenellated the walls. (Courtesy of the Kenan Research Center at the Atlanta History Center)

Milledgeville Capitol. The Milledgeville Capitol served as the center of state government from 1807 until 1868. Since 1879, it has been used by Georgia Military College for a variety of purposes. In 2001, after undergoing a major restoration, the former statehouse was the site of a ceremonial session of the Georgia Supreme Court and of the Georgia General Assembly. (Courtesy of Diane Kirkland and the Georgia Department of Economic Development)

ornamented with a gilded eagle. The interior arrangement was more advanced, with the legislative chambers sharing equal status on the second (top) floor. Broad hallways intersected at the exact center of the building, and committee rooms filled the rest of the floor. On the first (middle) floor were the offices of the executive branch. The bottom story was a basement that held the state arsenal until 1812. The interiors featured fanlight transoms over doors, pilasters and columns, decorative plasterwork, and faux finishes on plaster and pine. The architectural style of the original building is unknown. Building records indicate the use of Federal or Georgian decorative elements, as well as four "Hiptic arches" (probably pointed), which may have lent a Gothic flavor to the facades.[7]

The expanding apparatus of state government soon outgrew the available space in the Milledgeville Capitol, and within twenty years the statehouse was cramped. A two-phase expansion added wings to the north and south and transformed the exterior into a more elaborate rendition of the Gothic Revival style. The exterior walls were raised, crenellated, and stuccoed with faux mortar joints. New granite terraces flanking the main entrance added outdoor gathering places. The finished basement contained the state archives, law library, supreme court, and other offices. The Gothic styling was an unusual choice for a statehouse, because with the recent completion of the U.S. Capitol, Greek Revival was in vogue.

Despite the improvements to its statehouse, Milledgeville's position as capital was soon challenged. The city's economy fluctuated, hampered by westward migration, the exhaustion of cotton land, and, especially, poor transportation. Steamboats could navigate the Oconee River only part of the year, and road transport was slow and expensive. Rumblings of relocation began in the late 1820s, when Milledgeville's decline had become evident and Macon, at the fall line of the Ocmulgee River, was suggested as the new capital.[8]

Real trouble began in 1847, as representatives of a young town to the northwest began to agitate for the capital. Atlanta was at the center of what was emerging as the dominant form of overland travel: the railroad. The young city had rail links to Augusta, Macon, and Savannah, offering easy passenger access year round. At first, no one took the challenge from Atlanta too seriously; Macon seemed the more serious threat. Even Atlantans laughed at the idea, but according to diarist William N. White, their chuckles turned into a "storm of cheers" when the idea was presented at large town meeting in December. With a population of less than 2,500 and about twenty business establishments, Atlanta had both the energy of its residents and its rail links to the rest of the state. That was enough to engage the Georgia General Assembly in debate for the better part of two days, but in the end, House members voted 68–55 against relocation.[9]

A few years later, the assertive little city, by now home to four thousand residents, began a more prolonged effort. By 1853, the issue seemed serious enough for Governor Cobb to ask the legislature to take "decisive action," for "the constant agitation of that question ha[d] paralyzed the energies of the people of Milledgeville, and crushed their spirit of enterprise." Milledgeville

Downtown Atlanta, 1856. When Atlanta made its second attempt for the capital in the mid-1850s, it was a town of about four thousand people and far bigger than Milledgeville. This 1856 photograph of a community gathering is set against the backdrop of the railroad, the key to the city's growth. (Courtesy of the Kenan Research Center at the Atlanta History Center)

Richard Peters, 1848. Atlanta civic booster Richard Peters arrived in Georgia in 1835, $100 in debt. Among his early real estate investments was a $225 lot southeast of the center of town that he sold to the city for $5,000, which eventually became the site of the Georgia State Capitol. Peters was involved in virtually every civic undertaking in Atlanta for over forty years, including the successful effort to relocate the capital. (Courtesy of the Kenan Research Center at the Atlanta History Center)

Milledgeville, c. 1858. Just a few years after a decisive vote affirming its status as state capital, Milledgeville appeared to be a tranquil river town in the midst of cotton country. The statehouse, seen on the right, still dominated the small city after more than fifty years of modest but irregular growth. The source of its fluctuating economy does not appear in this illustration: its limited rail connections. (Courtesy of Olin & Uris Libraries Reference Services, Cornell University Library)

supporters scrambled to fend off relocation, claiming that inaccessibility was no longer a problem, since a rail connection had opened in 1851, and that relocation would cost taxpayers $500,000.[10]

Early in 1855 Atlanta sent fifty lobbyists to Milledgeville. All fifty were influential white men, most of whom managed several businesses while filling civic leadership positions. Like their peers in other small cities and towns across Georgia, these men knew that Atlanta's prosperity would increase their own. Among them was Richard Peters, who would play a significant role in Atlanta's quest for the capital.

That winter the General Assembly bantered several relocation proposals and passed a bill calling for a general election in October 1855 in which Georgia voters would choose between Milledgeville, Macon, and Atlanta. The vote was decisive, with almost fifty thousand choosing Milledgeville, thirty thousand Atlanta, and four thousand Macon. Railroad connections had made Atlanta an attractive location, but not enough to make voters want to expend the funds to relocate state government. Since the issue appeared to be settled, the legislature allocated thirty thousand dollars to repair and rejuvenate the Milledgeville statehouse and governor's mansion.

During the Civil War, the state capital relocation issue faded. In 1864, General William T. Sherman focused on Atlanta as he severed the rail connections that linked the upper and the lower South and, in the process, reduced to rubble block after block of the city's commercial buildings along the railroad tracks. Left standing were a handful of larger buildings, including several churches and the City Hall / County Courthouse. Returning citizens first erected makeshift structures and then slowly replaced them with two- and three-story brick buildings. In a capital-starved economy, commercial investment money was slow in coming. Civic leaders began to dream of the boost to the local construction, banking, and service industries that would result from the relocation of the capital city and the construction of a new Capitol.

The first Reconstruction Georgia legislature convened in Milledgeville to comply with the demands of the federal government and, by the end of 1865, ratified the Thirteenth Amendment, which abolished slavery. However, the following year the General Assembly refused

to ratify the Fourteenth Amendment, which gave blacks U.S. citizenship and, instead, passed "black codes" that limited the freedom of African Americans. Congress responded with the Reconstruction Act of March 1867, which required states to pass the Fourteenth Amendment, giving black males the right to vote, and then elect a new state government, with newly enfranchised adult black males voting. The act also placed Georgia in a temporary military occupation district, headquartered in Atlanta under the command of General John Pope.[11]

Atlanta's civic leaders took advantage of Georgia's postwar Reconstruction chaos to maneuver the relocation of the second constitutional convention to their city. When General Pope arrived in Atlanta to oversee a second Reconstruction, he stepped off his train to encounter a delegation of local citizens, including Richard Peters, which welcomed him cordially and lobbied him on the advantages of their city. Before leaving to visit the other states under his command, Pope called for Georgia's constitutional convention to be held in Atlanta. The decision stunned Milledgeville leaders, but Pope preferred to place the convention near his military headquarters and in a location where there was at least one Republican newspaper, the *Daily New Era*. Lodging was also an issue. Neither city offered racially mixed lodging at that time, but because

Federal encampment on the grounds of the Atlanta City Hall / Fulton County Courthouse, 1864. One of the few large downtown buildings to escape destruction by Sherman's troops was the Atlanta City Hall / Fulton County Courthouse, located on the future site of the Georgia Capitol. Fresh from the success of the Atlanta Campaign, Union soldiers established camp on the south end of the block and constructed fortifications around the building in September 1864. (Courtesy of the Kenan Research Center at the Atlanta History Center)

Atlanta, c. 1865. Atlanta's Civil War damage was extensive, but the city rebuilt quickly. When the constitutional convention delegates arrived in 1867, they found a city under construction and eager to welcome them as well as any opportunities for further growth. The cupola of the City Hall / Fulton County Courthouse, used as a temporary capitol in 1868 and the future site of the State Capitol, appears in the left background. (Courtesy of the Kenan Research Center at the Atlanta History Center)

of its size and larger Republican population, Atlanta would have extended a warmer reception to black delegates.

When the constitutional convention convened in the Atlanta City Hall / Fulton County Courthouse in December 1867, a biracial group of delegates gathered for the first time in Georgia history. White Democrats referred contemptuously to their "piebald" (two-colored) convention, making every effort to create a hostile environment for Republican (and black) lawmakers. The 1868 constitution was an uneasy mix of reforms and limitations. For blacks recently freed from slavery, it offered new protections, such as the abolishment of whipping for crimes, and new rights, such as a publicly supported education. However, the new constitution also retained the poll tax and, because it was clear that the right to vote carried with it the right to hold office, omitted a specific reference to the right of blacks to hold public office.

Meanwhile, Atlanta leaders got to work selling their city. The *Daily New Era* dismissed Milledgeville as "out-of-the-way" and its statehouse as "old and dilapidated" (despite its refurbishment six months earlier) while promising legislators that Atlanta offered a healthier environment as well as less wholesome diversions: "fresh, pure air and good water up here, and if they want the water

*Atlanta City Hall / Fulton County Courthouse,
c. 1870.* When the members of Georgia's biracial
constitutional convention met in Atlanta in late
1867, the Atlanta City Hall / Fulton County
Courthouse was the only building large enough
to accommodate them. A few months later,
the structure served as the location of the
1868 legislative session, the first in the state's
new capital, Atlanta. (Courtesy of the Kenan
Research Center at the Atlanta History Center)

mixed, we'll let them." However, Atlanta's main advantage was its location: "[W]hile it is not strictly a geographical center, it is, what is more important, *the* railroad center." Atlanta's initial proposal, along with an offer to use the City Hall / County Courthouse building for five years, came before the delegates on February 26, 1868. That night the city council unanimously agreed to a more attractive proposal, drafted by Richard Peters, which offered up to ten years of free meeting space as well as either the city's twenty-five-acre fair grounds or ten unoccupied acres. The convention delegates ignored a last-minute bid from Macon and named Atlanta as the state capital in the new constitution. The grateful city council promised, "[We will] spare no pains, in an honest and earnest effort, to fully comply with all the pledges we have made to you today." African American delegates were delighted and celebrated that evening with a "grand soiree and supper."[12]

Atlanta would be capital, however, only if the voters approved the new constitution. For Atlantans, the critical issue

was capital relocation. When the votes were counted in April 1868, the constitution had been ratified, Republican Rufus Bullock was the governor, Atlanta was the capital, and a biracial General Assembly would meet there in ten weeks.

Richard Peters, chair of the city's Committee on Capitol Removal, quickly refitted the City Hall / County Courthouse building into a temporary meeting space. Peters focused on interior alterations, enlarging two main meeting rooms into House and Senate chambers. Contracts were not finalized until late May, just five weeks before the legislative session. In mid-June, the *Daily New Era* reported with relief that work was underway and opined that the City Hall / County Courthouse "present[ed] quite as attractive an appearance as the old halls at Milledgeville."[13]

One of the citizens who had worked hardest for relocation was Hannibal I. Kimball. A native of Maine, Kimball had arrived in Atlanta in 1866 and soon threw himself into the relocation effort. With ratification, Kimball found an entrepre-

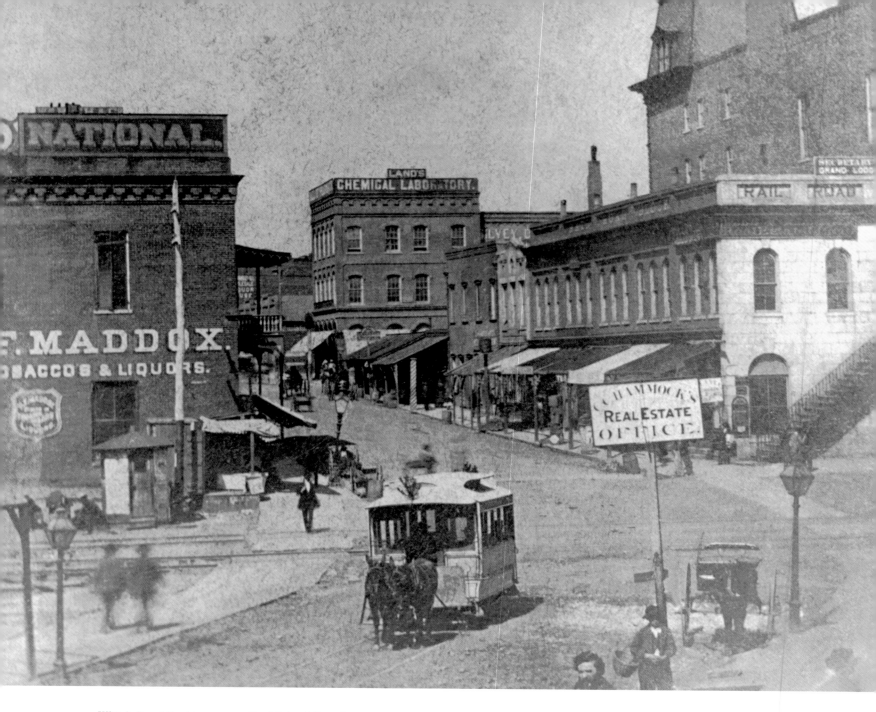

Whitehall and Peachtree streets, 1872. Richard Peters's business dealings were numerous and varied. He bought a stagecoach company in the 1840s and built Atlanta's first mass-transit system in the 1870s. His antebellum flour mill was the largest in the city, and after the war, he owned or had interests in a telegraph company, several railroads, and the Kimball House Hotel. This 1872 view of Whitehall Street includes one of Peters's horse-drawn streetcars (foreground) and his Railroad Block building (first building on the right). (Courtesy of the Kenan Research Center at the Atlanta History Center)

neurial opportunity at the corner of Marietta and Forsyth streets. There stood the shell of the Atlanta Opera House, a five-story commercial building begun in 1867 as a harbinger of the city's postwar recovery but abandoned when its owners had run out of funds. Originally intended to provide grand assembly space for performances and civic gatherings, the roofless structure was still the largest building in town. Kimball knew that the legislature would soon demand more spacious quarters and that he had the connections to influence their selection. His brother Edwin bought the Atlanta Opera House on June 2, 1868, for $31,750, and Hannibal began to campaign to have it refinished as the new Capitol. He faced little opposition, for the only other viable option, to enlarge the City Hall / County Courthouse, would displace city and county government.

Meanwhile, the 1868 General Assembly was about to convene. A train arrived from Milledgeville, its sixteen cars full of statehouse furniture and furnishings. The legislators arrived soon afterward. Assisted by the moderating influence of federal troops and a congressional mandate for open and fair elections, black voters across the state had helped to elect a number of Republican legislators and a governor—Rufus Bullock. Several legislators were African American: 3 of 44 senators and 29 of 175 representatives, including Bishop Henry McNeal Turner and Tunis Campbell. These two prominent leaders hoped that black representatives would be able to work with the governor and their moderate white colleagues in the Republican Party to weld together a coalition that could shape a new political order in post–Civil War Georgia.[14]

The first order of business introduced the Fourteenth Amendment, which former Confederate states were required to ratify to be readmitted to the Union. A biracial majority in each house duly voted for ratification. Having fulfilled the minimal federal requirement, white legislators went on the offensive and claimed that their African American colleagues did not have the right to hold public office. Ironically, many of the protesting legislators did not themselves have the right to hold office because they had qualified as candidates by falsely swearing that they had not held office prior to the war or taken part in the rebellion. Skirting federal law and their new state constitution, these legislators introduced bills that voided the election of black Republican representatives and replaced them with white Democratic runners-up. On September 3, 1868, the House voted to cast out twenty-six of its twenty-nine African American representatives "because of the condition of their race"; the Senate followed suit on September 12, when it voted to cast out two of its three African American members. (The four African American legislators who were not expelled were sufficiently light skinned that their opponents could not prove they were black.)[15]

The ejected legislators did not go silently. Senator Campbell called the action of his colleagues "illegal, unconstitutional, unjust, and oppressive." House representative Turner observed: "It is very strange, if a white man can occupy on this floor a seat created by colored votes, and a black man cannot do it." Governor Bullock spoke out on their behalf, saying that the constitutional

Hannibal Kimball, c. 1875. Corrupt carpetbagger or energetic city promoter? Historians disagree about H. I. Kimball, a flamboyant entrepreneur who arrived in Atlanta in 1866 and speculated in real estate and railroads. The owner of the Opera House Capitol used his influence with Republican Governor Rufus Bullock to persuade the legislature to lease the building for twenty years, despite shaky financing and structural problems. (Courtesy of the Kenan Research Center at the Atlanta History Center)

Senator Tunis Campbell, c. 1848. The 1868 General Assembly was Georgia's first biracial legislature, but only briefly. After ratifying the Fourteenth Amendment, which extended citizenship to African Americans and allowed Georgia to be readmitted to the Union, the legislators voted to expel the elected black representatives and senators. Senator Tunis Campbell and Representative Henry McNeal Turner left with angry words and dashed hopes for a new political order in Georgia. (Courtesy of the Moorland-Spingarn Research Center, Howard University)

convention had voted overwhelmingly to defeat a motion that only white men could hold office and that "since the framers of the Constitution made no distinction between electors, or citizens, on account of race or color . . . neither [could they] without violating it."[16]

The newly constituted majority in the legislature moved on to other issues. They thought that their Atlanta statehouse was shabby, even after its recent remodeling. The *Atlanta Constitution* ceased its glowing accounts of the City-Hall-as-statehouse and began to advocate for a twenty- to twenty-five-year lease on a completed Kimball Opera House. Faced with a choice between Kimball's ample building and an enlarged City Hall / County Courthouse, the legislature asked the city to finalize the arrangements for the Opera House Capitol. Council member Richard Peters handled the negotiations, and in late August the city signed a lease for six thousand dollars a year for five years. Kimball's building would be ready by the beginning of the legislative session the following January.[17]

With a ratified constitution naming Atlanta as the state capital and a signed five-year lease, Atlanta supporters were elated with the 1868 legislative session. Unhappy Milledgeville supporters continued to fight for their Capitol. For African American delegates, however, the session had been catastrophic; they had lost most of their representation in state government.

Transforming the Opera House into a capitol was difficult, especially when the parties involved disagreed over who would pay to outfit the building with lighting, plumbing, heating, furnishings, and decorative finishing. As finances grew shaky and tempers flared, Governor Bullock intervened and advanced $54,500 in emergency state funds. Kimball worked furiously and spent lavishly, completing most of the work by the opening reception on the night of Tuesday, January 12, 1869.

Thanks to the expulsion of its African American representatives the previous fall, the 1869 General Assembly presented a powerful voice of opposition to the Republican administration. The new legislature contained far fewer Republicans and only four black representatives. Its Democratic majority was hell-bent on thwarting any action taken by Governor Bullock, whose political support was based on African American votes. The conflict was apparent in the local press coverage of the first days in the new Capitol. The Republican *Daily New Era* had only superlatives for the new statehouse, while the Democratic *Atlanta Constitution* reported every operational glitch. Eventually, the *Constitution* succeeded in making the Opera House Capitol into a symbol of Republican corruption.

After the genteel opening-night reception, the 1869 General Assembly settled into its posh new surroundings, but the atmosphere in the chambers was tumultuous. While the white legislative majority sought to restrict further black political participation, Governor Bullock, supported by the efforts of Tunis Campbell and other African Americans, countered by traveling to Washington, where he lobbied Congress tirelessly throughout 1869 to reinstate the expelled

Portrait of Henry McNeal Turner, third floor.
Henry McNeal Turner and his colleagues
returned to the General Assembly in 1870,
reinstated by the U.S. Congress. However,
a fraudulent election later that year
deprived Turner of his seat. The numbers
of blacks in the Georgia legislature
declined dramatically in the 1870s as white
intimidation kept blacks from the polls.
A little over a century after his expulsion,
Turner became a permanent presence
in the Capitol with the hanging of this
portrait. (Courtesy of Diane Kirkland and
the Georgia Department of Economic
Development)

black legislators and eject their white Democratic replacements.
His efforts paid off; in December 1869 Congress reinstated
military rule in Georgia and authorized Bullock to recall a
session of those elected to serve in the 1868 legislature.[18]

The General Assembly that convened on January 10, 1870, in
the Opera House Capitol was the high point for biracial legislation in Georgia for almost one hundred years. The opening
session provided high drama, as heightened emotions caused
routine legislative debates and vote taking to turn violent. The
tense day began with the halls and galleries filling early with African American
spectators eager to witness the restoration of the black legislators. The sight
of black lawmakers and spectators incensed many whites, and the local white
press mirrored and magnified these feelings with condescending references
and unsupported accusations. The Republican president of the Senate made an
impassioned speech condemning those who opposed the national government
and supported instead "prowling bands of assassins."[19]

The opening session in the House turned into a fracas that revealed the
deepening split in the Republican Party between those who supported African American rights and those who were more concerned with cultivating
white support. Two men, each representing a Republican faction, confronted
each other during the organizational votes to select session leaders. When the
sergeant at arms tried to eject a member, the two drew pistols while spectators
cheered and shouted. Republicans struggled over the possession of the speaker's

Governor Rufus Bullock, c. 1870. Republican
Governor Rufus Bullock opposed the
expulsion of the elected black representatives
from the Georgia legislature in 1868. He
successfully petitioned the U.S. Congress to
require a third Reconstruction in Georgia,
which would reinstate the twenty-eight
expelled legislators. Consequently, Bullock
was pilloried by his Democratic opponents,
who used the unpopularity of the Kimball
Opera House Capitol to further tarnish
his reputation. (Courtesy of the Georgia
Archives, Small Print Collection, spc17-033)

stand, with one group blocking access to the podium. The session officially ended when one of the spurned members climbed onto a chair and moved to adjourn. The gallery was closed for over two weeks until the black-supported candidate won the speaker's chair.

With similar Republican leadership now in command of both chambers, the General Assembly reinstated the expelled African American legislators and removed the fraudulent replacement legislators. The legislature ratified the Fifteenth Amendment, which protected African Americans' right to vote, and reratified the Fourteenth Amendment (since the previous ratification was fraudulent). To ensure the continued political support of black citizens, the Republican legislature declared the poll tax illegal and halted its collection.

The achievements of the 1870 Georgia General Assembly were short lived. African American citizens had little time to influence legislative affairs before Democrats regained ascendancy. During the next election held in December 1870, "Klansmen, 'military companies,' and posses organized by county sheriffs, dominated the elections" and suppressed the black vote. Along with voter intimidation, elected black officials were constantly harassed. Historian Edmund Drago's survey of black elected officials in postwar Georgia shows that more than one-fourth were "threatened, bribed, beaten, jailed, or killed."[20]

In the next three elections, Georgia lost virtually all of its African American representatives as the number of elected black representatives fell from thirty-two in 1870, to thirteen in 1871, to eight in 1874, to one in 1876. This rapid decline happened despite federal oversight. Federal officials were not allowed to intervene at the local level, where county officials manipulated polling hours and conditions, nor did they try to prevent the Georgia General Assembly from assisting local efforts to disfranchise blacks. This interplay of state and local legal machinations, coupled with intimidation and violence, created a complex but effective system of disfranchisement. With fewer African Americans voting, Republicans could not afford to alienate their white support. Caught between their party's founding principles and their own political futures, many white Republicans abandoned their party or worked with the Democrats to further disfranchise black voters.[21]

In response to the short-lived Republican ascendancy, Democrats looked for any issue to discredit Governor Bullock and others who supported African American rights. The Opera

House Capitol made an ideal target, for both its financing difficulties and its ongoing maintenance and structural problems. Claiming financial irregularities, the Democratic-dominated legislature refused payment of Bullock's $54,500 advance to Kimball. The administration's opponents accused Kimball of shoddy workmanship and Bullock of corruption and charged the city of Atlanta with a lack of good faith. Eventually, the city offered the state $100,000 in March 1869 to cover the annual rent and the controversial advance, while still insisting that it had never intended to furnish, heat, or light the building. Kimball offered the structure to the state for $380,000 and volunteered to return the $54,500. In August 1870, the legislature accepted his price, based on an optimistic estimate that the building was worth $395,000 and would produce a $15,000–20,000 yearly rental income. The city would pay $130,000 and the state $250,000.[22]

The ink was barely dry when the legislators discovered that Kimball had not paid off a $60,000 mortgage, leaving the state to contend with the encumbrance. Enraged legislators began new investigations of the building's financing and state of repair. Condition reports came back generally positive, despite plaster cracks, bowing walls, and defects in the roof and tower. This did little to appease legislators, many of whom detested the building and had transformed it into a symbol of Republican dishonesty. City leaders, caught in the middle of this struggle and worried about the continued viability of the city as capital, agreed to take over Kimball's mortgage and to forgive the state's portion of the debt as long as the Capitol remained in Atlanta.

In the end, the Opera House made a poor statehouse. Georgia needed a custom-built capitol as well as a vote to settle the relocation issue permanently. In 1877, after the federal government withdrew its troops and ceded to the southern states the right to control their political processes, the Georgia legislature called for a convention to prepare a new state constitution. The convention convened in Atlanta on July 11, and its all-white delegation drafted a document friendlier to their interests. A

OPPOSITE PAGE *Kimball Opera House, 1878.* Georgia Democrats were on the attack from the start of the 1869 legislative session in the new Opera House Capitol. They used the building to symbolize alleged Republican corruption by exaggerating the problems with its financing and structural stability. (Courtesy of the Georgia Archives, Vanishing Georgia Collection, ful0649)

Bird's-eye view of Atlanta (portion), 1871. This portion of an 1871 sketch of Atlanta is centered on the railroad passenger station (MIDDLE CIRCLE). Three blocks to the south stands the Atlanta City Hall / Fulton County Courthouse (BOTTOM CIRCLE), where the 1868 state legislature met and where the Georgia State Capitol would be built in 1884–89. Four blocks to the west, the Opera House Capitol (TOP CIRCLE) stands on Marietta Street. (Courtesy of the Library of Congress)

key component was the county-unit system, which elected representatives to the state House of Representatives disproportionate to population. The 6 most populous counties were allowed three representatives each, the next 26 had two each, and the remaining 105 counties each were allotted one. The system assured white and rural dominance by giving disproportionate representation to small counties. Over time, the county-unit system would be extended and modified so that "unit votes" would be used to elect state senators and Georgia's U.S. congressmen.[23]

The issue of capital relocation surfaced two days into the convention. To counter other cities' relocation proposals, Atlanta offered the lot where the Atlanta City Hall / Fulton County Courthouse stood and sweetened the deal by adding what the *Atlanta Constitution* called "this magnificent present": "a Capitol Building as good as the old Capitol building in Milledgeville." This carefully worded promise suggested that the citizens of Atlanta would pay for the construction of a new statehouse, but their actual obligation was only for the assessed value of the abandoned building in Milledgeville.[24]

The main challenge to Atlanta's boosters was the very building in which the constitutional delegates were convened, the Opera House Capitol. Adding to the financing fiasco was the increasing urgency of the eight-year-old building's structural problems. An impending ceiling failure hovered over the Speaker's stand in the House chamber. The roof swayed under the weight of the state library, and the west wall bulged where a section of the foundation had failed. Shifting and settling had caused windows to jam, doors to drag, and plaster to fall in both chambers.[25]

For many legislators, the Opera House Capitol represented all that was wrong with Atlanta as well as the Republican Party; it became the basis of their argument that the city could not be trusted. The more sympathetic relocation committee concluded that although the state had been wronged, the city was not to blame. However, the minority report requested that the location issue be put to the voters separately, arguing that Atlanta's claim was too controversial to be left in the constitution and could cause its defeat. The convention delegates agreed and put relocation into a constitutional amendment, so that on December 5 voters could decide separately but simultaneously about the constitution and the capital location.

Preventing a return to Milledgeville looked like an uphill battle to Atlanta's leaders, who faced a difficult choice. If they attacked the new antibusiness, antiurban constitution, they might repel the critical rural votes they needed for the relocation. Atlanta boosters chose the Capitol. The relocation campaign was lively and heated, a nineteenth-century media blitz that eventually involved almost every newspaper in the state. Speakers stumped all over Georgia, but most of the discussion took place in the newspapers of the state's largest cities.

Despite an intense effort by both cities, Atlanta won a conclusive victory, winning the election with a majority of almost 44,000. Rival newspapers initially responded with critical comments about the result. The *Savannah Morning News* blamed everything from the weather to "the money so lavishly expended [by Atlanta] upon negro [*sic*] preachers and leaders in the 'black belt.'" The *Columbus Daily Enquirer Sun* warned that the state would end up footing the bill. However, competitor cities soon shifted gears and began to make conciliatory gestures. The Savannah paper pleaded, "[N]ow let us have peace." The *Macon Telegraph & Messenger* was "willing now to let by gones be by gones [*sic*]" and instead was "proud of [Atlanta's] progress and grandeur."[26]

Atlanta's civic leaders had some making up to do, too. The new constitution had been ratified, but not in Atlanta. Two days after the vote, the *Atlanta Constitution* emphasized that the contest had been closer than expected and blamed black voters for providing the critical votes that had swung support away from the constitution. Apparently while voting for the capital, African American Atlantans had also voted against a governmental blueprint that would further reduce their political influence.

Atlanta had won the capital but still lacked a capitol. It would take six years of increasingly tense negotiations to get construction underway. In August 1879, the General Assembly accepted Atlanta's offer of the City Hall / County Courthouse site, but instead of a monetary contribution, the state wanted the city to provide a 50 percent larger lot and wider streets and sidewalks. When the surrounding property owners refused to sell, the city again offered the state the lot as originally proposed, plus the cash value of the Milledgeville Capitol.

The state and city squabbled over the value of the Milledgeville statehouse for months before agreeing to arbitration and settling on a figure of $55,625. At this time, a statehouse typically cost at least $1 million, and usually much more; the free land and $55,625 were but a fraction of the actual cost. Fulton County representative Frank Rice agreed to make capitol funding his top priority for the upcoming session.

Rice introduced the Act to Provide for the Erection of a State Capitol Building, commonly called the Capitol Act, on November 3, 1882. The act called for a $1 million appropriation, an amount that represented two-thirds of the 1883 state revenue. Realizing they had been hoodwinked but that a new capitol was an urgent necessity, the legislators received Rice's

Frank P. Rice, c. 1885. Frank P. Rice led the effort to get the new statehouse financed and built. He served on the Atlanta City Council for most of the 1870s and was elected to the Georgia House of Representatives in 1882, where he introduced the Capitol Act of 1883. A shrewd businessman as well as an experienced politician, Rice knew how to minimize opposition to the erection of a monumental statehouse in Atlanta. (Reprinted from Walter Cooper, *Official History of Fulton County* [Spartanburg, S.C.: Reprint Co., 1978], 316)

bill with great amusement, but Rice fought for the bill every step of the way, meeting with every member of the General Assembly, appearing before committees, and giving impassioned speeches from the House floor. After tacking on several amendments, the House approved the bill on August 15, 1883. As he told the *Atlanta Constitution*, Rice maneuvered the vote carefully: "I knew exactly how many votes I had every day and I knew the day I got over the notch. Then I had the bill made the special order for a certain date. When that day came I checked my men as the clerk called the roll, and saw that I did not have the majority present. . . . I changed the date, I don't know how many times, but finally I got a majority of my men present. . . . The vote was 93 yeas, 58 nays and 24 not voting."[27] After volleying several amendments back and forth, the two legislative houses came to an agreement, and the Capi-

Detail of corner and dome. The 1883 Capitol Act required a statehouse plan that would accommodate all three branches of government comfortably. The act did not specify an architectural style, leaving that choice to the Board of Capitol Commissioners. Their preference would be a classical design reminiscent of the U.S. Capitol. (Courtesy of Diane Kirkland and the Georgia Department of Economic Development)

tol Act was signed into law by Governor Henry McDaniel on September 8, 1883.

Chafing under their cramped conditions in the Opera House Capitol, the Georgia General Assembly approved a new statehouse that would give them commodious quarters and also be large enough to house all of the functions and offices of state government. For the legislative branch, the act specified that it "shall contain a Senate Chamber and a Hall for the House of Representatives, with all the additional rooms necessary and proper for the full and comfortable accommodation of the Legislative branch of the Government; a sufficient number of committee rooms for the House and Senate." For the governor, there should be "an Executive office, with all the additional rooms necessary for the full and comfortable accommodation of all the various offices of the Executive Department." The judicial branch would have "a Supreme Court room, with all rooms in addition thereto, necessary for the proper accommodation of the Judges and officers of said court, and for the proper accommodation and security of the files and records of the same." The act also provided for other constitutional officers and functions, including the secretary of state, comptroller general, attorney general,

the Department of Agriculture, the Department of Education, the state library, and "the Treasurer and his assistants." Finally, the building was to be sufficiently substantial to provide "for the full and complete protection against burglaries and fire of the treasure, archives, library, records and files of the State."[28]

The Capitol Act provided for a great public building, but it also reflected the desire of a distrustful General Assembly to regulate the finances of the project as tightly as possible without getting involved in construction details. Twice the act stressed that the total expenditure could not exceed $1 million, a stipulation that was heeded carefully. The act also warned that the money could not come from any tax increase, a reassurance that was ignored later. No money would be released until Atlanta paid the promised $55,625. All construction decisions, from design to final payments, would be made by the Board of Capitol Commissioners, whose five members were appointed by its ex officio chairman, the governor.

Anticipating the commencement of a monumental public-works project, Atlanta supporters celebrated. The efforts of the fast-growing railroad terminus had paid off handsomely. Reconstruction politics had brought them the capital and the Opera House Capitol. Atlantans paid for relocation by accepting the 1877 constitution, which established the county-unit system that would ensure rural domination of state government for the next eighty-five years. After years of political strife, the persistent city boosters had $1 million to pump into the local economy that would create an architectural landmark of unchallenged significance for the state. The controversial converted Opera House would soon be abandoned for a custom-built capitol.

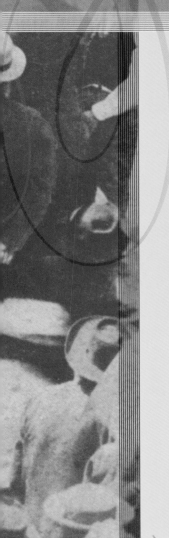

3

A BUDGET
CAPITOL

With the walls of the new statehouse rising from a sea of stone, it was

time for the first great public event at the Georgia State Capitol. Many

more ceremonies would follow, each adding another layer of meaning to

a structure intended to symbolize the state's democratic governance. On

this hot late-summer day, September 2, 1885, citizens gathered early to see

the laying of the Capitol's cornerstone in what promised to be a historic

event. Three hours before the rite was scheduled to begin, only a few guests

were able to find a spare chair under the huge canvas tent erected near the

northeast corner of the foundation. Most of the seating was reserved for

the dignitaries who were assembling at the Opera House Capitol six blocks

away for the first dedicatory march to the new statehouse site. A second,

similar procession would commence three and a half years later when the

completed State Capitol was ready for legislative occupancy.[1]

As the temperature rose, most of the spectators scrambled for shade or investigated the building site. They wandered around nine-foot-high granite foundation walls, eight feet thick at the base in order to bear the building's heavy load. They watched the impressive machinery, operating amid limestone-finishing sheds, railroad tracks and ramps, derricks, and stockpiles of granite and limestone.

A few blocks to the northwest, politicians, dignitaries, and members of various civic organizations were getting ready to march. Over twelve hundred Freemasons, easily recognized in their regulation white aprons and gloves, had come to witness the dedication ceremony that would be presided over by their leader, Grand Master (and state senator) John S. Davidson. Several hundred state legislators and dignitaries looked for their places in line, while mounted marshals got everyone organized. Promptly at 10:00 a.m., the Marietta Silver Cornet Band struck up, and the procession began to move along streets lined with cheering onlookers.

The expectant crowd at the new Capitol site had grown to at least six thousand. Boys and men climbed up into nearby trees for a better view and shade. Spectators gathered on surrounding rooftops, grateful for their position above the sweating throng. A huge barrel mounted on a cart displayed a banner that read "The Good Templar's Cup of Cold Water, Free to Everybody," and many accepted a cup of temporary relief.

Finally the heads of the first riders of the governor's horse guard appeared. The mounted column halted and opened its ranks to allow the marchers passage to the cornerstone area. When all the marchers were in their places, a one-hundred-voice choir rose and opened the ceremony with "My Country 'Tis of Thee." Governor Henry McDaniel, who also served as the chair of the Board of Capitol Commissioners, welcomed the crowd in a characteristically businesslike speech. The task of constructing a symbolic meaning for the civic landmark was given to keynote speaker Alexander R. Lawton of Savannah, a Confederate brigadier general who had been quartermaster general during the Civil War. After the war, Lawton had worked with John B. Gordon to organize the state's Ku Klux Klan, had served several terms in the Georgia legislature, and in 1882, had been elected president of the American Bar Association. Now a nationally recognized figure of regional reconciliation, Lawton used his address to construct a heroic version of the recent, successful power struggle by Democrats to gain political ascendancy in Georgia and to memorialize the building as a symbol of their victory.[2]

Lawton described Georgia's rapid growth in population and property and marveled at the technological advances of the first eighty years of the nineteenth century. He characterized the Civil War as a misunderstanding in which the North enjoyed all the economic advantage and slavery was "an important fac-

A. R. Lawton, c. 1885. The eloquent rhetoric of Alexander R. Lawton captured the jubilant mood the day of the cornerstone ceremonies with his proclamation: "On this spot may 'high passions, high desires unfold, prompting to noblest deed.' Then will it be no flippant boast that Georgia is indeed the Empire State of the South." (Courtesy of the Georgia Historical Society)

Cornerstone ceremonies, September 2, 1885. At least six thousand Georgians, many with raised umbrellas, waited under the hot midday sun in the midst of rising walls and construction equipment on September 2, 1885, to witness the laying of the Capitol cornerstone. In the center of the photo, a chain from a derrick holds a suspended piece of marble as it is lowered into place in the Capitol wall. (Courtesy of the Kenan Research Center at the Atlanta History Center)

tor and irritating cause." Reconstruction was a period when an "arrogant and angry power" took advantage of "helplessness and desperation." Now the "proper partition" between federal and state had been restored, and "all of [Georgia's] most important affairs [were] being controlled by state authority." Finally free of federal interference, white Georgians were "as loyal to that great government as any portion of the union, since [they were] no longer called upon to surrender [their] self-respect, nor to do violence to [their] most sacred sensibilities, in making that claim."[3]

This was the message that Georgia governors, legislators, and newspaper editors had championed for several years: a "New South" was rising from the ashes of the Old South of slavery. New South leaders proclaimed that, with the help of northern capital, their region would advance into peaceful prosperity through economic and industrial development. However, the tricky issue of race remained. Even as they looked north for financial assistance, New South leaders insisted on autonomy in working out the relationship between black and white citizens in the southern states, where over 90 percent of the country's African Americans lived. Now, in Georgia, Democrats, who were in complete control of state and local politics, claimed that they would take care of African Americans, whom they had disfranchised. Northern audiences, eager to make lucrative investments and to be freed of the difficult postwar task of policing the South, were receptive.

To achieve their goals, New South proponents had to construct a view of the recent past that allowed for reconciliation of the two regions without federal interference in the political affairs of the southern states. Lawton did this well, embracing nationalism by focusing on the soldiers' courage and citizens'

sacrifice during the war while lauding the "proper partition." He concluded by holding up the Capitol as a symbol of the New South, saying, "On this spot may 'high passions, high desires unfold, prompting to noblest deed.' Then will it be no flippant boast that Georgia is indeed the Empire State of the South."[4]

After a hymn ("When Earth's Foundation First Was Laid"), the ceremony was turned over to the Freemasons. The nondenominational, religious organization had been performing cornerstone ceremonies for public buildings for centuries. Tracing their roots to medieval stonemason guilds, Freemasons began accepting nonoperative members in the early seventeenth century and broadened their activities to include community service. They came to the United States, and Georgia, in the 1730s, and in 1793, U.S. president and Freemason George Washington officiated at the laying of the national Capitol's cornerstone.

Like many cornerstones, the Georgia State Capitol's was hollow. A copper box was placed in the eighteen-by-twelve-inch cavity, filled with items selected to represent the issues and events of the day. Most were documents, such as lists of elected state officials, copies of newspapers, and the Georgia Code for 1882. Among the other items were a Bible, a bottle of Indian Springs water, Confederate bills, and a photograph of a local baseball player. A crane lowered the massive piece of Georgia marble into the Capitol's northeast corner, the location favored by the Freemasons because it symbolized the passage from ignorance (the north represented darkness) to knowledge (the east represented light). The ceremony followed the Freemason's prescribed procedure exactly. Grand Master Davidson tested the stone and consecrated it before announcing the completion of the ceremony. After the benediction and a final hymn ("Now Our Festive Joys Are Over"), the crowd dispersed slowly as many spectators lingered to look over the construction site.

The ceremony received thorough coverage from most newspapers, bringing Lawton's New South message to all parts of the state. This delighted supporters of the new Capitol and its capital city, among them probusiness

Capitol cornerstone. The hollow marble stone placed in the northeast limestone wall of the Capitol bears a carving of the state seal. Inside the cornerstone is a metal time capsule containing documents and objects that commemorate the state and its new capitol. (Courtesy of Diane Kirkland and the Georgia Department of Economic Development)

Atlantans such as Henry Grady. As an orator and editor of the *Atlanta Constitution*, Grady was the most visible spokesman for the New South campaign and a key force in Georgia politics in the 1880s. Henry Grady's virtual handprints were all over the Capitol's cornerstone. In 1883, he had lobbied hard for Henry McDaniel's appointment to fill the unexpired term of Governor Alexander Stephens, who had died while still in office.

McDaniel's first significant acts as governor had been to sign the Capitol Act into law and appoint the five members of the Board of Capitol Commissioners, who were charged by the act to oversee the design and construction. After signing the act midday on September 8, the governor left for lunch and upon his return promptly announced his appointments. None of McDaniel's appointees had applied for the job and most had not even been recommended to him, but the governor's choices were not surprising. The group consisted of General Edmund Porter Alexander of Augusta, Major Benjamin E. Crane of Atlanta, General Phillip Cook of Americus, A. L. Miller of Houston County, and W. W. Thomas of Athens. All five were white male Democrats, and most were Civil War veterans and lawyers with political experience; one, W. W. Thomas, was an architect. Several had served on finance committees; several had ties to railroads and cotton mills. Representatives from Macon and Milledgeville were noticeably absent. Collectively the group had influence, experience, and political acumen. To assist the work of the commission, the governor appointed a clerk, "Tip" Harrison, to execute its decisions and to record minutes.

Grady's *Atlanta Constitution* opined that there was a "general impression" that the $1 million budget was "simply a starter and that the amount would be increased after the work was begun." Such speculation was not unfounded. A capitol was far more than a building housing the state government, and the commissioners envisioned a public monument that would announce to the world that Georgia (and particularly Atlanta) was poised to become a national leader. Other states spent far more for their capitols, and most went well over their budgets. The choice seemed clear: either spend more to build a capitol that would exceed expectations or build a budget capitol.[5]

However, in 1883 Georgia there was no choice, for the $1 million appropriation was already more than the state had to spend. Just after the General Assembly passed the Capitol Act, Georgia's fiscal year ended with revenues of $1.3 million and disbursements totaling almost $1.5 million. This lowered the preexisting state surplus from almost $700,000 to a little over $500,000, obviously not enough to pay for the Capitol.

YMCA building, Atlanta, Edbrooke and Burnham, 1890. Edbrooke and Burnham's classical design for the Georgia Capitol won them a prestigious commission, but it was not typical of their work. During their eighteen-year partnership, the architects usually produced High Victorian designs such as this structure, which once stood in downtown Atlanta. (Courtesy of the Kenan Research Center at the Atlanta History Center)

Whatever their vision, the commissioners knew they had to stick to their budget.

The great public building envisioned in the Capitol Act had to be large enough to house all the functions and offices of state government. To translate this agenda into a monument in stone, the Capitol Commission's first task was to select an architect whose design would inspire respect and confidence. The Capitol Act recommended a contest, so in October the commissioners sent notices to the major Georgia newspapers and the *American Architect and Building News*, asking for detailed building proposals that would include facade elevations, floor plans, perspective drawings, bidding specifications, and cost estimates.

Arriving at their January 16, 1884, meeting, the commissioners entered a room full of drawings and anxious architects, but not as many as they had hoped. According to the *Atlanta Constitution*, the Capitol commissioners began the selection process "in fine spirits," but their attitudes soon deteriorated when they saw what a million dollars would buy. Reportedly one commissioner felt that none of the plans was adequate "nor equal the dignity of the state" and that they should return to the General Assembly and request a larger appropriation. Of the ten submissions, just three were from Georgia. A proposal to design the largest building in the state required great staff expertise and time, and the chance of winning the competition was not high.[6]

After several frustrating days sorting out proposals that they deemed viable, the Capitol commissioners voted to bring in an outside expert to advise them on the final selection. They hired notable New York architect George Post to come to Atlanta to review the entries. By the time Post arrived on February 7, the commissioners had made enough progress to limit his review to three designs, only one of which was by a Georgia firm. Post's preference for classical style over High Victorian was clear in his report and doomed the plans of local favorites Humphries and Norrman. Post dismissed their design as "very picturesque," a term he used to express disapproval. He praised the elaborate, classically inspired plan of E. E. Myers, but found it too complex and costly. His favored entry, Edbrooke and Burnham's, was "more academic . . . [and] dignified, and more simple and elegant in detail than that of Myers: less picturesque but more monumental than that of Humphries and Norrman."[7]

Post provided the Capitol commissioners with an expert opinion that allowed them to select unanimously the out-of-state team of Edbrooke and Burnham. The winning design offered the right combination of low cost and high style. That style had to be "classical," by which the commissioners meant any rendition of Greek, Roman, Renaissance, or even Baroque Revival styles. Classicism offered several advantages over other styles of the time. First, it was "best suited, by reason of its imposing effect, to a building of a character so monumental as a State Capitol." The commissioners wanted plenty of bang for their buck. Second, the commissioners considered classical to be a traditional style immune to changing tastes, "more certain to meet the demands of a constantly progressive public criticism" than more modern styles. They wanted to avoid fads. Finally, the commissioners looked to Washington for inspiration and selected a classically inspired design with a central dome that emulated the national Capitol. Their choice was intended to symbolize the state's unity with the nation and its shared democratic traditions.[8]

The new Capitol may have been dressed in the latest style of classicism, but its body was Victorian. The building had a strong vertical thrust, a Victorian characteristic found especially in its defining element, the elongated dome. Most of the interior details were Victorian, in both form and material. However, the new Capitol was still noteworthy compared to what was typically being built

Georgia State Capitol, Hughson Hawley, 1886. Working from Edbrooke and Burnham's original drawing, renowned architectural renderer Hughson Hawley created this tinted sketch. According to the *American Architect and Building News* in 1893, the new Georgia State Capitol spoke "eloquently of a State rising, by her own efforts, from the impoverished conditions in which a most devastating war had left her, to a level with her more fortunate sisters." This was exactly the message that Georgia's leaders, especially those in Atlanta, wanted the architecture of the statehouse to send. (Courtesy of Edwin L. Jackson, Carl Vinson Institute of Government, University of Georgia)

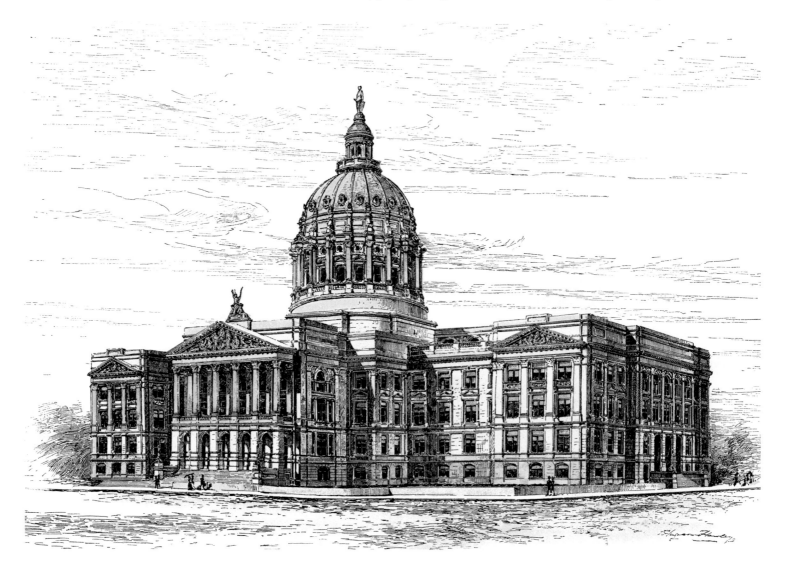

in Georgia in the 1880s, where picturesque, irregular designs predominated in institutional buildings.

As the local newspapers trumpeted the winning design, the commissioners finalized Edbrooke and Burnham's contract. The architects would receive five thousand dollars for the detailed plans, plus four thousand dollars per year to supervise construction. This amounted to about 3 percent of the construction cost, half of the current standard architectural fee. A local superintendent would oversee the work on site, but the architects were responsible for providing estimates, settling any cost differences, and giving final approval on both materials and work. Reconciling cost differences would prove to be the most difficult task.

Franklin P. Burnham, c. 1892, ABOVE, and Willoughby J. Edbrooke, c. 1890, RIGHT. Edbrooke and Burnham's long, prolific partnership (1879–96) was not the marriage of two equals. The more acclaimed Edbrooke handled client relations, while Burnham stayed at the drafting board in Chicago. (ABOVE Frederick John Prior, Columbian Exposition Dedication Ceremonies Memorial [Chicago: Metropolitan Art Engraving and Publishing, 1893], 618; RIGHT Courtesy of the National Archives and Records Administration)

Although two architects had won the competition, the job belonged to Willoughby J. Edbrooke, the more experienced partner who corresponded with the commissioners and attended their monthly meetings. The Georgia State Capitol was the turning point of Edbrooke's career in which he established his reputation as a designer of large public buildings. Two years later, President Benjamin Harrison would appoint him the supervising architect of the Treasury Department, responsible for the design and construction of federal buildings all over the country. For Franklin P. Burnham, the Capitol was the climax of a successful partnership and possibly of his entire career.

With the architects selected, the commissioners needed to find contractors. The Capitol Act allowed them to hire one general contractor, which would be easier, or to parcel out the work, which would be cheaper. The bid request set a budget of $800,000 and a July 15, 1884, deadline. Clerk Harrison, who complained that the bidding was sluggish, eventually received forty-four entries. All proved to be disappointments. Only two proposals bid on the entire project, and both ignored the $800,000 limit. Just as distressing, the cost of using Georgia marble for the exterior was quoted five times higher than Indiana limestone.

After three difficult days, the commissioners rejected the entire batch and rebid the project, hoping that the worsening economy would work to their advantage. This time they met with limited success; only one of the thirty new proposals fell below the $800,000 benchmark. Its bidder, Miles and Horn of Toledo, Ohio, had submitted five other bids, and their second-lowest figure, $862,756.75, was eventually chosen. The victory was tempered, however, by a major concession; the winning bid specified Indiana oolitic limestone rather than Georgia marble or granite.

With the acceptance of the winning bid on September 26, construction was scheduled to begin the following month. However, the success in finding a contractor who could build the structure within budget was overshadowed in the press by a vocal opposition, initiated by the fledgling Georgia marble industry over the choice of Indiana limestone for the building exterior. The *Atlanta Constitution* noted that the bids of the Georgia marble and granite producers were $215,000 and $342,000 higher than those for the Indiana limestone. Georgia's marble and granite industries were not ready in 1884 to supply stone in large quantities at a competitive cost. As the *Manufacturer and Builder* observed: "The building of the Georgia State Capitol, at Atlanta, develops the fact that granite can be quarried in Maine, brought to Savannah, and thence by rail to Atlanta, at less cost than it can be had at a quarry only sixteen miles away."[9]

Georgia quarrying interests fought the decision, launching a vigorous lobbying effort in an attempt to inject the decision into the political process. On October 15, local marble quarry owner Marcus A. Bell presented the commissioners with a petition requesting that they alter the contract to substitute Georgia marble for the limestone. The press took up the story, and soon a flood of angry letters began arriving on Harrison's desk. The commissioners felt the stress and devoted much of their first annual report to defending themselves on the issue.

Marcus A. Bell, c. 1885. Many Georgians took offense when the Capitol commissioners announced the Capitol would be made of Indiana limestone, but local marble man Marcus Bell got on the offensive. Waging his war in the local press and the Georgia General Assembly, Bell demanded the use of Georgia marble or granite because such a large contract would boost the state's fledgling quarrying industry. (Courtesy of the Georgia Archives, Small Print Collection, spc12-042)

Assisted by his son Piromis, Marcus Bell worked tirelessly both in the press and in the halls of the statehouse to promote the use of Georgia-quarried stone. His appeal to the General Assembly first attacked the issue on legal grounds and then turned to melodrama: "Let us now bring forth from its quarry bed some blocks of this soft, oolite limestone, with its fragments of wood, impressions of ferns, cycadeae and other terrestrial plants, and remains of beetles and many genera of reptiles, etc. and see how the bastard marble will appear. . . . We shrink back depressed, as beholding the ghastly relics of some sad decay."[10]

The quarrier's political campaign paid off when the Senate appointed a subcommittee to investigate. While extolling the superiority of their stone during six days of testimony in December 1884, the granite and marble businessmen of Georgia also admitted that their product could not be supplied within the appropriation. The sympathetic subcommittee supported the substitution and recommended a larger appropriation, claiming that the honor of the state was at stake. The more cautious full Senate merely asked the Capitol commissioners to report on the matter by the following July and meanwhile, to avoid any construction that would interfere with the possible later substitution.

When the commissioners next met in January 1885, a more pressing concern commanded their attention. Commissioner Benjamin E. Crane had died five days earlier, and Governor McDaniel immediately appointed Evan P. Howell, the influential editor in chief of the *Atlanta Constitution*, as his replacement. Turning to the Senate request, the commissioners simply asked Miles and Horn to figure up the cost of switching materials and otherwise to proceed with construction.

In June 1885, the commissioners defended their actions to the Senate. Delaying construction and substituting Georgia material would cost more than $200,000, and they had not slowed or stopped work because the request came from only one legislative body. The rebuffed Senate subcommittee demanded a legislative mandate to force the substitution and printed five hundred copies of their request, and again, the issue escalated in the legislature and the press. By now the *Atlanta Constitution* was calling the limestone "practically worthless," while the supplier, Salem Stone, was frantically submitting testimonials from all over the country. The commissioners responded with a second report, released to the public on September 1, 1885, that dismissed Georgia stone due to its cost and defended the quality of oolitic limestone.

The commissioners' second report was timed carefully to coincide with the cornerstone ceremony. The press covered the popular event lavishly, reporting every detail of the first public ceremony at the Capitol. Accompanying the favorable stories was the commission's report praising the quality of the stone that was waiting to be put into place. A week later, the Senate Committee on Public Property concurred and settled the issue by approving Miles and Horn's original contract.

The construction that led up to the cornerstone ceremony began November 13, 1884, after crews demolished the thirty-year-old City Hall / County Courthouse. After railroad tracks were laid from the main line of the Georgia Railroad a block to the north, railway cars filled with huge slabs of stone made

Evan P. Howell, c. 1895. Evan P. Howell had all of the usual credentials when he joined the Board of Capitol Commissioners in January 1885: lawyer, Civil War veteran, former state senator, and editor in chief of the *Atlanta Constitution*. At the dedicatory ceremonies on July 4, 1889, he represented the commission when he symbolically turned the Capitol over to the state. (Courtesy of the Kenan Research Center at the Atlanta History Center)

their way directly to the construction site, where they stopped at the northwest corner of Capitol Square. There they climbed a twenty-foot-high trestle and were straddled by a traveler, a huge engine that lifted stone monoliths as large as one hundred cubic feet. The traveler transferred the stone to an area where saws cut chunks of proper thickness before passing them to the rubbing bed. A giant revolving iron disk rubbed the stone smooth. The traveler picked up the stones and conveyed them to the cutting shed at the southwest corner of the site. There each slab was cut into smaller blocks and shaped to fit a particular place on the exterior wall. Immense "walking" derricks, one on each side of the building, hoisted the stones into place. As the building rose, three more derricks located inside the outer walls went up. Three elevators hoisted bricks and other building materials. The total cost of the heavy equipment was about forty thousand dollars.

A second rail line ran through the site along the east side of Capitol Square, and another crossed through the center of the lot until construction began. The proximity of Capitol Square to the Georgia Railroad, with a direct rail connection to the site, saved the extra cost of transferring stone and other heavy construction materials to tramways or drays. The grounds contained several sheds, including a blacksmith shop and the contractor's office. The size of the workforce and the skills of its members varied with each stage of construction. Five months before the cornerstone ceremony, the *Atlanta Constitution* reported

Salem Stone & Lime Company quarry yard, 1887. Railroad cars, destined for the new Georgia Capitol, are loaded with limestone from a quarry in Salem, Indiana. The stone yards, sheds, railroad tracks, and derricks seen here could also be found on the Capitol grounds during construction, where the stone was unloaded, cut, finished, and moved into place on the rising walls by "walking derricks." (Courtesy of Cornell University Library, Making of America Digital Collection, *Manufacturer and Builder*, December 1887, 253)

West elevation, proposed central, south, and north statuary, Edbrooke and Burnham, 1884. George Crouch relocated to Atlanta to do ornamental exterior statuary for the Capitol. As unanticipated expenses accumulated, the commissioners had to reduce costs. One such cut was to curtail the amount of statuary found on the front facade of the building. These three statuary groupings were eliminated, and Crouch redesigned the pediment relief carving to include allegorical figures. (Courtesy of the Georgia Archives, RG 1-8-30)

that almost four hundred men worked on the project and 175 wagonloads of granite arrived per day. Georgia's citizens had never seen construction on so grand a scale.[11]

The dressing of the limestone on site was relatively rough work compared to the sculptural skill required to carve the relief in the west front pediment and the column caps and other ornamental features of the Capitol exterior. George Crouch, a "monumental architect" who had worked on a Vanderbilt mansion, relocated his business to Atlanta when he was awarded the contract to do all the ornamental work on the statehouse. Crouch also worked in marble and executed monuments in Atlanta's Westview Cemetery.[12]

The new State Capitol was rising on a site where diverse industrial, commercial, and residential neighborhoods merged. To the northwest lay bustling downtown Atlanta's commercial core, divided by the railroad tracks that served its busy Union Station passenger depot. It was a red-brick area of three- and four-story hotels, retail buildings, and warehouses. Although there were several bridges across the railroad divide in the downtown, many pedestrians who came to the Capitol had to dodge trains and cross as many as nine sets of tracks. The area north and east of the Capitol contained a mixture of industrial sites and modest workers' housing, whose residents worked as carpenters, draymen, and other types of laborers.

Directly west and to the south of the Capitol, five large churches anchored an affluent neighborhood of wide, quiet streets and large residences. Those closest to the Capitol were home to doctors, bank presidents, clergymen, and other members of Atlanta's white elite. A few blocks away, the neighborhood became more middle class, populated by lawyers, teachers, and other white-collar workers, many of whom used the trolley to commute downtown.

As work progressed at an increasing rate after the cornerstone dedication, legislators had to find a way to create the cash flow needed to sustain the undertaking. The day after the ceremony, the *Savannah Morning News* speculated that the project would not stick to its schedule or budget. Atlanta's payment of $55,625 had long been spent, and during the next year, expenses would average $22,000 per month. Georgia's finances had not improved in the two years since the passage of the Capitol Act, and the state's surplus had fallen below $500,000. It was time to do the inevitable.

On September 22, 1885, legislators passed a temporary property tax, five cents on every one thousand dollars, to fund the construction. The bill moved unremarked through the House but caused lively debate in the Senate. Senator Davidson, the Mason grand master who had presided over the cornerstone ceremony three weeks before, defended the bill as chair of the Finance Committee. The bill passed 23 to 12, and over the next three years, the General Assembly quietly approved three more temporary tax bills that funded at least three-quarters of construction costs.[13]

With funding in place, construction proceeded smoothly, and the commissioners settled into a monthly routine. At each meeting they inspected the site, examined the architect's estimate, and ordered a requisition to pay approved expenses. The commissioners knew that their budget ceiling was absolute, so they focused on managing costs. As "extras" (unanticipated expenses) accumulated, the commissioners ordered Edbrooke to eliminate some of the more costly effects, such as exterior statuary and hardwood stair rails.

As the months passed, several principals in the project changed. Governor McDaniel did not run for reelection in 1886, and the newly inaugurated Governor John Gordon joined the board as its chairman. The most startling development was the death of contractor Charles Horn, who was shot while attempting to break up a fight at the Kimball House Hotel. Horn died instantly, leaving

Capitol Avenue, 1890s. The neighborhood south of the Capitol was a posh Atlanta address in the 1880s. Fine residences could be found along tree-lined streets like those shown here on Capitol Avenue, just a short walk from the statehouse. (Courtesy of the Kenan Research Center at the Atlanta History Center)

a wife, four children, and a flourishing five-year partnership with Miles. Miles continued to oversee the Capitol project himself and eventually formed another partnership.

Despite the turnover, work continued uninterrupted. The commissioners spent the rest of 1887 making minor construction decisions, such as choosing the type of wood and finish for each major space. Their easiest choice may have been between tile and Georgia marble for the flooring and wainscot. The American Marble Cutting Company of Marietta, Georgia, won the contract for the pink wainscot marble, the lavatories, and probably the marble floor tiles in the atria and hallways, as well as the steps for the grand stairways. With the public spaces featuring one and one-half acres of Georgia marble, Georgia long-leaf pine doorways and surrounds, and locally produced plaster throughout the building, the interior of the Capitol displayed an abundance of local materials and craftsmanship. This fact went unmentioned during the controversy over the buildings' exterior material but was emphasized in articles written about the Capitol after its completion.

Lighting was a more difficult decision. Still a novelty in the mid-1880s, electricity was first employed as a secondary system for illumination. Edbrooke and Burnham designed the building to use only gas, but later specifications mentioned an electrical starting system for the larger fixtures. The commissioners may have considered an even more ambitious approach, for commission clerk Harrison told the *Atlanta Constitution* in February 1888, "[I]t will be a grand sight when the interior of this dome is lighted with electric lights, the lantern brilliantly illuminated by electricity, and there is a flaming torch in the hand of the Goddess of Liberty that will be visible at night for miles and miles around." He might have been anticipating an effect that was cut for budgetary reasons, for wiring was not installed in the dome during construction. The modified electrical plan serviced the House, the Senate, the supreme court, and the attorney general's department, probably providing power for starting gas systems and possibly a few combination fixtures.[14]

As construction proceeded, the commission had to work out the normal expense conflicts between the architects and the contractors. In his November 1888 State of the State address, Governor Gordon announced that the commissioners were confident of delivering the building on time, but two weeks later, he requested an extension beyond the January 1, 1889, date required by the Capitol Act. The General Assembly gave

Visitors view the Georgia Marble Company yard near Tate, Georgia, 1896. Three years after their controversial selection of Indiana limestone for the Capitol exterior, the commissioners requested Georgia marble for the interior. The American Marble Cutting Company in Marietta, Georgia, won the contract for the wainscot, lavatories, and probably the floors and stairs, but the stone itself may have been supplied by the Georgia Marble Company in Pickens County. Here visitors view the yard by the railroad tracks where the quarried marble was loaded for shipment. (Courtesy of the Georgia Archives, Vanishing Georgia Collection, COB-632)

Stamped
Sheet Bronze, Copper and Zinc
Statuary

Copyright, 1896-1898, by W. H. Mullins
As to cuts contained in his various Catalogues
Copyright, 1904, by W. H. Mullins

Manufactured by
W. H. MULLINS
SALEM, OHIO, U. S. A.

W. H. Mullins Manufacturing Company brochure, 1904. Evidence suggests that Edbrooke and Burnham picked Miss Freedom from a catalog produced by the W. H. Mullins Manufacturing Company of Salem, Ohio, a firm specializing in all kinds of ornamental metalwork. The cover of the company's brochure illustrated the variety of its statuary. Each statue was formed by molding thick sheets of bronze, copper, or zinc around a metal frame. (Courtesy of the Salem Historical Society, Salem, Ohio)

Miss Freedom. Standing fifteen feet tall and weighing in at two thousand pounds, the female figure now known as Miss Freedom represents liberty and stands atop the cupola. The figure holds aloft a lighted torch in her right hand and clasps a sword in her left, symbolizing the struggle to protect freedom. The realization of this symbolism for all Georgians would take decades of struggle in the statehouse. (Courtesy of Diane Kirkland and the Georgia Department of Economic Development)

them until March 30, 1889, as long as the delay would cost nothing but time. With three more months to work, the commissioners were as determined to spend every bit of the remaining appropriation as they were resolved not to exceed it. There was little money left, less than $25,000 after Miles's final bill and salaries were paid.

Decorative painting was a top priority, since colorful stenciling would produce the most visual effect for the least cost. In May 1888, with a $5,000 budget, the commissioners requested bids for decorating the main public spaces and chambers in the building. The commissioners chose the Almini Company of Chicago, a well-established firm with a national reputation, to decorate the two legislative chambers, the state library, and the supreme court, all they could afford within budget. Work began that summer, and by November, when the cost figures were settled and the commissioners had more to spend, they were impressed enough with Almini to authorize three more contracts to paint offices. The work totaled $10,670, only $530 less than Almini's original bid, which included the rotunda and two atria instead of the smaller office spaces. The commissioners may have regretted their decision, but other, more functional, improvements competed for the remaining funds, such as adding rudimentary offices to the unfinished basement, which had been slated as a place of rough storage.

With construction nearing completion, the General Assembly faced an urgent request for an additional appropriation. The Capitol Act had not included funding for landscaping or furnishings, vital elements to complete the building's monumental effect. An empty building seemed far worse than a bare yard, so legislators focused on the interior. In November 1888, a furnishing commission recommended a modest budget of $75,000 to obtain furnishings that were "commensurate with its [the Capitol's] magnificent proportions and elegant finish" but would avoid "extravagant, glittering novelties."

The General Assembly appropriated $71,000, money that would be stretched as tightly as the building budget had been. In the House chamber alone, the bidding specifications called for 174 desks and chairs, 240 opera seats in the gallery, a Speaker's platform, a ninety-light chandelier and numerous other light fixtures, carpeting, and a variety of tables, desks, chairs, and benches. The bulk of the contract went to the Robert Mitchell Furniture Company of Cincinnati, Ohio, which was already under contract for the interior woodwork. The only local winner was M. Rich and Brothers, a thirty-two-year-old firm that would continue to flourish (as Rich's Department Store) in Atlanta for many years.[15]

With the end in sight, on February 10, 1889, the *Atlanta Constitution* trumpeted "THE CAPITOL! Which Georgia Has

Decorative painting. Uncertain of their bottom line, the commissioners first authorized decorative painting in the House and Senate chambers, the state library, and the supreme court chamber and then contracted out the rest of the decorative painting in small batches. Consequently, the interior dome, the atria, and the main corridors were not embellished with Victorian detail. (Courtesy of Diane Kirkland and the Georgia Department of Economic Development)

Detail of atrium. The two-color scheme of the Capitol's public spaces may have been less ornate than the commissioners would have liked, but the simpler approach had its own benefits. The austere tones accentuate the architectural complexity of the spaces, allowing for the interplay of light and shadow seen in this photograph. (Courtesy of Diane Kirkland and the Georgia Department of Economic Development)

Just Completed," with two solid pages of illustrations and stories. After the final inspection on February 26, the commissioners dined together at Evan Howell's home in West End, joined by the project principals, Henry Grady, and other local dignitaries. The dining table's centerpiece was a three-foot-long papier-mâché model of the building, complete with interior lighting, created by Edbrooke and Burnham. The following morning, they formally accepted the building, and that afternoon, the *Atlanta Constitution* ran an interview with Edbrooke. The architect claimed, "[T]he new capitol of the state of Georgia is incomparably the best capitol for the amount of money expended in the United States," and he praised the commissioners, who had "accomplished so much so modestly, so wisely and so well."[16]

The building did come in under budget. After Miles received his final check, the remaining balance was $118.43. The next day the *Atlanta Constitution*, whose editor was a Capitol commissioner, editorialized: "There is not only not a dishonest dollar in the building, there is not even a careless or ill-advised dollar." Although the $1 million budget had included neither furnishing nor landscaping, the hyperbole was justified. Corruption, delay, and slander plagued most statehouse construction projects. The Tweed Ring ensnared the New York capitol, construction on the Illinois capitol stalled for six years, and Connecticut's capitol took three competitions, two feuding architects, and eight years to build. The personality conflicts, slight delays, and peripheral controversies of the Georgia Capitol seem minor in comparison.[17]

At their last meeting on March 20, 1889, the Capitol commissioners authorized final payments, and each of the major participants submitted a report.

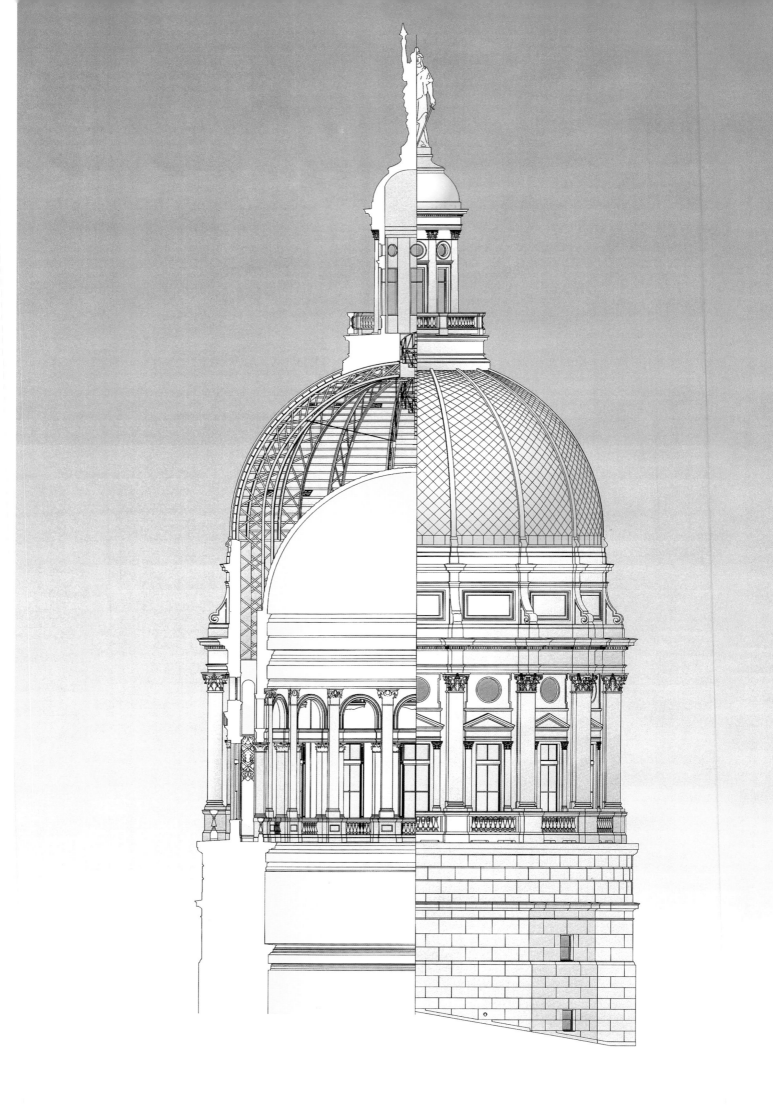

The commissioners attributed their success to the "harmony and singleness of purpose on the part of all concerned." Edbrooke and Burnham stressed the value of the structure; at just under 20 cents per cubic foot, the Capitol rivaled others built at twice the cost. In closing out the minute book, commission clerk Harrison wrote his assessment of the five-year project: "With this page closes the history of one of the best pieces of public work ever performed in the United States. A history of honest, conscientious discharge of duty, free from any suspicion of wrong doing, and the Building this day delivered will stand as a monument to the men who contracted for and caused it to be erected."[18]

Doing their best with limited funding, the Board of Capitol Commissioners gave Georgia all the statehouse a million dollars could buy. For a state still recovering from a devastating war, the Georgia Capitol was a monumental civic accomplishment. However, the budget called for every cent to be squeezed out of every dollar, and five years of design cutbacks had taken their toll. Modest decorative finishing and a meager furnishing budget resulted in less-than-breathtaking interiors, especially when compared with the showier capitols built by wealthier states. However, the effect of such decorative cost cutting paled in comparison to that of a more serious, structural modification. At some point during construction, wood covered with sheet metal was substituted for a stone dome. Years later, the long-term cost of this money-saving measure would become clear when decades of water leakage caused massive structural failure and the need for a major dome reconstruction.

In the late spring of 1889, any imperfections in the new State Capitol were not apparent to those who were moving into its offices. After the colorful woven carpets were laid and freshly polished furniture was installed in the grand public spaces and spacious offices, the locus of Georgia government migrated from Marietta Street to Washington Street. Once the state employees had settled into their new offices—officially they occupied the space as of June 15, 1889—a lull fell over the Capitol in advance of the legislative session in early July. Everyone working in the statehouse anticipated the next great ceremony, a symbolic march of the General Assembly from the old to the new Capitol, which would culminate in the official dedicatory ceremonies and initiate the annual burst of legislative activity in Georgia's temple of democracy.

4 A NEW SOUTH CAPITOL

Less than two years after its dedication, on April 16, 1891, the new Georgia Capitol was the center of national attention when Republican president Benjamin Harrison came to meet the people of the state. Harrison's visit to Atlanta was but one stop on the first national speaking tour by a president making "whistle-stop" addresses in cities and towns across the country. Stops on the southern leg of his tour brought the president to Knoxville, Chattanooga, Atlanta, Birmingham, Memphis, Little Rock, Houston, Galveston, San Antonio, and El Paso, all within the week beginning April 14. Because the press traveling with the president had access to the telegraph, his visits had both regional and national ramifications.[1]

The presidential stop at the Capitol while in Atlanta was but one of many indications that the statehouse was becoming what its proponents had envisioned, a signature building representing Atlanta, Georgia, and the New South. Immediately after its 1889 dedication, *Harper's Weekly* had featured the Capitol in a story with a drawing of the structure, asserting that the Capitol was "the best million-dollar edifice in America." The article also noted the expenditures lavished on the interior, where Georgia materials predominated: "[L]ess money was sent to Indiana for the limestone in the exterior than has been spent on the native marble tiles and wainscoting of the interior."[2]

In the years that followed, articles about Atlanta in national journals developed a popular story line about the Georgia statehouse. Typical of these accounts was a glowing article in the November 1891 issue of the *New England Magazine* by George Leonard Chaney, a northern Unitarian minister who knew both Henry Grady and Booker T. Washington. Chaney's description of the new Capitol presented the recurring themes that were already defining the new statehouse in the public mind. First, he connected the capitols in Georgia and Washington as kindred structures: "The new State Capitol is a really magnificent building. Without imitating the national Capitol at Washington, it is a distinct reminder of it." Chaney then elaborated on the two other strains of the popular Capitol

ABOVE *Souvenir ribbon commemorating Harrison's Atlanta visit, 1891.* The new Georgia Capitol hosted its first U.S. president on April 16, 1891, when Benjamin Harrison came through Atlanta on a whistle-stop tour of the South. Harrison stood in the rotunda and shook the hands of more than 2,500 citizens, some of whom sported souvenir ribbons commemorating the visit. (Courtesy of Diane Kirkland and the Georgia Department of Economic Development)

BELOW *Sketch from Harper's Weekly magazine, 1889.* The completion of the new Georgia State Capitol made national news. *Harper's Weekly* magazine editorialized that although "it was generally predicted that the building would never be finished within that limit," the Georgia State Capitol was "the best million dollar edifice in America." (Reprinted from *Harper's Weekly*, August 3, 1889, 623)

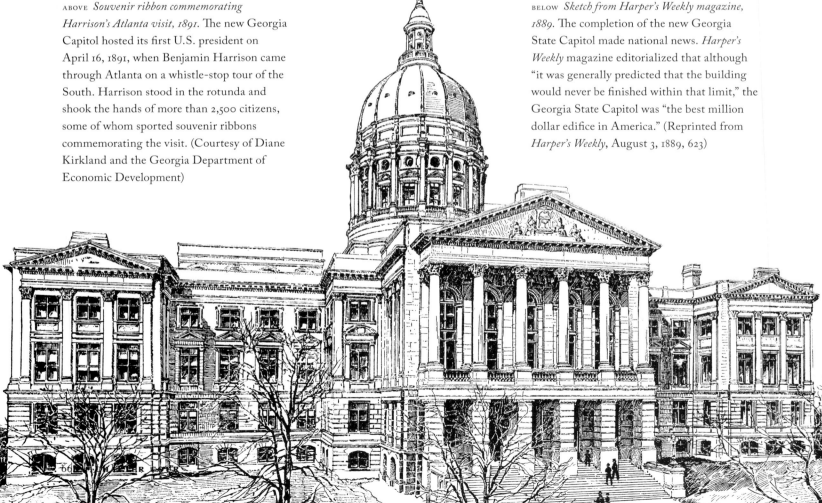

story: it was built within its million-dollar budget, and it was constructed mostly of Georgia materials. Observers like Chaney who described Atlanta in national magazines used the city and its Capitol to represent the successful reunification of the states in the aftermath of the Civil War.[3]

When Republican president Harrison visited Atlanta in 1891, the issue of reunification was still controversial. Citizens and politicians, split along party and geographic lines, battled over the issue of black disfranchisement. Harrison came to the South in an effort to downplay the conflict. He had come to Atlanta twenty-seven years earlier as a captain under the command of General William T. Sherman and had led Union troops in the Battle of Peachtree Creek. Now in his return as president, he began his brief visit with a trip to the battle site, located off Collier Road beyond the most distant suburbs of the 1890s. When the president returned to the Capitol for an evening reception, over twenty-five hundred citizens crowded on the steps of the west entrance and across the front plaza awaiting his arrival. The official welcoming committee, led by Governor William Northern, gathered at the north entrance. The group included several notables who were responsible for the new Capitol:

Bird's-eye view of Atlanta (portion), 1892. The newly constructed Georgia Capitol (BOTTOM CIRCLE) dominated the Atlanta downtown. To the northwest a new Victorian building is projected on the site of the former Capitol (TOP CIRCLE) on Marietta Street; it would burn down in late 1893. Union Station (MIDDLE CIRCLE) served as the arrival point in Atlanta for important Capitol visitors, including presidents Benjamin Harrison and William McKinley and, posthumously, Confederate president Jefferson Davis. (Courtesy of the Library of Congress)

commission member General Phil Cook (then serving as secretary of state); commission secretary Tip Harrison; contractor W. B. Miles; and Capitol Act author Frank Rice.

The president did not have much time to admire the grand architecture. He was ushered immediately through the north atrium and into the rotunda, where the crowd waiting to meet him surged in from the Washington Street entrance. Since his sole purpose at the reception was to greet the public, Harrison began to shake hands quickly and efficiently. As each person approached, he reached out, grabbed a hand, shook it once, and turned for the next. The press of the crowd kept people moving. Reporters noted that the president seemed well practiced with the routine: "He looked at each one with an invariable smile . . . and very rarely seemed interested in what he was doing. . . . Fifty a minute, fifty a minute."[4]

Like the opening reception at the Capitol dedication, the evening statehouse event for Harrison relaxed the color line, and the president shook hands with several African Americans. The issue of race relations was raised repeatedly as Harrison journeyed through the South, specifically his party's pending legislation that would prevent southern states from restricting black voting. With sectional passions enflamed over the issue, Harrison had crafted a message intended to gain the support of voters in both the North and the South. Throughout the regional tour, the president spoke eloquently in favor of the supremacy of the law, of equality before the law, and, most significantly for his southern white audience, of majority rule.[5]

In Atlanta, Harrison delivered his message of regional conciliation from his railroad car at Union Station just before his departure the morning after the reception. In a masterly stroke of political spin, the president claimed that emancipation now made it possible in Georgia "not only to raise cotton, but to spin and weave it." He then spoke of common purposes that united both regions and went on to declare to a cheering crowd: "[L]et us bravely and generously give every other man his equal rights before the law." White Georgians could embrace the call for "equal rights before the law" because they knew that the laws being crafted in the nearby statehouse would ensure their continued political and social preeminence.

Except for rare incidents like President Harrison's reception in the Capitol, strict but informal rules of etiquette regulated the interactions between black and white southerners in the late nineteenth century. By the early 1890s, however, the rise in urban population and intercity transit brought the races into closer proximity with each other. White citizens began to call for laws that would restrict African American access to trains, trolleys, restaurants, restrooms, theaters, and other public accommodations. Southern legislatures responded by passing a series of Jim Crow laws that claimed equality of treatment but in reality established a second class of citizenship. Georgia

President Harrison in El Paso, 1891. President Harrison continued his whirlwind cross-country tour by train, stopping for public appearances in other cities in the South and the West. Here he appears in El Paso, Texas, less than a week after his Atlanta stop. (Photograph by George Elbert Burr; courtesy of the George Elbert Burr papers, 1885–1972, in the Archives of American Art, Smithsonian Institute)

made its first contribution to Jim Crow law in 1891, when its legislature passed the nation's first statewide streetcar segregation law.[6]

When the General Assembly convened in the fall after President Harrison's April 1891 statehouse visit, the passage of legislation requiring the separation of the races was a high priority. Segregated railroad-coach laws had been passed and upheld in a U.S. Federal Court case. When the House Committee on Railways met in a fourth-floor committee room in early October, its members sought a way to expand the Jim Crow railroad provision to include trolleys. The problem, as they saw it, was logistics: unlike passenger trains, which could designate each railroad car as "white only" or "black only," electric trolleys consisted of single cars with bench seats. Spokesman Joel Hurt, the entrepreneur who developed Atlanta's Inman Park neighborhood and introduced the city's first electric trolley, offered an alternative to creating separate compartments. He suggested that conductors be granted police powers to compel blacks and whites

West entrance columns. The monumentality of the new Georgia Capitol attracted national acclaim as well as visiting dignitaries. The west entrance colonnade provided a dignified backdrop for grand public ceremonies. (Courtesy of Diane Kirkland and the Georgia Department of Economic Development)

Electric trolley, c. 1895. The earliest electric trolleys in Atlanta were open air with bench seats. The first Jim Crow law in Georgia, passed in the Capitol in 1891, required streetcar conductors to order black and white passengers to sit separately on trolleys and trains. (Courtesy of the Kenan Research Center at the Atlanta History Center)

Electric trolley passing by the Capitol, c. 1910. The Capitol was located on several trolley lines at the turn of the century, making the streetcar a popular method to travel to the statehouse. By this time trolleys had increased in size, been enclosed, and added a center aisle. (Courtesy of the Kenan Research Center at the Atlanta History Center)

to sit separately, allowing for flexible boundaries depending on the mix of passengers. The Georgia General Assembly took Hurt's recommendation and on October 21 passed the state's first Jim Crow law.[7]

When the legislation moved from within the Capitol onto the streets of Georgia's cities, African Americans responded immediately by organizing boycotts of trolley companies that attempted to enforce racial segregation. Black opposition delayed implementation of the law in several cities and eventually brought the issue back to the Capitol, where the state court of appeals reviewed it.[8]

Built intentionally to symbolize state government, the Georgia Capitol was a building where the actions of government were on display. Consequently, the activities in and around its walls took on important symbolic meanings. Early ceremonies had linked the building with the New South's twin creeds of economic development and local governance. Visits by prominent national leaders added the gloss of nationalism and unity. Each legislative session identified the important issues of the day and set the tone of the public discourse surrounding them.

Every public event brought citizens to the statehouse, where they linked the building with the ceremonial functions staged there. Many more read about these events and absorbed the interpretations that were presented by the press. Each event added another layer of meaning to the Capitol and further ingrained its role as the symbol of the democratic order of the state. Never was this process more apparent than during another highly choreographed presidential visit in the early 1890s.

On the afternoon of May 30, 1893, the four-year-old Georgia Capitol was inundated by crowds far greater than any ever assembled there before. The two major public rituals that preceded this event—the 1885 cornerstone laying and the 1889 dedication ceremony—had handsome turnouts but nothing to match this day in either numbers or emotion. Thousands had come to view the casket of Jefferson Davis, the former president of the Confederate States of America, whose posthumous appearance would consecrate the Capitol with new meaning.

When Davis died in 1889, his body was interred temporarily in New Orleans. In the spring of 1893, after a monumental tomb had been completed in Richmond, his remains were transported to their final resting place in the old Confederate capital. Atlanta boosters, not wanting to miss an opportunity

Jefferson Davis procession in Atlanta, 1893. When the remains of Jefferson Davis, former president of the Confederacy, passed through the South, the train stopped in Atlanta on May 30, 1893. This *Atlanta Constitution* sketch captures the procession of the Davis casket to the Georgia Capitol, where its presence symbolically joined the new statehouse with the Old South. (Courtesy of the *Atlanta Journal-Constitution*; *Atlanta Constitution*, May 30, 1893, 2)

for a major civic event in their city, arranged for a stopover with a parade and public viewing in the Capitol. After the train arrived at Union Station, a crowd of over five thousand onlookers watched as Davis's casket was placed on a wagon at the head of a procession consisting of a column of uniformed Confederate veterans, over two hundred carriages filled with dignitaries, and hundreds of marchers. Prominent among the dignitaries was former governor John B. Gordon.

When the march arrived at the Capitol, the casket was carried up the west steps and into the north atrium, where it was placed at the foot of the Benjamin Harvey Hill statue. This statue, the first major sculpture to enter the new statehouse, memorialized the gifted orator who had helped to popularize the term "New South." Seven years earlier, in 1886, the ailing Jefferson Davis had helped to dedicate this statue at its original outdoor location at the southern meeting point of Peachtree and West Peachtree streets. In 1890, Governor John Gordon, who had worked closely with Hill after the war to restore Democratic political power, had arranged to move the statue into the Capitol. Now, for the thousands of Georgians who gathered to pay tribute to Jefferson Davis, the placement of his casket beneath the Ben Hill statue represented a tangible link between the Confederacy and the new southern political order.

Davis's casket lay atop a caisson, whose inscriptions me-

Statue of Benjamin Harvey Hill. This marble statue of Benjamin Harvey Hill, a New South leader who had helped to craft the postwar political order, was placed originally at the intersection of Peachtree and West Peachtree streets. There in 1886, the ailing Jefferson Davis joined Atlanta civic leaders for its dedication. Four years later, Governor John Gordon relocated the memorial to the Capitol. (Courtesy of Diane Kirkland and the Georgia Department of Economic Development)

morialized his Confederate past: "Great in War, Greater in Peace," "Our Warrior Statesman," "A Patriot Always," and "Representative of the Lost Cause." The *Atlanta Constitution* claimed that forty thousand people passed by the casket, an unlikely figure but indicative of how mobbed the atrium and third- and fourth-floor galleries must have been. The hugely popular Davis was the embodiment of the Lost Cause movement, the postwar veneration of the Confederacy that would gain strength in the decades ahead.[9]

Newspaper accounts included sentimental vignettes of old veterans who wept and kissed the casket and a widow who "reached out a withered hand and patted it . . . lovingly and tenderly," saying, "[M]y husband was with him, you know." Once again the color line was relaxed; news accounts included a description of an elderly African American man, who approached, "hat in hand, and humbly asked his permission" to place a bunch of flowers he had brought at the foot of the catafalque. Permission granted, he laid them there and said, "Young marster died fer him, and he died brave." Later in the article, to emphasize the African American acceptance of the southern social and political order, the reporter described an almost identical incident.[10]

The newspapers devoted much attention to Jefferson Davis's daughters, who remained in a parlor of the Kimball House and received socially prominent Atlanta women while their father lay in state. Reporters noted that their "sweet, gentle and unaffected manners completely won every heart." The separation of the adult daughters from the activities at the Capitol typified the popular perception of respectable women as meek, acquiescent creatures whose place was in the parlor and kitchen, not in legislative halls. After Davis's casket was returned to the depot, just before the train de-

Jefferson Davis's bier under the statue of Benjamin Hill, 1893. The casket of Jefferson Davis was placed in the north atrium of the Capitol beneath the statue of Benjamin Hill. Thousands of Atlantans mobbed the statehouse in order to pass by the casket and pay their respects. (Courtesy of the *Atlanta Journal-Constitution*; *Atlanta Constitution*, May 30, 1893, 2)

parted for Richmond, a soldier approached Miss Winnie and handed up his bugle, asking her to "consecrate" it by laying her hands on it. She complied, commenting as she did, "When it calls for your men to charge I know that they will always respond."[11]

By bringing the remains of Jefferson Davis to the Georgia Capitol, the state's political leaders were engaged in an act of consecration themselves. The monumental new Capitol provided the ideal stage for such grand public pageants. As the heroes of the Confederacy and the postwar Redemption period began to pass away, celebrations of their lives and monuments to their legacy at the Capitol helped to revive public memory and create lasting symbols. In the coming decades, state leaders would honor this recent but influential past by dedicating statues, hanging portraits, and arranging funerary celebrations in and around the statehouse.

The empty walls and halls of the new statehouse offered an irresistible opportunity to present a narrative of Georgia's past and a picture of its place in the evolving union of states. First to be installed in the new Capitol were the oversized portraits of Revolutionary era icons—Washington, Jefferson, Franklin, and Lafayette—and Georgia founding father James Oglethorpe, all of which had been commissioned in the mid-1820s for the Milledgeville Capitol. They

Jefferson Davis internment procession in Richmond, 1893. After the stop in Atlanta, the remains of Jefferson Davis continued on to Richmond, the former capital of the Confederacy. There crowds gathered to view the final procession that accompanied the casket to Hollywood Cemetery, where it was interred beneath a life-size statue of Davis. (Courtesy of Valentine Richmond History Center)

Capitol portrait. Portraits of national and state heroes and politicians adorn the rotunda and corridors of the Capitol, giving the building the feel of an art gallery. (Courtesy of Diane Kirkland and the Georgia Department of Economic Development)

Portraits in the Capitol rotunda. Portraits in the Capitol rotunda include the five oldest in the collection. They represent the founding of Georgia in 1733 (Oglethorpe) and its incorporation into the United States after the American Revolution (Washington, Jefferson, Franklin, and Lafayette). For the new Capitol, the General Assembly added portraits of leaders who had shaped post-Reconstruction democracy in Georgia. (Courtesy of Diane Kirkland and the Georgia Department of Economic Development)

Portrait of Robert Toombs, rotunda. The first portrait bought for the new State Capitol was one of Robert Toombs, purchased in 1891. Toombs served as the secretary of the Confederate States of America. Refusing to take the oath of allegiance to the United States after the war, Toombs lost his eligibility to hold public office. However, he still managed to dominate Georgia politics, especially as a leader in the 1877 convention that wrote a new state constitution after the end of Reconstruction. (Courtesy of Diane Kirkland and the Georgia Department of Economic Development)

were joined by the portraits commissioned in the mid-1880s of Benjamin Harvey Hill and Alexander Stephens, white political leaders who linked the Old and the New South in Georgia.

In the new Capitol, the Georgia General Assembly continued to select icons that laid the groundwork of the post-Reconstruction era, starting with an oversized portrait of Robert Toombs. Elected to the U.S. Congress from Georgia before the Civil War, Toombs resigned to serve the Confederacy as a brigadier general in the army and in the cabinet as secretary of state. After the war, Toombs refused to apply for a pardon and instead advocated continued defiance of the federal government. The placement of Toombs's portrait in the Capitol symbolized the continuing resistance of state political leaders to any federal oversight in post-Reconstruction Georgia.

As the statehouse walls began to fill with portraits, the halls also began to play a role in presenting Georgia to its citizens and visitors from other states. The Opera House Capitol had housed a display of Georgia's agricultural products and mineral deposits promoting the economic development opportunities in the state. With these artifacts available for placement in the new statehouse, the legislature established a state museum as part of the Office of the State Geologist in late 1889. The museum's rock specimens were placed in display cases in Capitol corridors and expanded in the mid-1890s with items from state exhibits that had been gathered for Atlanta's 1895 Cotton States and International Exhibition. Beginning with these few artifacts, the state museum would add other displays in the Capitol corridors representing Georgia's economic, social, and political history. Over time, the display cases and portraits gave the statehouse interior the look of both a science museum and an art gallery.[12]

Portraits of George Washington and James Oglethorpe, rotunda. Portraits of Revolutionary icon George Washington and Georgia's founder, James Edward Oglethorpe, painted by C. R. Parker in 1825–26, were originally hung on the walls of the legislative chambers in the Milledgeville Capitol. The elaborately decorated chamber walls in the new Capitol did not provide a suitable backdrop for these portraits, so they were placed on the less ornate walls of the rotunda. (Courtesy of Diane Kirkland and the Georgia Department of Economic Development)

Filled with visitors, legislators, lobbyists, citizen groups, the press, and various hangers-on, the Capitol hummed with the activities of hundreds of people each day of the General Assembly. The Capitol Act had created a place for the business of the people of Georgia. During the legislative sessions, bills traveled the steps and corridors of the statehouse on their quest to become the law of the land. Drawn up and registered in the offices of the House and the Senate on the third floor, the bills were then taken by their sponsors to fourth-floor committee rooms for consideration. From there, they were carried back downstairs to the great halls of the House and the Senate where they were debated and voted on. If approved by majority vote, a bill went downstairs to the second-floor office of the governor, who signed them into law. Finally, the new law traveled to the third floor for permanent filing in the state library. In time, laws that were challenged in the courts made their way to the state

court of appeals and the state supreme court on the third floor. Justices heard arguments in the courtroom and deliberated nearby in their chambers before rendering a final opinion, which was sent down the corridor to the state library.

Although it would be called new for almost a decade, the Capitol quickly showed signs of the interior wear and tear of annual legislative sessions, the day-to-day activities of state government, and major civic pageants, and the exterior assaults from Georgia's climate. From its opening day, the Capitol was in need of ongoing maintenance and repair. Once the work of the Capitol Commission was completed in 1889, the responsibility for the building's condition rested on a single employee who operated without the advice of an architect, the oversight of the Capitol Commission, or an annual budget. The keeper of public buildings and grounds, a position that predated the construction of the new Capitol, was a gubernatorial appointment that also included a martial role as the adjutant general of the Georgia Volunteers and the chairman of the Military Advisory Board. John McIntosh Kell, a sixty-seven-year-old veteran of the Confederate Navy, held the dual patronage appointment when the Capitol opened in

1889. His keeper responsibilities included signing the bimonthly paychecks for the watchmen, porters, and workmen who were responsible for maintenance and security, but he seemed far more interested in his military duties.

In December 1890, the legislature appropriated eighteen thousand dollars for the landscaping of the Capitol grounds with stone walls and walkways. The enabling legislation established a representative oversight committee consisting of the governor, the president of the Senate, the speaker of the House, the comptroller general, the treasurer, and the secretary of agriculture. After the grounds were landscaped, the committee was dissolved. The typical method of making changes to the Capitol became a piecemeal approach with funds appropriated in response to a request, either from one of the many occupants to make accommodations to suit a particular department's needs or from the keeper of public buildings and grounds for a specific repair that was not part of the annual appropriation. The statehouse became a divided structure because each branch of government treated its portion of the building as a separate fief-

Capitol and grounds, c. 1890.
A legislative appropriation in December 1890 provided eighteen thousand dollars to landscape the bare Capitol grounds with stone retaining walls, steps, walkways, and plantings. An oversight committee supervised this last major project of the Capitol construction. (Courtesy of the Kenan Research Center at the Atlanta History Center)

Capitol office, 1915, and state chemist's office, 1909. Office space in the new Capitol varied in size and finish, but maintenance was a constant challenge. A tiny budget and limited authority made the job of keeper of public buildings and grounds all the more difficult, and within a few years the Capitol showed signs of neglect. (Courtesy of the Georgia Archives, Vanishing Georgia Collection, ful1082-94, ful1081-94)

dom. As the building aged and departments grew, the legislature would appropriate funds for renovation and repairs without an overall plan or budget.[13]

The consequences of this uncoordinated, underfunded approach soon became apparent. When roof leaks appeared within a year of the Capitol dedication, the legislature approved funding in 1890 for the first of what would be a long history of roof repairs. In September 1891, only five months after President Harrison's visit to the Capitol, the *Atlanta Constitution* reported on the unkempt conditions in the building, where interior walls were dirty, dust was everywhere, and the marble floors were filthy with dirt tracked in from the city streets.[14]

With its leaky roof and unkempt interior, the Capitol lost its luster of newness in the early 1890s. During these years, disagreements arose over who might use the Capitol's halls and meeting rooms for public gatherings when they were not in use by the legislature. Civic groups regularly requested permission to meet in the numerous committee rooms, the commodious library, the dignified Senate chamber, and especially the large House of Representatives chamber. Most of these requests were granted as long as they did not interfere with legislative or other governmental activity. Yet in early 1895, when the state leaders of the women's suffrage movement requested to hold an evening meeting at the Capitol, Governor William Y. Atkinson refused, declaring "it would be unconstitutional to allow women to use it." The occasion was a joint meeting of the national and state convention of the American Women's Suffrage Association, the first time the national body had met in the South. With the Cotton States and International Exposition scheduled to open in the fall, Atlanta was enjoying some national exposure and seemed the perfect choice for women seeking to bring attention to their cause of suffrage. Denied access to the Capitol, the female conventioneers, including Susan B. Anthony, gathered at local hotels in February 1895.[15]

The Atlanta press was no more receptive to their message than the governor had been. On the eve of the convention, the local press advanced two popular arguments against universal suffrage. The first had been voiced by male opponents in every

Mary McLendon, c. 1913. Women's rights and temperance brought advocate Mary McLendon to the Capitol as a lobbyist from 1895 to 1921. In her keynote address to the American Women's Suffrage Association in 1895, she used the newly constructed Capitol to symbolize the exclusion of women from the political life of the state. (Courtesy of the Kenan Research Center at the Atlanta History Center)

state: "If women have the desire to make themselves felt in politics, they can through their fathers, husbands, brothers, and sweethearts." The second claim, based on race, was more distinctively southern and reflected white efforts in Georgia to restrict black voting: "[I]t would send every Negro woman to the polls while the whites would stay home."[16]

The keynote speaker at the convention was Georgian Mary Latimer McLendon, the tireless champion for suffrage who would roam the Capitol corridors for almost three decades advancing her cause. In her address, McLendon used the new Capitol, crowned by the figure of a woman, to drive home her political message:

> If Georgia women could vote, this National Convention could hold its session in our million dollar Capitol, which rears its grand proportions on yonder hill. Crowning its loftiest pinnacle is the statue of a woman representing Liberty, and on its front the motto, "Justice, Wisdom, and Moderation." It was built with money paid into our state treasury by women as well as men. . . . [Yet] it is with difficulty that women can secure a hearing before a legislative committee to petition for laws to ameliorate their own condition.[17]

Excluded from meeting in the Capitol, McLendon and her fellow advocates also experienced great difficulty in getting a

Atlanta celebrates the victory, 1898. President William McKinley appears between Jefferson Davis and Abraham Lincoln in the center of the *Atlanta Constitution's* front-page illustration marking the president's Atlanta visit. Although the "Peace Jubilee" was designed to celebrate the end of the Spanish-American War, McKinley struck a strong note of regional reconciliation as a secondary theme. His entourage included General Joseph Wheeler (upper left corner), a hero in the recent war who had also defended Atlanta as a Confederate major general in 1864. (Courtesy of the *Atlanta Journal-Constitution*; *Atlanta Constitution*, December 11, 1898, 1)

House or Senate committee to hear their grievances. In 1899, they enjoyed a small, incremental victory when the Georgia association was granted permission to hold meetings in the Capitol. However, the state's suffragists would have little success in amending the laws that restricted their rights as citizens until they secured their most basic right—the vote.[18]

The hall of the House of Representatives served as an important symbolic battleground many times in the course of its history. By virtue of its size, the House chamber was the place where governors gave addresses to joint sessions of the House and the Senate, some of which marked major turning points in Georgia's history. The same room hosted speeches by national leaders that marked milestones in regional and national history.

One of these occasions took place in 1898, when President William McKinley journeyed to the Capitol as part of his Peace Jubilee celebrating the end of the Spanish-American War. McKinley used the recent war, a popular effort that had united the nation, to help heal the South's lingering wounds from an earlier, more divisive conflict. Among those traveling with the president was the immensely popular general Joseph Wheeler. A former Confederate major general who defended Atlanta in 1864, Wheeler had served in Congress as a representative from Alabama in the 1880s and was commissioned as a major general in the U.S. Army during the Spanish-American War. As a hero of two wars, Wheeler had become a living symbol of regional reconciliation and drew a large audience for the president. McKinley brought another popular hero of the Spanish-American War in his entourage, General Henry Lawton, who as a Union captain had been awarded the Congressional Medal of Honor for his bravery during the Battle of Atlanta. The two former foes now stood with the president as victorious compatriots in the recent conflict.

On December 15, 1898, President McKinley, members of his cabinet, and his generals made their way through a crowd of onlookers near the west entrance and walked briskly up the Capitol steps. The president proceeded to the third-floor hall of the House of Representatives, where members of the House and the Senate stood to greet him as he entered. A newspaper reporter caught the gravity of the occasion: "The scene was as unique as it was unparalleled. The chief executive came in the presence of a legislative body with his head uncovered, walking by the side of Governor Candler, and together the head of the state and the chief of the nation ascended the stand and took the seat of the speaker and the one to the right." The joint session was called to order, but "it required several minutes to stop the applause and cheers that came from the overcrowded galleries."[19]

When the president rose to speak, the applause was deafening. He began with a frank declaration: "Sectional lines no longer mar the map of the United States. Sectional feeling no longer holds back the love we bear each other." Using the Spanish-American War as his reference, McKinley pledged first to care for those who were disabled in combat and to honor those who had died and were interred in national cemeteries. Then he went a step further, declaring to the packed hall: "[The] time has now come in the evolution of sentiment and feeling under the providence of God, when in the spirit of fraternity we should share with you in the care of the graves of the Confederate soldiers." In the aftermath of the Civil War, the federal government had honored deceased Union soldiers and veterans by maintaining cemeteries where they were buried, while southern states had assumed the obligation for their Confederate dead. McKinley's gesture sought to unite North and South in the veneration of their Civil War dead, for the graves of the former rebels would now receive the care, respect, and funding of the federal government.[20]

President McKinley's speech to the General Assembly resonated in a statehouse where Georgia's political leaders were customizing interior walls and halls with portraits and statues of men who had fought in the Civil War and then helped to shape the post-Reconstruction political order. A few years later, the death of one of these key figures, John B. Gordon, inspired a movement to add the first memorial to the Capitol grounds. As governor during the construction of the statehouse, Gordon had chaired the Capitol Commission. As the keynote speaker at the Capitol dedication ceremonies in 1889, Gordon had consecrated the building by proclaiming it "a fit memorial of the indomitable will and recuperative energies of this great people." Four years later, as a U.S. senator, he returned to the Capitol to accompany the body of Jefferson Davis in another consecration, one that linked the Capitol to the Lost Cause of the Old South. On January 13, 1904, Gordon made his final return to the Georgia Capitol, this time to lie in state.

Like Jefferson Davis's, Gordon's casket arrived at the depot on a train draped

President McKinley entering the Capitol, 1898. President William McKinley, hatless and in partial shadow in the lower right-hand corner of the photograph, ascends the steps of the west entrance to the Georgia statehouse on December 15, 1898. In his address to a joint session of the General Assembly in the House chamber, he called for the federal government to assume care of Confederate graves, another symbolic gesture toward regional reconciliation. (Courtesy of the Library of Congress)

John Gordon's bier entering the Capitol, 1904. By the time Confederate general and statesman John B. Gordon died in 1904, the ritual for public mourning at the Capitol was well established. Huge crowds gathered on January 15, and the public outcry soon focused on the need to memorialize the popular leader with a monument on the Capitol grounds. (Courtesy of the Kenan Research Center at the Atlanta History Center)

in black, where a somber crowd had gathered. Aging veterans served as an honor guard and carried the casket to a waiting hearse, which joined a lengthy procession to the statehouse. At the Capitol, another, larger crowd watched the arrival of the carriage and parted as the casket was carried slowly inside. The corridors were draped in black crepe, and black and white streamers hung from each balcony opening. Gordon's casket was placed on a bier in the center of the rotunda, surrounded by wreaths, potted plants, flowers, and Confederate flags. Family, friends, and civic leaders viewed the body privately for several hours before a steady flow of mourners began to pass through the rotunda. The veneration continued until the next day, when militiamen cleared a path through the teeming west plaza so that Gordon's pallbearers and family could process across the street to a memorial service at Central Presbyterian Church. After the service, huge crowds remained to witness the departure of Gordon's remains, which were taken for interment in Oakland Cemetery.[21]

John Gordon was not yet buried when political and civic leaders began to clamor for a monument in his honor on the grounds of the Capitol. Such a monument presented an opportunity for a symbolic merging of the Old and the New South in one figure. The sculptor chosen to render Gordon's image, Solon H. Borglum (1868–1922), had made his reputation sculpting heroic bronzes representing the taming of the West. His ability to capture horses as well as humans was an asset, for Borglum was commissioned to create an equestrian figure that cleverly combined Gordon's Old and New South associations. Gordon was depicted as he appeared in his later political life, but dressed in Confederate uniform, mounted on his favorite warhorse, while reviewing veteran troops.

The day of the unveiling, May 27, 1907, began like previous celebrations at the Capitol, with a parade. Hundreds of school children witnessed the occasion, and again men and boys "perched up on convenient telephone poles like so many blackbirds." All around the northwest corner of the grounds, "eager, expectant throngs" filled "every window on every floor from the front entrance of the Capitol back to the Hunter street [Martin Luther King Jr.] side, on the projecting ledges." The ceremonies lasted nearly three hours, culminating when Gordon's two daughters released the drape that covered the equestrian statue.[22]

Gordon's statue was placed on the most prominent corner of Capitol Square facing the heart of the downtown. The five-foot

oblong base of the statue had two bas-reliefs on its sides, one depicting Gordon in the battle of Spotsylvania and another in civilian dress with the caption: "GOVERNOR—PATRIOT—SENATOR." On the backside of the statue, a synopsis of Gordon's career emphasized his military heroism and his many elected offices, without mentioning his role as state leader of the Ku Klux Klan in the immediate aftermath of the Civil War.

In May 1907, the Capitol was approaching the end of its second decade. John Gordon's mounted figure stood looking toward the center of Atlanta, at the corner where the members of the 1889 General Assembly had turned as they had processed into their new statehouse almost twenty years before. Much had changed in Atlanta in the ensuing years. Skyscraper construction had brought buildings that rivaled the Capitol's domination of the skyline. Automobiles were beginning to replace carriages on the city's streets, signaling a new age of transportation. State government was growing in size, filling up the Capitol as it expanded to provide new services to Georgians. The building had become an important stage on which the theater of post-Reconstruction Georgia politics was being acted out. With the addition of interior portraits and now exterior statuary, the Georgia statehouse represented the ascendancy of the Democratic majority.

5 A MEMORIALIZED CAPITOL

When Governor Joseph Terrell addressed the exuberant throng gathered on the Capitol grounds for the dedication of the Gordon statue on May 27, 1907, he articulated a new vision for Capitol Square. In the eighteen years since the completion of the statehouse, an expanse of lawns and walkways had created a parklike setting for the landmark building. Now, with a monumental statue of John Gordon adorning the grounds, it was possible to envision additional memorials that would ring the Capitol and add new layers of symbolic meaning to the statehouse. To loud applause from his audience on the northwest lawn of the square, Governor Terrell gestured to the southwest corner, where he called for a statue of "gallant Georgia leader General James Longstreet, while on the southeast corner he suggested one to commemorate the great valor of the private [Confederate] soldier." Representative Joe Hill Hall from Bibb County, who followed Terrell to the podium, picked up this theme by advocating a fourth memorial to a southern Civil War hero, "that great military chieftain, Robert E. Lee."[1]

Capitol and grounds, c. 1917. The John B. Gordon monument brought sweeping changes to the Capitol grounds. Not only were the pathways redesigned to accommodate the equestrian statue, but its presence inspired a vision of a statehouse surrounded by heroes of the Confederacy. (Courtesy of the Kenan Research Center at the Atlanta History Center)

The Atlanta press played up the speeches by Terrell and Hall with much of the enthusiasm it had mustered for a new Capitol. In accounts of the audience's fervent response to additional memorials, reporters offered the news that the Gordon Monument Commission, chaired by Governor Terrell, would soon be reconstituted as the Southern Monuments Commission, with the task of creating a ring of memorials around the Capitol.[2]

However, the rhetoric of Terrell and Hall had but a short-term effect. As was the case with the Capitol itself, cost was a major impediment to new statuary. The new memorials would beautify the grounds and honor Confederate heroes, but the project competed with the more pressing needs of the statehouse, where ongoing maintenance and space demands for expanding bureaucracies were chronic challenges. In the ensuing decades, many grand designs to enhance the Capitol and its surrounding blocks would be put forth, but as each new plan developed, the implementation was put off in favor of lower-cost alternatives.

In the face of tight public funding, the Southern Monuments Commission never produced results, in part because of the difficulties the Gordon Monument Commission had faced in its private fundraising. The Gordon Monument Commission formed in 1904, the result of an inspirational appeal by General Clement A. Evans during his remarks at a celebration of Robert E. Lee's birthday held in the Capitol on January 19, 1904. At the beginning of the twentieth century, Lee's birthday was one of many celebrations that white southerners used to memorialize what they characterized as the heroic military struggle for the Lost Cause of the Confederacy. In Atlanta, the organizers

behind the Capitol event were the Atlanta camp of the Confederate Veterans
and the Atlanta chapter of the United Daughters of the Confederacy. Both
groups were legacy societies that had organized in the previous fifteen years
to keep the memories of the Lost Cause alive.[3]

The day after Evans's speech, in a typical act of Atlanta boosterism, a large
committee made up mostly of local residents, met in the mayor's reception room
in City Hall to form the Gordon Monument Association. With no specific site
in mind for the memorial, the committee set a goal of $25,000
for the Gordon statue (roughly $500,000 today). Twice before,
Atlantans had organized memorial associations to raise funds
for statues in their city. The first, honoring Benjamin Hill,
had been erected in 1886 on the corner of Peachtree and West
Peachtree streets and was moved into the Capitol in 1890. The
second, memorializing New South hero Henry Grady, was
dedicated October 21, 1891, in a ceremony that began with a

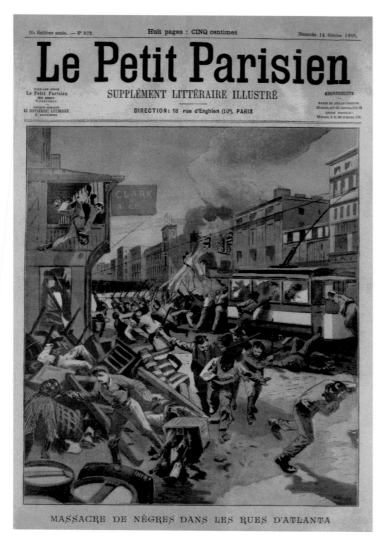

Le Petit Parisien

SUPPLÉMENT LITTÉRAIRE ILLUSTRÉ

DIRECTION: 18 rue d'Enghien (10e), PARIS

MASSACRE DE NÈGRES DANS LES RUES D'ATLANTA

Atlanta Race Riot, 1906. The legislature of 1907 convened in a tense political climate. Hoke Smith won the heated 1906 gubernatorial contest with the promise of disfranchising Georgia's black voters. Soon after, a race riot broke out in downtown Atlanta, in which white mobs attacked African Americans and their businesses. The 1907 General Assembly was expected to make good on Governor Smith's campaign promise, as well as pass a statewide prohibition on alcohol. (Reprinted from *Le Petit Parisien*, October 14, 1906; courtesy of the Kenan Research Center at the Atlanta History Center)

march from the Capitol to its prime location on Marietta Street near the site of the old statehouse.

Atlanta boosters were less successful in raising funds for a third statue in their city. After two years, the association had $6,000 cash in hand and $4,000 in pledges, well short of the $25,000 goal. In an effort to get state support for the project, the association staged an artistic competition and in May 1906, exhibited six models in the Capitol. The exhibition in the statehouse had its intended effect, for the following August, the legislature passed a bill to create the Gordon Monument Commission and to appropriate $15,000 of public funds for an equestrian statue to be erected on the Capitol grounds.

In the first three quarters of the twentieth century, major monuments would be added to the Capitol grounds one at a time, but not at public expense. Each effort would be led by an individual commission that raised private funds for the cost of the statue. Each new monument would be unveiled in a grand public ceremony. All the statues would honor Georgians who had held elective office, all but one of whom had served as governor. Smaller memorials honoring Georgians of more varied achievements would begin to fill the exterior grounds and interior spaces, as the Capitol itself came to function as a memorial to the state's honored dead.

The legislature that convened in July 1907, just two months after the unveiling of the Gordon monument, began work during a time of great turmoil in Georgia. Ten months earlier, Atlanta had been the site of a race riot during which white mobs attacked and killed dozens of African Americans and destroyed their businesses in the downtown. The riot came in the aftermath of a heated gubernatorial contest between Hoke Smith and Clark Howell, which, aided by inflammatory articles in the white press, had incited antiblack sentiment among whites. Hoke Smith won the election with the support of Tom Watson, the fiery leader of Georgia's Populist movement and champion of poor whites, and with a pledge to limit African American voting. At the same time, a major political campaign was underway to impose prohibition statewide, an effort in which women were playing a major role.

The 1907 General Assembly faced a legislative docket that revealed the two different directions in which women and blacks were headed in Capitol politics. Prohibition enabled women to emerge as a potent force in the political life of Georgia. From the opening of the 1907 session, women could be seen roaming the corridors, packing the legislative chambers' galleries, and lobbying representatives and senators. That session the issue was statewide prohibition, and the women were working at the behest of the Women's Christian Temperance Union. They hoped to convince the male legislators to prohibit the sale of intoxicants in Georgia by passing the Hardman-Covington-Neal Bill. One of the foremost lobbyists, Mary McLendon, was familiar to many legislators, who had encountered her resolve in her previous efforts for women's suffrage.

Thanks to a local option law passed more than twenty years earlier, 124 of Georgia's 144 counties had voted themselves "dry." The remaining "wet" counties, where liquor could be consumed or purchased for easy transport to dry counties, contained or were near large cities. Support for the bill was strong, but urban businessmen were fighting vigorously to maintain the local option.[4]

By 1907, Georgia women had developed a sophisticated approach to political participation. While legislators debated the Hardman-Covington-Neal Bill, women massed in the statehouse to make sure the men did the right thing. The Women's Christian Temperance Union led the charge, coordinating a widespread network of influential individuals, churches, and organizations. Marshaling the public relations tactics of their day, the prohibitionists issued statements to the press, produced and distributed thousands of leaflets, and gathered and presented a multitude of signatures on petitions from localities around the state.

The outbreak of passions on each side of the temperance debate in the House of Representatives on July 24, 1907, demonstrated that Georgia women were ready for the rough and tumble politics of the statehouse. Most spectators arrived early that morning, expecting to witness the historic vote that would give final legislative approval to statewide prohibition. Dressed in heavy skirts and long sleeves, temperance women filled most of the gallery seats, undeterred by the stiflingly hot and humid conditions inside the statehouse. Many of the men present in the balcony were opponents of prohibition and, given the tenor of the crowd, ignored social etiquette and kept their eyes downcast so they would not feel obligated to offer their seats to standing women. In one atrium, temperance women set up tables with fried chicken, stuffed eggs, sandwiches, and lemonade for "dry" legislators. Across the rotunda in the opposite atrium, the whiskey interests offered food and beverage to their supporters. All the legislators would need sustenance, for the "wets" were planning a filibuster to thwart or at least stall passage of the bill.[5]

Just before the 9:00 a.m. opening, Mary H. Armour, president of the Georgia Women's Temperance Union, slipped into a front-row balcony seat secured by her allies. In the well below, Speaker John Slaton gaveled the session to order. Slaton had a difficult day ahead. Instead of a quick, decisive vote, the speeches of the "wets" kept the House in session long after

ABOVE *Editorial cartoon depictions of the selling of prohibition badges and of ladies serving lunches, 1907.* The first day of the House's prohibition debate, July 24, 1907, was hot and humid. Temperance supporters crowded the corridors distributing white ribbons, the symbol of prohibition support. They also set up tables to serve lunch to their legislative supporters. (Courtesy of the *Atlanta Journal-Constitution; Atlanta Constitution*, July 26, 1907, 1)

LEFT *Ladies in the House gallery, 1907.* The House gallery filled at 8:00 a.m., two hours before the session convened. The mostly female temperance supporters grew restless as they watched the male legislators debate on the House floor below. (Courtesy of the *Atlanta Journal-Constitution; Atlanta Constitution*, July 26, 1907, 1)

HON. SEABORN WRIGHT.
Presentative from Floyd County.

Caricature of Seaborn Wright, 1907. Well into the evening, ardent prohibitionist Representative Seaborn Wright challenged his legislative colleagues to end their filibuster, and pandemonium broke out in the galleries. Speaker John Slaton responded by ordering all spectators from the chamber. (Courtesy of the *Atlanta Journal-Constitution*; *Atlanta Journal*, July 4, 1907, 6)

Legislators' fistfight in the House, 1907. When debate resumed around 10:45 p.m., there was an exchange of words between prohibition foe Joe Hill Hall and Seaborn Wright, and the two legislators began to brawl beneath the Speaker's podium. After their peers pulled them apart, the House adjourned. Atlanta police helped to clear the Capitol of the agitated crowd. (Courtesy of the *Atlanta Journal-Constitution*; *Atlanta Constitution*, July 26, 1907, 1)

the sun went down. As the day dragged on, the spectators, described in press reports as "a seething, smoldering mass," grew impatient and tried to cheer on the efforts of the "dry" legislators. However, the "iron hand" of the Speaker held them back, as Slaton threatened to clear the gallery at the first outburst. Emotions remained in check until just after 10:00 p.m., when Representative Seaborn Wright, the floor leader for prohibition, rose and asked if the Speaker was "helpless as a child" to stop the minority filibuster. He then rallied his fellow prohibitionist legislators, declaring, "Men, let us do our duty and stand like men." His declaration unleashed the pent-up passions of the gallery, which erupted with cheers that resounded from the walls and ceiling of the hall.

The gaveling Speaker Slaton ordered the gallery cleared as the spectators booed and hissed, shouted and threatened. Armour left as ordered, proclaiming, "Yes, we will leave, but if we do not get this legislation at once, there will be an uprising of the people." Armour left the Capitol and marched straight to the offices of the *Atlanta Constitution*, where she decried the behavior of her opponents in the legislature, repeated her "uprising of the people" quote, and warned the General Assembly that "the time for foolishness ha[d] passed."[6]

Back in the House chamber, Speaker Slaton had attained order, but the prohibitionists crowding the halls outside continued to agitate for a swift vote. At 10:45 p.m., Representative Joe Hill Hall, a "wet" supporter, rose to condemn the continuing disruption in the corridor by declaring, "We are tonight in the midst of anarchy." When Representative Wright interrupted him, Hall thundered back that, after the gallery-clearing scene that Wright had just caused, he was surprised that Wright had "again raised his voice on this subject" in the assembly that night. Wright responded fiercely, "In the name of God Almighty I do raise it here and now," to which Hall retorted with equal fury that Wright was "no longer worthy to occupy a seat in the house." Wright cried, "You are a liar, sir," and rushed toward the podium where Hall was standing.

Speaker Slaton watched in amazement as a fistfight between the two men broke out beneath his rostrum and other legislators ran toward the front of the chamber. Once again, Slaton called for the sergeant at arms to restore order. The representatives who were closest to the combatants separated them and escorted them to their seats. A tense calm overcame the House chamber as the legislators quickly passed a motion to adjourn and headed for the exits. Further altercations in the packed hallways were prevented only by the arrival of reinforcements from the Atlanta police, who quickly cleared the Capitol of the agitated crowd.[7]

Cooler heads prevailed the following day as legislative leaders scheduled the final vote on the prohibition bill for July 30. When that day arrived, the galleries remained locked, but once again, prohibitionists massed at the Capitol, gathering in the corridors, rotunda, and atria "to the point of suffocation."

When Representative Massengale, an ardent prohibitionist, burst from the House chamber and announced the successful 139 to 39 vote to the awaiting throng, "there rose a shout that reached and reverberated through the building, and which was reinforced by still another." Pandemonium ensued as women hugged one another and children waved handkerchiefs. Armour declared, "[T]his is the grandest day Georgia ever saw," and led fifteen hundred supporters out of the Capitol, down its front steps, and toward City Hall on Marietta Street, where they gathered under the statue of Henry Grady, a fellow prohibitionist. There on the widest boulevard in downtown Atlanta, the antiliquor enthusiasts sang the doxology to celebrate their victory.[8]

As Georgia women savored their political success with the 1907 legislature, the tenuous grasp on the vote held by African Americans was being pried loose. Spurred on by Governor Hoke Smith and his ally Tom Watson, legislative committees advanced a disfranchisement bill through both the House and the Senate with ease. In contrast to the hundreds of women who had swarmed the Capitol just two weeks earlier, black Georgians did not go to their statehouse and were virtually absent from the debate over their right to vote. The only effort to dissuade the legislature came in the form of an eleven-page pamphlet published by twenty-two prominent African American businessmen, ministers, and educators from cities across Georgia. The authors argued that that the disfranchisement amendment was undemocratic, unconstitutional, unjust, and uncivil, and that its consequence would be that the "Negro race would be subjugated to a complete state of political serfdom." In vain, Georgia's white politicians were asked to live up to their earlier New South promises to "deal with absolute fairness between [their] white and black citizens" if blacks withdrew themselves from politics.[9]

Governor Smith made good his campaign promises and paid his political debt to Tom Watson by championing the Williams-Felder Bill. The proposed legislation would add an amendment to the Georgia Constitution restricting the right to register to vote to

"Suggested by the New Law," 1907. After the passage of prohibition, the *Atlanta Constitution* published a cartoon that contemplated its effects. A new state seal representing PROHIBITION replaced the male soldier with the outspoken temperance activist Carrie Nation. A racist caricature of a black man with liquor bottle and razor was identified as "The Real Cause of it All." (Courtesy of the *Atlanta Journal-Constitution*; *Atlanta Constitution*, August 19, 1907, 1)

> any male who was sane, had no criminal record, had paid all taxes since 1877, had met the existing residency requirements, *and had satisfied one of the following existing conditions* [emphasis added]: (1) had served honorably in wars of the United States in the forces of the Confederate States, (2) had descended from persons who had such service records, (3) was of "good character" and could understand the duties of citizenship, (4) could read and write in English any paragraph of the state and federal constitutions or could understand and give a reasonable interpretation of any paragraph of such constitutions, or (5) owned at lease forty acres of land or property assessed for taxation at a value of $500.[10]

Although the Williams-Felder bill did not mention race, the editorial writers in white newspapers were explicit about the intentions behind the proposal. The *Savannah Tribune* noted: "The principal purpose of the bill is to disqualify the ignorant and venal negro [*sic*] voters of Georgia, preserving to the white man the right to vote. It will eliminate at least 90 per cent of the negroes [*sic*] of Georgia as voters, and will not disqualify a single white man."[11]

On August 13, 1907, the Williams-Felder Bill came to the House floor for debate and passage. Representative William Rogers, the lone African American representative in the Georgia General Assembly, sat at his desk quietly as the debate progressed. Rogers, who hailed from coastal Liberty County, was one of the few African Americans who had not withdrawn himself from the political arena. The rhetoric that surrounded him was heated and rushed; adjournment was only four days away.

Now the time had come for Rogers to take a stand. As he rose to speak, the low buzz of the many private conversations among legislators in the House chamber continued. Rogers began with a deceptively simple argument to his white colleagues, one that did not sound out of character for the black representative: "There is not a man here that does not love both the old soldier and the old slave. Let us treat them and their children alike." "In the

Statue of Tom Watson. As a national Populist leader in the 1890s, Tom Watson ran for president and built an army of fervent supporters in Georgia. Populism collapsed with the turn of the century, but Watson continued to influence Georgia politics. In 1906, his support put Hoke Smith into the governor's suite, based on the campaign promise that black Georgians would lose their right to vote. (Courtesy of Diane Kirkland and the Georgia Department of Economic Development)

Caricature of Representative Joe Hill Hall of Bibb County, 1907. The voice of Representative Joe Hill Hall was heard often during the 1907 legislative session. At the dedication of the Gordon statue on May 27, he called for a statue of Robert E. Lee on the Capitol grounds. On July 24, his heated words as a prominent "wet" led to a fistfight with "dry" legislator Seaborn Wright. On August 12, he spoke passionately against the disfranchisement bill because he argued that it could be used to restrict white voting. (Courtesy of the *Atlanta Journal-Constitution*; *Atlanta Constitution*, July 30, 1907, 1)

interest of fairness" he moved to expand the list of grandfather qualifiers to include "those held in involuntary servitude January 1, 1863," as well as their descendants. When his fellow legislators heard the motion, some of the side conversations came to an abrupt halt. Caught off guard by what they considered an outrageous change, one that would include the very citizens they intended to exclude, Roger's colleagues greeted his call with a chorus of laughing nays that voted down his motion. Representative Rogers was the sole supporting aye.[12]

Representative Rogers was not chastened but stood again to present a second motion. This time he was not so self-effacing.

To his colleagues' surprise, Rogers moved to add language to the bill that would clarify the amendment's intent, a preamble stating that "this was a white man's government, and providing for the enfranchisement of all whites and disfranchisement of all negroes [sic]." This time there was no laughter, just silence.[13]

On its face, Rodger's motion merely echoed the popular understanding of the law's intent. The *Atlanta Journal* hailed the passage of the bill as a victory for the "people of the state, who were anxious to rise and assert once and for all in unmistakable terms that this was a white man's country and the prevailing rule should be that of the Anglo-Saxon race." However, for an African American to state the bill's intention so explicitly was an act of public defiance. The legislators wasted no time in voting down the motion, Rogers's vote again being the sole aye.[14]

The Williams-Felder disfranchisement amendment to the Georgia Constitution passed in August 1907, was ratified by Georgia voters in October 1908, and soon had its intended consequences. The percentage of eligible black males who registered to vote in Georgia plummeted from 28.3 percent in 1904 to 4.3 percent in 1910. Keeping African Americans off the voting rolls also eliminated their ability to vote for local officials and prevented them from serving on election or school boards or juries. Deprived of their most basic civil rights and struggling against agricultural decline, African Americans voted with their feet. Thousands left Georgia for better economic opportunities

and greater political freedom in the cities of the North and the Midwest. Between 1910 and 1930, African Americans declined from 45 percent to 37 percent of the total state population, and their absolute numbers decreased by over 100,000.[15]

After the close of the 1907 legislative session, William Rogers committed his final act of protest by resigning his position in the Georgia House of Representatives. The color line at the Capitol hardened. For the next half century, every elected official in the Capitol would be white. African Americans did work at the Capitol, but in servile positions as porters, shoeshine men, and cleaners. On occasions when other African Americans were permitted to attend meetings in the legislative chambers, they sat segregated in the galleries while whites gathered on the floor below. When viewing legislative debates, black spectators were shunted into a side section of the House or Senate galleries. The color line also extended to the Capitol's public facilities. Restrooms on the main floors were off-limits to African Americans. Lavatories for blacks were located in the basement, marked by "colored" signs.

By the early years of the new century, the basement of the Capitol had evolved into a makeshift maze of additional offices and storage. As government expanded, the demand for office space packed the statehouse ever more densely. A 1905 House committee reported that crowding was obstructing the work of many departments, recommended more expensive repairs, and mentioned the need for an annex. Above the basement level, additional desks were moved into existing offices, and legislative committee rooms were converted for office use. Even the

THE 1907 LEGISLATURE PASSES INTO HISTORY

"*The 1907 Legislature Passes into History.*" Weary legislators head into history after the eventful 1907 legislative session. Among the bills they had passed were the Hardman-Covington-Neal Bill, which extended prohibition statewide, and the Williams-Felder Bill, which disfranchised African American voters. (Courtesy of the *Atlanta Journal-Constitution*; *Atlanta Journal*, August 18, 1907, 1)

hallways began to fill. With only a few benches in the wide corridors and around the atrium stairwells, there was plenty of display space for the expanding state museum.

Since its origin as a geological collection in 1890, the state museum had grown rapidly, and by 1910, the fourth-floor corridors were filled with over fifty display cases. Slabs of polished granite jutted from the walls, and marble columns with heavy Corinthian capitals competed with the cases for floor space. Most of the new exhibits were promotional, recycled from those created by the General Assembly in 1903 with a thirty-thousand-dollar appropriation to create exhibits for the St. Louis Exposition and others to follow. These former fair exhibits established the tone of the Capitol Museum for many decades to come. Many focused on the economic potential of Georgia's natural resources, the raw materials that awaited industrial development. Agriculture was heralded in displays such as a seven-hundred-boll cotton stalk, while others celebrated Georgia fruits, woods, and grains. A small collection of "relics" grew into several collections of fossils, Native American artifacts, and Civil War memorabilia. When the federal government returned its captured Civil War flags in 1905, Georgia added as many as thirty-three Confederate battle flags to its Civil War collection. By 1910, the museum filled the Capitol corridors and had matured into a popular tourist attraction.

The keeper of public buildings, now managing an overused, aging property, became a busy man. By 1909, Keeper J. L.

Barron was producing detailed annual reports that included salaries for an engineer, a fireman, a watchman, porters, and laborers. In response to two decades of wear and tear, he ordered new carpets in the House and Senate chambers and repairs that required painting, plumbing, bricklaying, and carpentry. However, because of budgetary restrictions, many of Barron's recommendations, including his call for an annex to provide additional office space, went unheeded by the General Assembly.[16]

The aging Capitol continued to attract visitors, both social and political. In the second decade of the twentieth century, the Leo Frank case filled the statehouse more than once with angry protesters. After Atlanta factory worker Mary Phagan was brutally murdered in April 1913, plant superintendent Frank was tried in a courtroom one block west of the Capitol, where he was convicted and sentenced to death by hanging September 1, 1913. The local press supported the decision, feeding on the public's insecurity regarding "foreigners" and crime. As the legal appeals wore on the following year, the press frenzy intensified. The incendiary voice of Tom Watson entered the fray, as his newspaper, the *Jeffersonian*, called repeatedly for extralegal action. Frank's case moved into the Capitol. Appeals were heard in the Supreme Court Room, the Prison Commission held clemency hearings in the state library, and Governor John Slaton conducted commutation hearings in the anteroom of the governor's suite.[17]

Capitol Museum, 1922. The state museum grew rapidly in the early twentieth century. New exhibits, many taken from displays developed for state exhibitions, filled corridors and attracted a growing number of visitors. (Courtesy of the Georgia Capitol Museum)

State chemist's office, c. 1908. The Capitol's interior filled quickly, and by 1909, the keeper of public buildings was requesting an annex to provide additional office space. Basement offices such as this state chemist laboratory were grim and makeshift. (Courtesy of the Georgia Archives, Vanishing Georgia Collection, ful1083-94)

With each step in the legal process, crowds gathered at the statehouse. While the Prison Commission deliberated whether to commute Frank's sentence, a crowd of over 2,500 gathered on the Capitol steps to hear speeches advocating Frank's execution. The crowds came back on Monday, June 14, 1915, when the governor announced his commutation of Frank's death sentence to life in prison. Slaton had seen elevated emotions in the Capitol when he presided as Speaker of the House over the Prohibition debate, and now, eight years later, his decision ignited a firestorm of outrage. Bedlam broke out in the city, and the statehouse became a forum for protest. Around noon, an excited throng burst into the governor's office, only to find that he was not there. The crowd repaired to the Senate chamber, where they listened to impassioned speeches denouncing the decision. That evening, the governor called up the state militia and declared martial law when a mob marched on his home near Peachtree Street and West Paces Ferry Road.

Inauguration day brought outgoing governor Slaton back to the Capitol,

Former governor Slaton and Governor Harris leaving the Capitol, 1915. Outgoing governor John Slaton was booed, hissed, and threatened when he left the Capitol after the inauguration of his successor Nathaniel Harris. Several days earlier Slaton had commuted the death sentence of Leo Frank, a Jewish factory manager who was convicted of murdering shop worker Mary Phagan. Frank's appeals, clemency hearings, and commutation all occurred inside the Capitol. (Reprinted from Nathaniel E. Harris, *Autobiography: The Story of an Old Man's Life with Reminiscences of Seventy-five Years* [Macon, Ga.: J. W. Burke, 1925], 358)

where an enraged crowd created a harrowing situation. Onlookers in the packed House gallery hissed and booed Slaton as he performed the symbolic duty of passing the state seal to incoming governor Nathaniel Harris. As the two left the building together, a man in the throng of onlookers outside threatened Slaton with a lead pipe. The attacker was apprehended quickly, and John Slaton got into his automobile and was driven away from the Capitol and out of Georgia politics.[18]

Few Georgians realized it at the time, but the politics in the statehouse that Slaton left behind in 1914 were about to change significantly. That year, Mary McLendon, who had been advancing the cause of women's rights for over twenty years, formed the Georgia Women's Suffrage Party and finally got a suffrage bill advanced to a committee hearing. However, the success of women in advancing the temperance cause in the General Assembly did not assure their victory in other political debates. As support for the women's vote grew nationally, Georgia legislatures remained entrenched.

McLendon directed the suffrage campaign with the same strategies that had served her well in her temperance efforts. Suffrage supporters distributed forty thousand pages of leaflets and fliers, sent news releases around Georgia and the nation, deluged legislators with suffrage literature, and massed advocates at the Capitol when the issue was considered. McLendon arranged for Rebecca Latimer Felton, her sister and a national advocate for women's rights, to speak for the franchise at the first Senate committee hearing on the subject. The opponents to women's suffrage recruited their own advocate.

Dolly Blount Lamar, the daughter of the popular Georgia congressman James Blount (1837–1903) and historian for the United Daughters of the Confederacy, testified, declaring "that women's place was in the home bearing children, not in the political arena," and that the Nineteenth Amendment "was really the Fifteenth Amendment in disguise and that it would foster racial equality by giving Negro women the vote." With women of the white elite divided on the issue, male legislators in Georgia found it easy to vote against suffrage. The 1914 bill died in committee.[19]

Elsewhere in the United States, the push for women's political rights was succeeding. On June 4, 1919, Congress approved the Nineteenth Amendment and sent it to the states for ratification. In the Georgia Capitol, however, antisuffrage sentiment remained strong. Representative Jackson of Jones County introduced the ratification bill to the Georgia General Assembly with the expressed purpose of defeating it. In an impassioned speech to his colleagues, Jackson concluded that "women were temperamentally disqualified for the exercise of the political franchise and that he would never agree to place them on equality with man at the ballot box." On July 19, 1919, the House voted down the Nineteenth Amendment by a substantial majority, followed by the Senate on July 24. The following day, the *Atlanta Constitution*, which had changed its position on the matter, editorialized that the "time is coming—and it is not far distant—when the men who have been most conspicuous in opposition to it will be ashamed of and apologetic for the records made on this issue."[20]

Postmistress Grace Hamby Brewer, c. 1917. Prior to gaining the vote, Georgia women did hold a few select positions in state government. Grace Hamby Brewer, seated here at her desk in the Capitol, served as postmistress in 1917–18. (Courtesy of the Georgia Archives, Vanishing Georgia Collection, rab256)

Senators in the Senate chamber, 1911. Although women could not vote or hold elected office, they did work in the Capitol in administrative roles. Here the 1911 Senate poses with a lone female secretary (foreground). (Courtesy of the Georgia Archives, Georgia Senate Composites, 1911)

Two years later, with the national ratification of the Nineteenth Amendment expected by the end of the legislative session, the *Atlanta Constitution*'s prediction proved true. Male members of the 1921 General Assembly adjusted quickly to the new political reality in which women could vote them out of office. On August 13, they voted overwhelmingly to permit women to vote in all elections and to hold public office. Regarding the change in attitude among the male legislators, the author of *History of Woman Suffrage* observed wryly: "These legislators were so courteous and obliging the women could scarcely believe it was a Georgia legislature." With the vote, came immediate changes in both the Georgia legislature and the Capitol itself.[21]

In November 1921, three months after a woman's right to vote in Georgia had been secured, Mary McLendon died. Women's rights and temperance groups in Georgia organized to create a permanent memorial to honor their tireless leader for her work in the halls of the Georgia Capitol. They commissioned a five-foot-high marble drinking fountain, which, without official action by the General Assembly, was installed and dedicated on March 18, 1923. Now the political work of women was memorialized in the Capitol. After the installation of the McLendon fountain, legislators would bow below her marble relief to receive a cooling drink of water, paying homage to the leader of the fight for women's suffrage in Georgia. The McLendon memorial has since been moved

Senator Susie Tillman Moore,
c. 1940. Women won seats in
the House of Representatives
soon after the female vote was
secured, but change came more
slowly to the Senate. The first
woman elected to the Senate
in her own right was Susie T.
Moore of Tifton, Georgia, in
1932. Prior to Senator Moore,
two women had been elected
to replace their deceased
husbands. (Courtesy of the
Georgia Archives, Small Print
Collection, spc31-042)

Fountain commemorating Mary McLendon. After more
than twenty-five years of passionate advocacy, Mary
McLendon lived to see Georgia women granted the
vote in 1921. After her death in November of that year,
women's rights and temperance groups organized
quickly to create a memorial to her in the Capitol. This
fountain was installed in March 1923, three months
before Georgia's first elected female representatives
took office. (Courtesy of Diane Kirkland and the
Georgia Department of Economic Development)

to a prominent position in the Capitol facing the grand staircase in the center
of the south atrium, but since the relocation did not provide a source of water,
the memorial no longer functions as a fountain.

Three months after the dedication of the McLendon memorial in the Capitol,
on June 28, 1923, Representatives Viola Ross Napier from Bibb County and Bessie Kempton Crowell of Fulton County walked up the Capitol steps, climbed
one of the grand staircases, entered the House chamber, and took their seats
as the first women to serve in the General Assembly. Representatives Napier
and Kempton were pathbreakers who advanced their professional and political
careers in Macon and Atlanta, cities with growing opportunities for women.
Kempton was a reporter for the *Atlanta Constitution*. An attorney, Napier had
been to the Capitol as the first woman to argue cases before the Georgia Court
of Appeals and the Georgia Supreme Court. After the General Assembly passed
legislation opening the practice of law to women in 1916 (one of the legislative
changes long advocated by McLendon's suffragists), Napier had been among
the first group of women to be admitted to the Georgia bar.

Upon their arrival in the House, Napier and Kempton wasted no time in
taking up their legislative duties, introducing bills separately and as cosponsors.
The political careers of Napier and Kempton proved that women could gain
political office and influence legislative outcomes, but it would be fifty years
before women's political power would flourish. Napier won reelection once,
and after her 1926 defeat, spent the rest of her career as Macon's city clerk.
Kempton was reelected three times and served until 1931. Georgia women won
their first Senate seats in the late 1920s and early 1930s. Margaret Johnson and
Tassie Kelley Cannon were elected to replace their deceased husbands in 1927
and 1931, but the election of 1932 brought the first woman to serve in the Senate
in her own right, Susie T. Moore of Tifton.[22]

As women entered and changed statehouse politics, the area around the
Capitol showed signs of a different kind of progress. As many as four hundred

tourists a day came to see the bustling city of Atlanta from atop the Capitol dome. They waited in line at the third-floor entrance to the stairwell that wound its way between the interior wall of the rotunda and the exterior walls of the drum and the dome. Emerging in the cupola, they stepped out onto an exterior balcony that offered a breathtaking 360-degree view of the city.

Visitors in the early 1920s looked out onto a city in flux. To the northwest, stood four large churches—Second Baptist, Central Presbyterian, Immaculate Conception, and the Cathedral of St. Philip—whose towers and pinnacles rose above the surrounding structures. The stately single-family homes whose residents had supported these institutions were subdividing and disappearing, as their former middle- and upper-class occupants moved to newer housing in the burgeoning suburbs. Soon two of these anchor churches—Second Baptist and St. Philip's Cathedral—would abandon their downtown locations to follow their congregations to northside neighborhoods.

The view from the Capitol dome to the north revealed the continuing influence of the

Interior of the Capitol dome, c. 1933. Climbing up the interior staircases of the Capitol dome to view the city from the cupola was a popular pastime in the early decades of the twentieth century. Visitors walked up 232 steps, taking three sets of spiral stairs and a series of straight stairways between the inner and outer domes. (Courtesy of the Library of Congress)

railroads, where trains moved along the many rows of tracks, and passenger and depot buildings lined the right of way. Much of the railroad gulch disappeared under viaducts, wide bridges spanning the tracks at various points, including Washington Street, just north of the Capitol. Beyond the railroad, a new skyline of office towers was emerging. The Fourth National Bank Building, the Empire Building, the Flatiron Building, the Grant Building, and the Candler Building towered over the three- and four-story storefronts of the late nineteenth century.

To the south of the statehouse, residential neighborhoods spread out into the distance. However, by 1916, state government had expanded out of the Capitol and into surrounding leased residences. In 1919, Governor Hugh Dorsey introduced a proposal to look at the statehouse comprehensively and to plan for a "Capitol campus." The recommendation was a proper build out for the first floor and the acquisition of land for the development of a Capitol campus. The General Assembly ignored Dorsey's report, but the glare of publicity would soon prod its members into action.[23]

By the early 1920s, deferred Capitol maintenance was presenting problems of public safety. The situation became newsworthy in early 1923 when a pane fell out of one of the north clere-

Composite view of downtown Atlanta from the Capitol dome, early 1920s, looking west, northwest to north, and north to northeast. Visitors who arrived atop the Capitol dome in the 1920s were rewarded with dramatic views of the downtown. These composite photographs to the west, north, and east reveal a downtown core of skyscrapers, church spires, railroad facilities, factory smokestacks, and two- and three-story commercial storefronts. (Courtesy of the Georgia Archives, Vanishing Georgia Collection, ful0929a,b,c,d,e,f-84)

story windows into the interior, plunging fifty feet to the marble floor below. The *Atlanta Journal* investigated and ran a front-page story deploring the sorry condition of the Capitol. Besides the safety hazards of falling glass and failing plaster, the article described severe deterioration and neglect. The legislature took note and began funding more repairs, and a joint committee began to look into converting the basement into office space.[24]

For the next few years, repairs progressed slowly, one appropriation at a time. Appeals for a more systematic approach were almost an annual feature of the Governor's message, but it would take another media exposé before a comprehensive approach was taken. Early in 1929, the *Atlanta Constitution* called the Capitol "an outrage and a disgrace" and described its "dirty and dilapidated" and dangerous condition in colorful detail.[25]

At the request of Governor L. G. Hardeman, chief custodian W. T. Thurmon gathered bids and prepared a request. Hardeman shepherded the $250,000 appropriation through the House and Senate personally. The General Assembly approved the request, reserving $55,000 of the appropriation to purchase nearby properties for future expansion. Finally, a decade after Governor Dorsey's recommendations, funding was provided to remodel the first floor, renovate the entire building, and begin the creation of a governmental campus.[26]

Work began in September 1929. The basement became a fully functioning first floor, with the addition of new offices, upgrading of existing ones, and the enclosure of the staircases to create storage space. The entire building was rewired, the water system reworked, and the elevator replaced. Interior walls and ceilings were replastered and painted.[27]

View of the main dome from the cupola. Visitors looking out from the Capitol dome enjoyed panoramic views of the city. If they dared to lean out over the balcony railing, they would have seen this unusual perspective of the Capitol's main dome and the city streets below. (Courtesy of Diane Kirkland and the Georgia Department of Economic Development)

Dedication of the Joseph E. Brown statue, 1928. Joseph E. Brown's memorial was the second major monument placed on the Capitol grounds. Located on the southwest corner, the statue was financed through a bequest from Brown's son Julius, who requested that it include Brown's wife, Elizabeth. Brown was Georgia's Confederate "war governor" as well as a U.S. senator. (Courtesy of the Georgia Archives, Vanishing Georgia Collection, ful0176)

By the end of the third decade of the twentieth century, many of the chronic problems inside the Capitol had been addressed. The 1920s also saw changes outside, when the legislature authorized the placement of two new monuments on the Capitol grounds. Joseph E. Brown's statue would be erected in three years, funded by the will of his second son, Julius. Slowed by fundraising, the monument to Tom Watson would not be unveiled until 1932.

In 1925, the General Assembly accepted an offer in the will of Julius E. Brown to fund a statue on the Capitol grounds that would honor his parents, Governor Joseph E. Brown and his wife, Elizabeth. Brown had played a critical role in orchestrating Georgia's secessionist vote in 1861 and governed the state during the Civil War. After the war, he was pardoned and served as a Republican political appointee to the state supreme court. He returned to the Democratic Party and was elected by the General Assembly to serve in the U.S. Senate in the 1880s. After his death in 1894, his son Joseph Mackey Brown followed in his footsteps and served as Georgia governor from 1909 to 1913.

When accepting the Brown family gift, the General Assembly also gave the executor of the estate the authorization to execute the design and erect the statue. The second major monument on the Capitol grounds was assigned a prominent location in the southwest corner. On October 27, 1928, a bronze statue of the Confederate "war governor" and his wife was dedicated amid great pomp and pageantry. In what is as much a family memorial as a political statement, Brown is depicted standing with his arm tenderly encircling his wife's seated figure. The Georgia General Assembly called her "every sense a fit mate for her husband, of modest demeanor, shunning public display, she was yet, a quiet force."[28]

By the end of the 1920s, the State Capitol and Capitol Square looked and functioned better than they had in years. The building was arranged more efficiently, and many of its systems had been improved. The grounds featured a new monument to another Confederate hero. In addition, the legislative halls and courtrooms were now opened to women, making the Capitol a more democratic place. However, beneath the newly painted surfaces and fresh female presence lay some underlying conditions that had not improved. The wooden and metal dome support system, still untouched since its installation in 1889, was slowly failing and would continue to cause serious structural problems. Similarly, many of Georgia's citizens were still denied the vote, overcome by a web of obstacles that stood between them and the ballot box. The next decade would bring a bold new force into Georgia politics and the statehouse, but it would bring little relief to Georgians or their statehouse.

A CIVIC CAPITOL

On August 28, 1932, the front pages of the Atlanta newspapers featured a
visionary plan that would transform the motley assemblage of buildings that
surrounded the Capitol and create a grand civic space with the statehouse as
its centerpiece. A four-column perspective drawing of "Atlanta's Civic Center"
projected eight new municipal and state facilities around a "Central Park" facing
the Capitol, joined by the recently constructed Atlanta City Hall (1928) and the
Fulton County Courthouse (1914). The Atlanta City Planning Commission was
the source of the $11,600,000 improvement plan, which was endorsed by Mayor
James L. Key, promoted by the chamber of commerce, and sent to the city council
for approval. In the midst of the Great Depression, such visionary plans for
rebuilding city centers were a common first step in attracting federal funding to
projects that would help to revive the local economy.[1]

The Central Park at the heart of the proposal would replace three churches and other structures occupying the block opposite the west front of the Capitol. Beneath the block's terraced gardens, the plan featured a new accommodation for the automobile age: underground parking for up to one thousand cars. Since the City of Atlanta had created the plan, municipal buildings predominated. The proposed new structures included a fire headquarters, a police headquarters and jail, and a City Hall annex with a small plaza. For Fulton County, the plan projected an addition to the 1914 building and an annex with a second small plaza. The state would gain an office building to the north of the statehouse and another to the east. The most striking new building was a monumental auditorium on the block south of the Capitol and east of City Hall. The plan also called for the realignment of Capitol Avenue to improve the north-south flow of vehicles, a change that would reduce the size of the northeast corner of the Capitol grounds.

The 1932 plan was the culmination of a generation of proposals intended to reshape Atlanta's downtown to accommodate the increasing population and its use of motorized vehicles. In the third decade of the twentieth century, the Georgia Capitol and the surrounding central city were in the midst of major transformations. Atlanta had become a city with regional headquarters of national corporations whose offices were located in skyscrapers, along with the local banks that had built many of these structures. The downtown had major department stores, hotels, restaurants, and first-run movie theaters. With auto ownership on the rise, cars were replacing the trolley as the means of travel and creating a need for specialized parking facilities. As the city became denser, so did pedestrian and motorized traffic.

The railroads, with their sprawling tracks and grand depots, continued to dominate the downtown and ensnarl traffic. City planners devised schemes to move the city above the tracks, by building a series of viaducts and plazas that would both beautify the downtown and allow the free flow of pedestrian, trolley, automobile, and truck traffic. The first of these plans was advanced in 1909 by architect Haralson Bleckley, who proposed covering over the railroad tracks from Central Avenue west to Spring Street and creating a series of plazas lined with skyscrapers. Bleckley's plan fell victim to the ownership of air rights by the railroads, which did not want to allow construction over their tracks. While Bleckley's plazas were not built, the city did explore other ways to bridge the railroad tracks. Worsening downtown traffic congestion pushed the city in 1924 to commission the John C. Beeler Organization to produce a comprehensive study of Atlanta's traffic needs. The Beeler Plan recommended additional viaducts to speed vehicular movement and increased parking for downtown workers and shoppers. The plan then went further, pre-

Planning Commission designs for Civic Center Plan, 1932. In 1932, the Atlanta Planning Commission announced in newspaper headlines a Civic Center Plan for the ten-block area surrounding the Capitol. It proposed a terraced park with underground parking to the west of the statehouse and a monumental auditorium to the south. Among the buildings called for in the plan were a second Fulton County Courthouse, a fire headquarters, a police headquarters and jail, and two state office buildings. (© 2006 The Atlanta Journal-Constitution; reprinted with permission from the *Atlanta Journal-Constitution; Atlanta Journal*, August 28, 1932, 7)

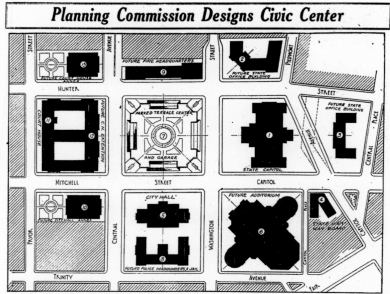

Planning Commission Designs Civic Center

CITY, COUNTY AND STATE BUILDINGS WOULD BE GROUPED around a small park under the civic center scheme made public Saturday by the City Planning Commission. The park would comprise the block bounded by Washington, Hunter and Mitchell Streets and Central Avenue. The City Hall, Courthouse and State Capitol, already located in this vicinity, would be supplemented by other public buildings as they are needed. Immediate construction in this neighborhood of a Police Station and an Auditorium are recommended by the commission. This drawing is a map showing the arrangement of public buildings.

Georgia Capitol, c. 1935. In this 1935 view of the Georgia Capitol from the southwest, a trolley travels down the center of Mitchell Street, flanked on either side by parked automobiles. On the left side appears Second Baptist Church, now the site of the upper portion of Georgia Plaza Park. The block on the right, now the site of the State Judicial Building, was the proposed location of the monumental auditorium in the 1932 Civic Center Plan. (Courtesy of the Kenan Research Center at the Atlanta History Center)

Beeler Report of 1924. An illustration from the 1924 Beeler Report proposed new ways of accommodating cars, buses, and trucks in downtown Atlanta. In response to the increased density of high-rise developments, people would travel underground on moving sidewalks. The artist's vision shows Peachtree Street looking north to Five Points, where shops line the "subsurface moving platforms." (Reprinted from John A. Beeler, *Report to the City of Atlanta on a Plan for Local Transportation* [Atlanta, Ga.: Foote & Davis, 1924], 83)

senting a vision of a new downtown where underground moving sidewalks would carry people through the heart of a high-rise city.

Built at a time when its occupants and visitors walked or rode in trolleys or carriages, the Capitol now needed to accommodate arrivals by automobile. State government also needed more office space. The 1883 Capitol Act had assumed that one building could provide ample space for all state government functions. Two generations after its completion, the statehouse had been renovated to accommodate expanding state departments, but it was no longer large enough. The state had begun to acquire land on the block to the south of the Capitol for an annex, the first phase of what would become a Capitol campus. Similarly, city and county governments also needed office space for their expanding departments. All these governmental buildings would require automobile parking for officials and visitors alike. The city's Civic Center Plan was a scheme to serve these

Governmental Complex Plan of 1927. Beginning in 1909, architect Haralson Bleckley drafted several "City Beautiful" designs for monumental complexes in downtown Atlanta. This 1927 schematic, which the chamber of commerce published in its journal the *City Builder*, has many of the elements of the plan adopted by the City Planning Commission the following decade: a central plaza flanked by the Capitol and state, city, and county buildings. (Reprinted from *City Builder*, September 1927, 19)

demands. However, unlike fifty years earlier, when they had wooed and won the capital, Atlanta's business and political leaders no longer had enough influence in the statehouse to bring the Civic Center Plan to fruition.

On September 14, 1932, just over two weeks after the front-page projection of the city's plan, Eugene Talmadge won the gubernatorial nomination in the Democratic primary, which was tantamount to election. Talmadge had served as commissioner of agriculture from 1927 to 1932. His arrival in the Capitol as governor ushered in three decades of political turmoil during which civic and political leaders in the capital city had little sway in the Capitol.

Eugene Talmadge made his mark on Georgia politics as a mercurial rural Democrat who inherited the mantle of Populist demagogue Tom Watson. Dynamic with a wily charm, Talmadge built his support on a foundation of white supremacy, a system upheld by local courthouse officials and their followers in the state's rural counties. During his three terms as governor from 1933 to 1937 and from 1941 to 1943, Talmadge cottoned to his rural constituency at the expense of Atlanta's chamber of commerce, proudly proclaiming that in his electoral victories he never carried a county that had streetcars.[2]

As commissioner of agriculture and governor-elect, Talmadge was an invited speaker on December 4, 1932, at the unveiling of the Tom Watson statue, which was erected in the middle of the great plaza in front of the west entrance to the statehouse. Authorized seven years earlier, the statue had been delayed by efforts to find a sculptor who could catch the fiery oratorical powers of its subject. J. S. Klein's statue, depicting Watson with fist raised in the midst of an oration, now stood guard outside the main entrance of the Georgia Capitol. John T. Boifeuillet, the keynote speaker, proclaimed that the statue would "speak to future races of men of Watson as a leader who with words governed the multitudes of human beings and controlled their will."[3]

Talmadge, supported by the poor white rural vote that Watson had courted and enflamed, now had his chance to control the will of state government. After being sworn in, the new governor sent the 1933 General Assembly a set of proposals based on the promises made during his renowned stump speeches. In response to the economic hardships of the Great Depression, Talmadge promised Georgia's voters that he would reduce property and automobile taxes as well as utility rates. His legislative package recommended a lower millage rate on ad valorem property taxes and a dramatic reduction in the cost of an auto tag. The popularity of Talmadge's campaign promise of a "three-dollar tag" revealed how thoroughly the automobile had taken over as a means of transportation for ordinary Georgians. He also asked the members of the Public Services Commission to lower electricity rates. During the legislative

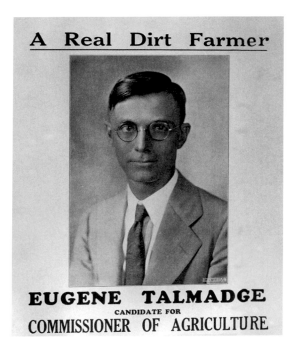

A Real Dirt Farmer

EUGENE TALMADGE
CANDIDATE FOR
COMMISSIONER OF AGRICULTURE

LEFT *"A Real Dirt Farmer," 1926.* Eugene Talmadge established a rural white base of voters in his 1926 campaign for state agricultural commissioner. Being a "real dirt farmer" was his ticket to the Capitol, where he was a dominant presence for two decades. (Courtesy of the Georgia Archives, Vanishing Georgia Collection, geo126-83)

BELOW *Capitol and Central Presbyterian Church.* Bleckley's plan for a government complex would have removed the buildings around the Capitol and surrounded it with more open space. Instead, a smaller plaza was built east of the Capitol, and the 1883 Central Presbyterian Church still stands adjacent to the statehouse. (Courtesy of Diane Kirkland and the Georgia Department of Economic Development)

session of 1933, Talmadge failed on both accounts. The governor was not able to muster a majority in the General Assembly, nor could he persuade the independently elected public services commissioners to lower utility rates. However, the legislators and commissioners soon discovered that Eugene Talmadge played the political game by his own rules.

After the 1933 General Assembly adjourned and left town, Talmadge remained in the Capitol and took the first of several unorthodox steps that proved his willingness to use almost any means to achieve his goals. He issued an executive proclamation that suspended all state taxes until the next session of the General Assembly, which was two years away (to save costs during the Depression, the legislature met every other year). Talmadge replaced the legislatively approved taxes with a new set that included his promised three-dollar auto tag. Faced with losing his appointment, the motor vehicle commissioner agreed to the governor's demand to lower the fee, even though he felt obliged to collect the taxes required by the state law that the legislature had just enacted.

Talmadge's next goal, to gain control of the powerful State Highway Department, took more muscle to achieve. The behemoth department expended 51 percent of the state budget and was overseen by the Highway Board, whose members were legislatively appointed. The quasi-independent department awarded huge construction contracts and employed a potential army of patronage workers around the state. Highway tax funds had helped to construct the new (1931) Highway Building, the first office building built on what would become the Capitol campus. It stood across the street from the southwest corner of the statehouse, on the east side of the site where a monumental municipal auditorium was once projected to rise in the 1932 Civic Center Plan. To Talmadge, the department was a plum waiting to be plucked.

Responding to the state's financial difficulties, Talmadge ordered a cut in the department's budget, but then went on to demand the dismissal of five engineers. Highway Board chairman and civil engineer J. W. Barnett refused to fire the employees, since compliance would allow the governor to intrude into the board's hiring-and-firing function, the basis of its professionalism, power, and independence. Rather than simply remove the recalcitrant Barnett, Talmadge chose a more dramatic tactic. He declared martial law.

"Talmadge Orders Military Control of All Activities," 1933. On June 20, 1933, Governor Eugene Talmadge ordered troops to occupy the Capitol and its surrounding buildings as the first step in establishing his control over quasi-independent state agencies. He used Georgia National Guard troops to oust the head of the State Highway Board, whom he replaced with a loyal supporter. (© 2006 The Atlanta Journal-Constitution; reprinted with permission from the *Atlanta Journal-Constitution; Atlanta Constitution,* June 20, 1933, 1)

On June 20, 1933, Georgians awoke to front-page newspaper photographs of uniformed troops from the National Guard massed on the steps of the Highway Department Building. The *Atlanta Constitution* headline proclaimed: TALMADGE ORDERS MILITARY CONTROL OF ALL ACTIVITIES. The lead sentence of the article read: "Making himself dictator of virtually all functions of state government, Governor Eugene Talmadge Monday declared martial law over the state highway department, the comptroller general's office, the state treasury, the secretary of state and the office of supervisor of purchase." The use of the term "dictator" in April 1933 conveyed a disturbing implication, since Adolph Hitler's rise to power was also front-page news. Having placed National Guard troops in and around the Capitol and the Highway Department, Talmadge presented a list of charges against the Highway Board, dismissed Barnett "for aiding and abetting" insurrection, and ordered Adjutant General Lindley W. Camp to remove Barnett bodily from his office. Using military language that suggested he was quelling a revolt, Talmadge placed his ally Jud P. Wilhoit in "supreme command" of the department. Talmadge also took control of the Public Services Commission by ordering the dismissal of its members after serving as prosecutor, judge, and jury in a mock trial he conducted in the hall of the House of Representatives.[4]

Talmadge now controlled two state government entities that had been established by law to function independently. The federal government took notice. When Talmadge took control of the Highway Department, the Federal Bureau of Roads suspended Georgia's project funding until it was clear that the department was properly managed and supported with state funds. Because of the need to restore federal funding to state road projects, Talmadge ended martial law on July 29, after thirty-nine days of occupation. This action restored the flow of highway funds, but it did not resolve the governor's problems with federal programs in Georgia. In early 1934, Franklin Roosevelt responded to Talmadge's resistance to New Deal programs by federalizing relief operations in Georgia. Instead of funding state agencies to provide relief, the federal government established its own organizations and staffed them with out-of-state recruits. To Talmadge, each one of these imported workers was a "carpetbagger" and a lost patronage appointment.

Despite the federal intervention, Talmadge was in a powerful position when the General Assembly convened in 1935. The legislators were deeply divided between those who supported the New Deal programs and the Talmadgites, who opposed them. They deadlocked over the state budget. Rather than call a special session to work out the problem, Talmadge opted to run state government on the appropriation that had been passed for the previous (1934–35) fiscal years. In order to do this, the governor needed the cooperation of two elected officials, Comptroller General William B. Harrison and State Treasurer George B. Hamilton. Both refused, arguing that they needed authorization from a current appropriation bill before they could move funds collected in tax accounts into the operational accounts of state agencies.

By February 1936, several departments were running out of money, and Talmadge resorted to his strong-arm tactics. This time he was a bit more circumspect, having learned that a newspaper photograph of uniformed troops in the Capitol was not the way to win a public relations battle, especially at a time when papers often featured images of Nazi soldiers in Germany. Talmadge sent several of his beefier "boys" to warn Harrison and Hamilton that they needed to vacate their Capi-

Governor Eugene Talmadge swearing in constitutional officers, c. 1934.
Governor Eugene Talmadge swears in elected constitutional officers in January 1933 or 1935, including (left to right): Manning Jasper Youmans, attorney general; George B. Hamilton, state treasurer; John B. Wilson, secretary of state; and William B. Harrison, comptroller general. Talmadge would later force Hamilton and Harrison from office in a dispute over the state budget. When Hamilton refused to leave his office, state troopers carried him out of his office and deposited him outside of the Capitol. (Courtesy of the Georgia Archives, Vanishing Georgia Collection, ful0740-83)

tol offices. Comptroller General Harrison agreed to vacate, departing quietly as Talmadge's appointed replacement arrived to assume his position.

State Treasurer George Hamilton was not so docile. When a Talmadge disciple barged into his second-floor Capitol office on February 26 and ordered him to vacate, Hamilton placed a pistol on his desk and replied: "I am constitutionally elected to this office, and I have the means to protect it." Talmadge, waiting across the north atrium in the governor's suite, bellowed for Adjutant General Lindley Camp when he learned of Hamilton's resistance. Talmadge ordered Camp to direct soldiers under his command to take the Office of Treasurer by force, but this time they were not to wear their uniforms.

Later that afternoon, Camp and six National Guardsmen in civilian dress entered Hamilton's offices to find the state treasurer working at his desk. A crowd of fifty to one hundred people gathered to witness the expulsion. When Hamilton refused to leave, the adjutant general and one of his soldiers walked behind the treasurer's desk and hoisted Hamilton out of his chair. Followed by the other five guardsmen, they carried the state treasurer out of his office, through the atria, out the door, and down the Capitol steps. During Hamilton's ejection, spectators watched Hamilton's treasury assistants flee the building and assumed they were running in fear of the governor's soldiers. In fact, Hamilton had previously instructed his assistants to remove the state's financial instruments and deposit them with local banks. J. B. Daniel, Talmadge's appointed replacement, slipped quickly into the warm chair while several soldiers in civilian dress remained on call outside the office door.

The dramatics in the Capitol were not over yet. Before his departure, Hamilton had set an eighty-hour timer on his office vault, where the state bonds and other securities had been stored. Treasurer-designate Daniel called in locksmiths, who worked six and a half hours with blowtorches to cut open the vault door, only to discover that Hamilton had removed the financial instruments.[5]

Treasurer Hamilton was able to prevail in the short run because the Atlanta banks refused to honor State of Georgia checks signed by Daniel. Meanwhile, each side pressed its case in the state courts with mixed results. When the dispute finally reached the Georgia Supreme Court on the third floor of the Capitol, Hamilton was expected to win the case. Talmadge gained the upper hand when he successfully pressured four of the six justices to disqualify themselves from the proceedings, claiming a conflict of interest because they had ties to the banks that were involved. With the power to designate replacement judges, Talmadge appointed four replacements, who promptly decided the case in his favor.

For the next eighteen years, the damaged door of the treasurer's safe served as a physical reminder of the Talmadge-Hamilton dispute. The voters of Georgia returned Hamilton to his office in the Capitol in 1937, and he continued to be a presence in the statehouse long after Eugene Talmadge. When the Capitol was renovated in 1956, Hamilton supervised the replacement of the damaged door, which he called the "the last relic of the fracas."[6]

The white press treated Eugene Talmadge's strong-arm tactics as a kind of tragicomedy. His down-home humor and ability to sound like a country boy disarmed and sometimes

Inauguration of Governor E. D. Rivers, 1939. The arrival of E. D. Rivers in the Capitol increased the flow of federal dollars to Georgia, some of which helped to refurbish the statehouse and construct a new State Office Building. (Courtesy of the Kenan Research Center at the Atlanta History Center)

charmed the white reporters who covered him. Regardless of his predilection to take liberties with the law, Talmadge's rank-and-file supporters remained fiercely loyal, because, as Robert Sherrill says, "he made them feel like people, fit for laughter, supreme over the black man at least, and sharing with him the sly knowledge that since only the rich could profit from government, the poor man was foolish to take government seriously."[7]

However, others in the white electorate were becoming concerned over Talmadge's extralegal maneuvers and his strident opposition to federal assistance programs. When Talmadge used his anti–New Deal platform to run against popular Democratic incumbents in the United State Senate in the 1936 and 1938 Democratic primaries, he lost by a healthy margin. Georgia voters did not want to move the Talmadge show to the national Capitol.

With Talmadge out of the governor's office and looking for a national platform, Georgians elected the pro–New Deal administration of E. D. Rivers. In two terms (1937–41), Rivers helped to attract federal dollars to the state, fostering a number of governmental construction projects in Atlanta in an effort to satisfy the need for office space and to reduce unemployment. However, these New Deal projects proceeded without regard for the 1932 Civic Center Plan. In 1936, the city used federal funds to help renovate the thirty-year-old Municipal Auditorium at Courtland and Gilmer streets and add a new "WPA"-style marble-clad entrance building facing Courtland.

(This is now Alumni Hall at Georgia State University.) The site that had been proposed for a new auditorium, almost directly south of the Capitol, was developed in 1938–39 as the six-story State Office Building (now the Legislative Office Building). Designed by A. Thomas Bradbury, the marble-clad building echoed the style of the 1931 State Highway Department Building to the east. The construction of the new State Office Building signaled the end of a coordinated state-city-county effort to shape a downtown civic center.

The Rivers administration also used forty thousand dollars in federal funds, matched by a state contribution of twelve thousand dollars, to refurbish the Capitol before the legislative session of 1939. In May 1938, painters erected scaffolding in the rotunda in order to replace the "dull grey" color of the dome with cobalt blue and a horizon edged in yellow. The pilasters in the rotunda were painted ivory and ochre, and four shades of cream covered the walls in the rest of the public areas. The legislative chambers were modernized. A checkerboard pattern of inlaid asphalt tiles replaced the carpets. The Trinity Furniture Shop of Atlanta stripped the legislators' desks to their original color. New ventilation and lighting systems were installed, and Venetian blinds replaced the "old fashioned shades." Scaffolding covered the exterior of the statehouse to permit reworking of the roof and dome.[8]

Elected governor again in 1940, Talmadge returned to the Capitol believing that he still wielded the political power of his previous stints in the statehouse. The governor overestimated

Governor Eugene Talmadge in the House of Representatives, 1941. Governor Eugene Talmadge delivers an address in the House of Representative. Behind him, the intricately carved wooden back of the original dais can be seen, along with the more recent additions of Venetian blinds covering the windows. (Courtesy of the Lane Brothers Collection, Special Collections Department, Georgia State University Library)

his power when he targeted ten college educators in state colleges and the University of Georgia, accusing them of fostering integration. Claiming that they violated segregation laws, the governor demanded the removal of the president of Georgia Teachers College in Statesboro, the dean of education at the University of Georgia, and eight other university system employees. When the Board of Regents refused to fire them, Talmadge reacted in his usual autocratic way. He dismissed the members of the Board of Regents and had their replacements fire the offenders.

Talmadge calculated that his popularity would allow him to intrude into the operations of the state's system of higher education, but soon he discovered that he had to answer to the education establishment outside Georgia. Citing the governor's blatant political interference in the operation of the state's public system of higher education, the Southern Association of Colleges and Schools suspended accreditation for the entire state university system. Talmadge was not worried about the accrediting agency, but he was surprised by the reaction of his white constituents. Despite the Atlanta newspapers' unfavorable responses to his earlier tactics, Talmadge had not faced widespread popular opposition before. This time his actions were viewed as undermining the University of Georgia, whose football team had a wide following in the state, and public disapproval was immediate and intense.

On the morning of October 15, 1941, a major political demonstration at the Capitol began when approximately one thousand University of Georgia students arrived in a motorcade from Athens. Stretching over four miles, the colorful and noisy procession inundated the downtown and circled Capitol Square before the students alighted and joined a crowd waiting for them on the west Capitol plaza and lawn. Placing a bust of Talmadge on top of the head of the statue of Tom Watson, the students sang and cheered their protests. Three student representatives entered the building and sought out the governor in his executive office. Since Talmadge was not there, they presented the assistant attorney general with a petition. The crowd disbursed quietly, and the students returned to Athens.[9]

The university fiasco cost Talmadge the 1942 gubernatorial election. He lost to Ellis Arnall, a former state attorney general and legislator from Newnan who, at thirty-six, became Georgia's youngest governor. Like all statewide-elected officials, Arnall was a segregationist, but his more moderate approach made him a liberal by the standards of 1940s Georgia. During his two terms in office, Arnall eliminated the state debt and rewrote the state constitution.

The Atlanta Chamber of Commerce worked with the City of Atlanta to take advantage of a friendly face in the Capitol's executive suite. They jointly produced a new visionary plan to reshape the downtown with an expanded governmental complex of state, county, and city buildings; a transportation nexus with a grand new railroad passenger station connected with a heliport; and an automobile parkway covering the railroad tracks running through the heart of the downtown. It was another grand scheme only partially implemented as Atlanta grew in the decades after World War II.

Arnall sought to eliminate some voting restrictions, including the poll tax. The governor did not want to hinder registration at a time when the Depression and the economic restrictions of World War II had reduced the numbers of white voters. Talmadge agreed, arguing that the white-only Democratic primary was sufficient to maintain white control of the electoral process. With the support of his main opponent, Arnall pushed his bill through the 1944 session of the General Assembly.[10]

The elimination of the poll tax had an unintended consequence. It removed a major impediment to black voter registration at a time when the Democratic primary was under challenge in the federal courts because it excluded blacks from selecting candidates who would be on the ballot in the general election.

Georgia's restrictions on black voting were beginning to show their age by 1944. The state's African American population was no longer overwhelming rural and under the control of landowners and county courthouse officials. Increasing numbers of urban blacks were registering and voting in general and special elections. The elimination of the poll tax removed the financial impediment to registration. The white-only Democratic primary, which determined the outcomes of elections because the Republican Party did not offer viable candidates in the general election, remained the major legal barrier to the effective participation of African Americans in state and local politics.

Many black Georgians believed that they had won the right to vote in the Democratic primary of April 1944, when the U.S. Supreme Court had struck down the white primary in Texas in *Smith v. Allwright*. That opinion should have opened the Democratic primary in Georgia as well, but African Americans discovered on the July 4 primary date that they would need another federal court decision before they could help to determine the outcome of elections in Georgia. After he was

Talmadge counterdemonstrators at the Capitol, 1941. During his third term as governor, Eugene Talmadge confronted another independent state agency—the Board of Regents and the state university system. After he dismissed the board members and fired a popular dean at the University of Georgia, the school lost its accreditation. Over one thousand students demonstrated on the Capitol grounds. Here, Talmadge massed his own counterdemonstration. (Courtesy of the Lane Brothers Collection, Special Collections Department, Georgia State University Library)

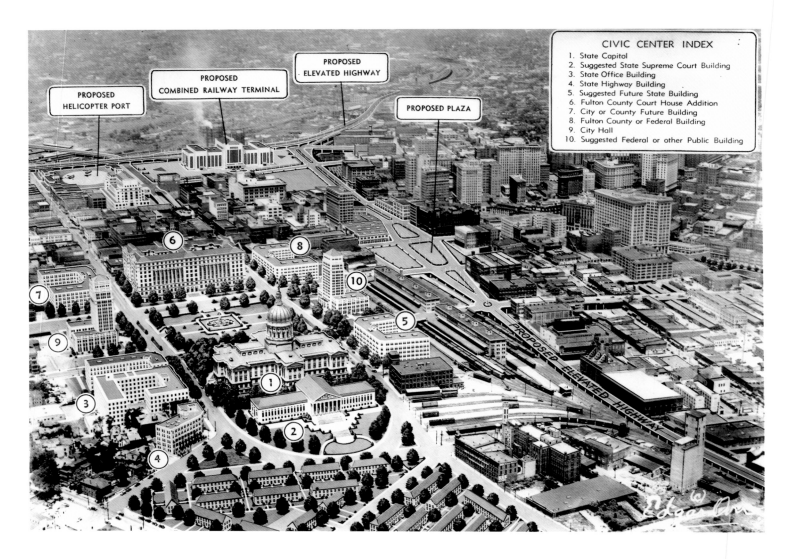

CIVIC CENTER INDEX
1. State Capitol
2. Suggested State Supreme Court Building
3. State Office Building
4. State Highway Building
5. Suggested Future State Building
6. Fulton County Court House Addition
7. City or County Future Building
8. Fulton County or Federal Building
9. City Hall
10. Suggested Federal or other Public Building

PROPOSED HELICOPTER PORT

PROPOSED COMBINED RAILWAY TERMINAL

PROPOSED ELEVATED HIGHWAY

PROPOSED PLAZA

PROPOSED ELEVATED HIGHWAY

Civic Center Plan of 1944. In 1944, the City of Atlanta and the chamber of commerce continued to promote a civic center near the Capitol as well as new postwar transportation facilities. A classical addition for the Georgia Supreme Court (2) would extend Capitol Square across Capitol Avenue. A new state office building (5) would occupy the entire block to the north of the statehouse. (Courtesy of the Tracy O'Neal Collection, Special Collections Department, Georgia State University Library)

denied his ballot in Columbus, Georgia, Primus King went to federal court and initiated a legal contest that would, in the second half of the twentieth century, undermine the electoral foundations of white domination in the Georgia Capitol. After two years of litigation, on March 7, 1946, newspapers across the state announced that the U.S. Fifth Circuit Court of Appeals had ruled that Primus King was eligible to vote in the Georgia Democratic primary election, effectively killing the white-only restriction. Nascent voter-registration organizations in African American communities across the state responded to the court ruling with drives to increase the numbers of black registered voters.[11]

This sudden challenge to white political supremacy and an unexpected threat to the Talmadge dynasty produced a gubernatorial election that set a high-water mark for Talmadge-machine theatrics in the Georgia Capitol. Representing the hardest-core opposition to integration, Talmadge supporters responded with a call for purges of black rural voters from registration lists and, when necessary, for the use of violence and intimidation to block them from actually voting. According to Laughlin McDonald, white boards of registrars responded to Talmadge-machine demands and issued subpoenas en masse in over thirty counties, ordering African American voters to appear and explain why they should not be disqualified from voting. "There was no way the Talmadge people could have known the qualification of the thousands of voters whom they challenged, but that was irrelevant. What they did know was that they were black, and that was enough." As a result, an estimated 15,000 to 25,000 black Georgians were purged from the voting rolls in advance of the 1946 Democratic primary. Less subtle methods were also part of the Talmadge strategy. The white newspaper in Greene County warned its majority black population not to vote because the "KKK will ride again" and that "all power acquired by the ballot will be lost by terrorism." The threat of violence was real. In Taylor County, Marceo Snipes, the sole black who voted in the primary, "was called out from dinner and shot by four white men."[12]

Talmadge succeeded in controlling the ballot in Georgia's rural counties by suppressing the black vote and turning out the white vote to counter the more moderate urban vote in the state. Although he came in second in actual votes, Talmadge won the Democratic primary with the help of Georgia's county-unit system. Candidates for statewide offices were elected by a majority of 410 county-unit votes. Depending on their size, each of Georgia's 159 counties was assigned from one to three

unit votes. The 38 largest, more urbanized counties were represented by 168 unit votes, while the 121 smaller, more rural counties had 242. Since the majority of unit votes came from rural counties, the efforts to suppress the black vote there paid off handsomely, especially in those counties where more than half the population was African American.[13]

Talmadge would not live to take the oath of office. By Election Day, he was in such poor health that his supporters began to plan for a successor. The obvious candidate was his son Herman, who had helped direct his father's campaign. Herman surreptitiously arranged to have several hundred write-in votes cast in his name during the general election, so that he would come in second to his father. The senior Talmadge won, and in the same general election, Georgians elected their first lieutenant governor, Melvin E. Thompson. The 1946 State Constitution had created the position and provided that the lieutenant governor would become acting governor in the case of the death of the governor. With the serious illness of the governor-elect, it appeared that Thompson, a non-Talmadge man, would be the next governor.

Six weeks after the election, on December 21, 1946, Eugene Talmadge died of a liver condition. The familiar ritual of public

African Americans registering to vote, 1946. When the Democratic primary was opened to Georgia's African Americans in 1946, thousands of city residents registered to vote as Democrats. In Atlanta, seventeen thousand African Americans registered in three months. Here blacks wait in the "Colored Only" registration line at the Fulton County Courthouse, one block from the Capitol. (Courtesy of the Lane Brothers Collection, Special Collections Department, Georgia State University Library)

mourning followed the next day. In less than six hours, approximately ten thousand people filed past Talmadge's casket in the Capitol rotunda. The statehouse was partially closed the day after the governor-elect's funeral, but behind closed doors, those competing to be named governor gathered there to plan strategy, and the saga now known as Georgia's Three Governors Controversy began to unfold in the Capitol.

The state constitution addressed the issue of gubernatorial succession but was not explicit about what to do if the governor-elect died *before* taking office. The dueling political factions each offered its own interpretation: the incumbent governor should hold office until his successor was chosen and qualified (favored by outgoing Governor Arnall); the lieutenant governor-elect should automatically become the governor-elect (Lieutenant Governor–elect Thompson's claim); and the General Assembly should choose the second-place vote getter in the general election (the Talmadge camp's argument).[14]

At Governor Arnall's request, the state attorney general issued a ruling on January 4, 1947, that, in the absence of a duly elected successor, the governor should retain his office until Lieutenant Governor Thompson was sworn in, at which time Thompson should assume the office of governor. Armed with this legal interpretation, Arnall announced his resignation on January 11, effective when Thompson was sworn in as lieutenant governor. However, the Talmadge faction in the General Assembly had other ideas. Under the leadership of Speaker of the House Roy Harris, they countered with their plan to place son Herman in the governor's chair. On January 13, the General Assembly convened and adopted a resolution for a joint legislative session to examine the election returns and announce the winners for each statewide office.

On the morning of January 14, the joint session of the General Assembly convened in the hall of the House of Representatives. The Capitol was as crowded as it had been for the 1907 prohibition vote. More than fifty correspondents from all over the world were on hand to cover the proceedings. Herman Talmadge had inherited his father's political organization, including the beefy "Talmadge boys," who swarmed the second- and third-floor corridors awaiting instructions. Talmadge recalled the scene: "[T]here were several thousand people there in the Capitol, 90 percent of them my friends—some of them armed, some of them drunk." When the House chamber filled with unauthorized visitors, the morning session became so chaotic that arriving senators could not find the extra seats that had been provided for them. After an hour of confusion, the joint session was adjourned until the afternoon, and the floor was cleared. Most of the six hundred people who jammed the gallery held their seats through the two-hour recess.[15]

When the joint session reconvened and the gubernatorial votes were counted, everyone was flabbergasted to learn that Herman Talmadge had come in fourth place, behind his father and two other write-in candidates who had narrowly edged him out. The Telfair County delegation, which represented the Talmadge home county, immediately challenged the count of their votes. In the ensuing confusion of the recount, an envelope containing fifty-eight additional Telfair County votes miraculously appeared. The Telfair representatives claimed that it had been mislabeled as containing ballots for the lieutenant governor rather than for the governor. To the surprise of only the most naive, the additional votes were just enough to propel Herman Talmadge into second place in the gubernatorial contest.

The drama of the recount kept the legislature in session into the early morning hours of January 15. When the results were finally announced, the Talmadge boys in the gallery, easily identifiable by their trademark white shirtsleeves and red suspenders, let loose a great cheer. The legislatively designated governor wasted no time in assuming the reins of power. The young Talmadge took the oath of office immediately and without ceremony, delivering his inaugural speech ad lib. Then,

surrounded by legislators, family, and his usual hangers-on, he paraded down the grand staircase to the governor's office.[16]

Anticipating a physical confrontation, Ellis Arnall had locked the door to the governor's office around midnight. When the entourage encountered a locked door, Talmadge's men smashed the lock and rushed into the governor's reception room. Speaker Roy Harris triumphantly led the young Herman Talmadge through the crowd and demanded that Arnall leave the office, to which Arnall replied: "[T]he governorship belongs to the people and cannot be decided by the legislature." Claiming that he did not want to create disorder, Talmadge left the suite, leaving his supporters behind in an agitated state. Those remaining tried to push their way into the inner office, where Arnall was standing, but the governor's executive secretary, P. T. McCutchen Jr., and one of his aides barred their way. As Governor Arnall retreated behind the door of his private office, the mob surged forward, and in the melee, an Arnall aide had his jaw broken. The crowd retreated into the Capitol corridors, where, coaxed by agitators, they milled about, cursing and shrieking. Despite the violence, the initial encounter between the two governors was a draw.[17]

A few hours later on the morning of January 15, both men

Swearing in of Herman Talmadge in the Georgia House of Representatives, 1947. After the death of Eugene Talmadge, a five-act drama that came to be known as the Three Governors Controversy unfolded in the Capitol. In act 1, the Talmadge majority in the General Assembly voted to confirm a rigged vote tally that gave first place in the general election to Herman Talmadge. In the early morning hours of January 15, 1947, Herman Talmadge was sworn in as governor in the Georgia House of Representatives. (Courtesy of Herman Eugene Talmadge)

Arrival of Herman Talmadge and his entourage at the governor's office, 1947. Act 2 began when outgoing governor Ellis Arnall refused to relinquish the governor's office to Herman Talmadge. Arnall called Talmadge a "pretender" whose selection by the General Assembly was unconstitutional. He said that he would remain in his Capitol office until Lieutenant Governor–elect Melvin E. Thompson was sworn in. Then, following the constitutionally mandated succession process, Thompson would take the oath of office as governor. (Courtesy of Time & Life Pictures, Getty Images)

reported for work in the Capitol. What had been the governor's office were now the governors' offices. Arnall remained in the private inner office, while Talmadge controlled the reception area and worked from what had been the office of the executive secretary. Each man tried to perform his duties normally, Talmadge making appointments and Arnall swearing in judges. Afraid to leave his office empty, Arnall skipped lunch. After Arnall departed for the day, Talmadge ordered the locks changed for the entire governor's suite.

The next morning Talmadge, with a .38 Smith and Wesson tucked in his belt, walked triumphantly into the inner office

around 7:00 a.m. When Arnall arrived, he had to push his way through Talmadge supporters to reach the inner office door. The newly appointed executive secretary barred his way and told him to wait in the reception room. Arnall left the suite and set up an office in the rotunda, using an information booth as his desk. Meanwhile, hysteria mounted in the Capitol throughout the day. Competing gangs of supporters grappled; a highway patrol officer loyal to Arnall suffered a broken jaw.

The next morning, January 17, Arnall arrived at the rotunda to find a large crowd and one of Talmadge's stalwarts sitting at his desk. James M. Dykes, a 237-pound legislator from Cochran, asked Arnall if he would like an appointment with the governor. When Arnall responded that *he* was the governor, the "smile faded from Dykes' face, and the Talmadge lieutenant shook his finger at Arnall and shouted: 'Ellis, you remind me of a hog in the slops. You've got your head in the trough and you just can't stop.'" Arnall relocated to his law offices in the downtown Candler Building, as Talmadge jeered, "I understand he's holding down the bathroom in the basement now."[18]

With Arnall out of the statehouse, the stage was set for the third claimant to the governorship. On January 18, M. E. Thompson took the oath of office as lieutenant governor and announced his intention to serve as acting governor. When Thompson took his oath as governor two days later, Arnall resigned and removed himself from the fray. Thompson proceeded to the governor's office to demand that Talmadge vacate the premises. With neither giving ground, the two men departed, agreeing that the matter would be settled by the courts.

The struggle that began in the third-floor House chamber and continued on the second-floor in the governor's suite and the rotunda finally would be resolved back on the third floor in the supreme court chamber. Both Talmadge and Thompson claimed that they would abide by the decision of the court, but until then, the two claimants struggled over control of state government. When Talmadge addressed the General Assembly on January 21, almost half its members left the chamber in protest. In the days that followed, popular opposition to Herman Talmadge increased. Two thousand students staged a mass demonstration, marching to the Capitol and hanging an effigy of Herman Talmadge from the statue of Tom Watson. The same statue had served as a platform for the bust of Eugene Talmadge, placed there in protest a few years before.[19]

ABOVE *Ellis Arnall in his office in the Capitol rotunda,
1947.* Act 3 followed when Herman Talmadge locked
Ellis Arnall out of the governor's office on January
16. Arnall then moved to the Capitol rotunda, where
he carried out his duties at what had been an information desk. The next day, a Talmadge crony took over
the rotunda desk and refused to budge when Arnall
arrived for work, so the displaced Arnall removed
himself to his law office in the Candler Building,
where he tried to manage the affairs of state. (Courtesy of the Kenan Research Center at the Atlanta
History Center)

RIGHT *Governor Melvin Thompson and Governor Herman Talmadge, 1947.* Act 4 commenced on January
20, when Melvin Thompson took the oath of office as
governor and Ellis Arnall, as he promised, resigned.
Here Thompson (center, holding hat) leaves the governor's office after meeting with Herman Talmadge
(right) to assert his claim. The two decided to let the
courts decide who should hold the office. In the in-
terim, each asserted gubernatorial powers. (Courtesy
of the Georgia Archives, Vanishing Georgia Collection, geo036)

Reporters getting the state supreme court ruling in favor of Thompson, 1947. The final act came on March 19, 1947, when the state supreme court declared Thompson the governor. Here reporters line up in the Capitol to receive the written opinion of the court. Two weeks earlier, the *Atlanta Journal* had unmasked the fraudulent votes that had given Talmadge his slim lead in the general election. (Courtesy of the Georgia Archives, Vanishing Georgia Collection, geo038)

ABOVE *Georgia Supreme Court justices, c. 1945.* The justices of the Georgia Supreme Court pose for a formal picture in the Capitol in the mid-1940s. Presiding is Chief Justice Reason Chesnut Bell (third from right), who served as chief justice in 1945–46, remained on the court, and in 1947 helped to decide the outcome of the Three Governors Controversy. (Courtesy of the Georgia Archives, Vanishing Georgia Collection, clq266)

RIGHT *Statue of Eugene Talmadge.* The Eugene Talmadge statue was dedicated on September 23, 1949, with the now legitimately elected governor Herman Talmadge presiding. Herman Talmadge proved to be a far less confrontational politician than his father; he went on to have a long career in the U.S. Senate. (Courtesy of Diane Kirkland and the Georgia Department of Economic Development)

Talmadge may have occupied the governor's office physically, but without clear title to the position, he could not manage the affairs of the state. State Treasurer George Hamilton, the man Eugene had forcibly removed from office eleven years earlier, froze state funds, which left the state with less than thirty days' worth of money. Hamilton was ordered by the courts to accept checks in early February, but Talmadge was still stymied. He could not execute state contracts or conduct official business without the state seal, whose emboss was required on all official state documents. The guardian of the seal was Secretary of State Ben Fortson, who had been elected to his office in the same tumultuous 1946 election. Fortson refused to relinquish the seal to anyone until the conflicting claims to the office were resolved in the courts.

As appeals worked their way through the state court system, both sides waited for the state supreme court to resolve the case. Talmadge felt particularly confident because he had secretly conferred with a supreme court justice who had assured him that a majority of the court agreed with his arguments.[20]

Meanwhile, on March 2, the Atlanta press broke a story that would undermine the Talmadge position in the case. The *Atlanta Journal* used a banner headline to declare: "TELFAIR

Aerial view of the Capitol complex looking north, 1950. By 1950, the block south of the Capitol (below it in this photograph) is dominated by the massive State Office Building, which towers over a hodgepodge of smaller buildings and surface parking lots. Two other prominent governmental buildings, Atlanta City Hall and the Fulton County Courthouse, rise to the west. The "City Beautiful" plans of the early twentieth century have yet to be realized. (Courtesy of the Tracy O'Neal Collection, Special Collections Department, Georgia State University Library)

DEAD WERE VOTED." Investigative reporters (who would win Pulitzer Prizes for their work) had reviewed the names on the list of write-in votes from Telfair County that had propelled Herman Talmadge into second place in the legislative count and concluded that they were almost totally fraudulent. Only 2 of 103 listed names belonged to actual voters. Some voters were dead or had moved out of the county, 34 of them voted in alphabetical order, and several totals were inflated. In hindsight and unashamed by the revelations, Herman Talmadge admitted that "his man in the county" might have fixed things if it was "too much trouble to pass the word." With the electoral fraud unmasked, the Georgia Supreme Court weighed in on March 19, upholding Thompson's claim to the office five to two. Talmadge vacated immediately, telling reporters as he left the Capitol, "The court of last resort is the people of Georgia. This case will be taken to the court of last resort."[21]

Two years later, Herman Talmadge rallied his forces to defeat Thompson in a special election to complete the term of his deceased father. Talmadge won easily, capturing majorities in both the popular and the county-unit votes. In 1948, Herman Talmadge returned triumphantly to the statehouse, elected on a white supremacist platform that was almost identical to his father's.

The decade ended, appropriately enough, with the September 23, 1949, dedication of a monument to Eugene Talmadge. With the now-vindicated governor and son presiding, the Talmadge faithful assembled on the southeast corner of the Capitol grounds. The twelve-foot bronze figure of Talmadge, his hand outstretched to emphasize his point, depicted a commanding politician with a strong sense of purpose. The plaque beneath identified its subject as a farmer, lawyer, and statesman. The back panel's inscription—"I may surprise you—But I shall not deceive you"—may have been a difficult claim for either Talmadge to defend, but the dedication ceremony was not the day for accountability. The speakers of the day celebrated a new hero on the Capitol grounds, as they paid homage to him and took jabs at his political enemies.

With the addition of the Talmadge statue, the Capitol grounds were beginning to fill up. A monumental governmental center had yet to be constructed around the Capitol, but additional office space and automobile access needs identified in the 1932 Civic Center Plan remained. A Capitol campus was emerging, but not in the form that Atlanta's civic leaders had promoted in the 1920s and 1930s. Instead of new municipal facilities, state office buildings were taking over the blocks to the south of the Capitol. In just a few years, the Capitol would be surrounded by new state office buildings. The statehouse itself was also headed for a transformation. Several generations of modernizations had not addressed its structural problems, especially the rotting wooden support system in the dome. The postwar explosion of the capital's population would bring sweeping changes to the Capitol and its surroundings and, after many confrontations, to the composition of the General Assembly itself.

THE HONORABLE JIMMY CARTER

SEAL OF THE PRESIDENT OF THE UNITED STATES

39TH PRESIDENT OF
THE UNITED STATES OF
1977

7 A CONTESTED CAPITOL

On the morning of August 7, 1958, an unusual procession arrived at the Capitol. Although most people now came to the statehouse by automobile, these forty-three men, women, and children, arrived in a horse-drawn wagon train. Dressed in nineteenth-century garb, they had begun their journey four days earlier in the mountains of north Georgia. They carried a precious cargo, forty-three ounces of gold that had been gathered at the behest of the Dahlonega Chamber of Commerce. The purpose of the symbolic march was to bring Georgia gold to the Capitol, where it would be used to gild the dome as the crowning act of its renovation. Governor Marvin Griffin greeted the delegation and accepted the gift that would bring about the most noticeable change that the Capitol had undergone in its seventy-year history.[1]

Wagon train approaching the Capitol, 1958. In the summer of 1958, a wagon train bearing forty-three ounces of gold made its way from Dahlonega to Atlanta, providing colorful publicity for the final stage of the extensive and expensive Capitol renovations underway. On August 7, Governor Marvin Griffin accepted the gold from costumed citizens on the statehouse steps. (Courtesy of the Chestatee Regional Library System, Madeline K. Anthony Collection)

Governor Griffin was at the helm of state government at a time of major political and social upheaval. As governor, Griffin rallied a rural white base to protect what he euphemistically called "the southern way of life," a Jim Crow political, social, and economic order. At the same time, Griffin sought to modernize the functioning of state government by renovating the Capitol and adding new office buildings to the emerging Capitol campus. Griffin knew firsthand about the need for expansion; as lieutenant governor in 1950, he had struggled to manage the legislative agenda. Committees could not meet to work through proposed legislation because the Capitol's committee rooms had long since been converted to office space. Griffin wanted to build a new facility for the judiciary, move the justices and their clerks out of the statehouse, and convert their courtroom, library, and offices on the third floor to legislative use. The major roadblock to this plan was budgetary. In 1950, the Georgia Constitution did not permit the state to incur debt, which was a necessity in financing major capital projects.[2]

At the same time, it was becoming clear that the Capitol itself required major capital expenditures. Secretary of State Ben Fortson was the most vocal proponent for a major Capitol renovation. First appointed to the office in 1945 and elected with opposition in 1946, "Mr. Ben" was reelected thereafter without opposition until he died in office in 1979. Throughout his career, he worked to make the Capitol an educational facility and visitor destination as well as a working statehouse. Fortson brought the needs of the Capitol to Governor Herman Talmadge, who was willing to support state funding to improve the appearance of the exterior. At Talmadge's behest, the General Assembly authorized modest funding in the early 1950s for repairs. The exterior limestone, blackened with six decades of grime, was sandblasted, a corrosive technique no longer recommended for use on historic buildings. The windows, whose wooden surrounds had not been painted in the memory of most Capitol observers, were covered in a hue that matched the exterior stone, rather than the two-tone gray and red rust of the original treatment.[3]

Fortson also persuaded Talmadge to support the restoration of the statehouse art collection. The Athens Lumber Company spent two years working on ninety-eight portraits. Some were so dirty that removing the darkened varnish revealed elements that had been lost to view for many years. Many canvases were torn, contained holes, or needed new frames. The last restored portrait was installed on April 8, 1954.[4]

Although the Capitol renovations were only skin deep, Governor Talmadge was much more effective in solving the problems of Capitol overcrowding. Working with Lieutenant Governor Griffin during the 1951 session, Talmadge introduced legislation creating the State Office Building Authority (SOBA), the predecessor of the current Georgia Building Authority. Designed wholly to fund construction of new state buildings, the authority was allowed to issue bonds, which were used to finance new building construction. The bonds would be paid back with the rents from occupying agencies and departments. With the power to borrow money and a revenue stream to pay back construction bonds, the authority initiated a decade of major construction on Capitol Hill that produced a campus of state office buildings with a gold-domed statehouse as its centerpiece.

Chaired by Governor Talmadge, the members of SOBA included the lieutenant governor, the state auditor, the attorney general, and the chief justice. At their first meeting in August 1951, they considered the construction of new buildings, which would cost up to $7 million. One of their first decisions was to affirm the concept of a Capitol campus surrounding the statehouse. When Chief Justice H. W. Duckworth proposed that a new judiciary building be built away from the Capitol, the authority denied the request. Two years later, the author-

Capitol dome, 1957. By 1950, the need for repairs to the Capitol was becoming obvious. An assessment report revealed severe structural damage caused by a cost-cutting decision made during construction. Although it was designed to be executed in stone, much of the dome's original structure had been fabricated in wood and brick and covered in metal painted to match the surrounding limestone. An arrow points to a large hole in the ribbing of the dome that allowed rainwater to flow freely into the building. (© 2006 The Atlanta Journal-Constitution; reprinted with permission from the *Atlanta Journal-Constitution*, February 10, 1957, E1)

ity awarded a construction contract for a large building that would fill this need and others. The seven-story, L-shaped structure would fill the corner of Capitol Square Avenue and Washington Street. Designed to appear and function as two buildings, the Judicial Building would run along Capitol Square and face the Capitol's south facade. The structure's other half, which would contain the Labor Department and other offices, would extend along Washington and face west. The architect, A. Thomas Bradbury, designed the structure to blend with his earlier State Office Building, which stood on Capitol Square Avenue directly to the east.[5]

The bond issue funded two other state building projects in the mid-1950s, also designed by Bradbury. The Agriculture Building was constructed on the block to the north of the Capitol, and a major extension of the State Highway Department Building was added to the back along Trinity Avenue. These structures, completed in 1956, matched the architect's other state buildings, all of which were faced in white marble, styled with a restrained classicism, and massed at a scale that complemented rather than competed with the Capitol.

In the mid-1950s, transportation planners were working on another major construction project in the vicinity: the north-south downtown connecter of Interstates 75 and 85 and the huge cloverleaf interchange with east-west Interstate 20. The planners faced the challenge of providing automobile access to the expressways without isolating the statehouse from its surrounding buildings.

In September 1955, Auditor General B. E. Thrasher publicly opposed plans that would have turned the streets to the north and south of the Capitol into major thoroughfares leading to and from expressway ramps. Thrasher was able to stop the construction of one of the ramps, but the need for automotive access resulted in the redesign of several streets in the Capitol district. All four streets surrounding the statehouse were converted into one-way thoroughfares, and to facilitate the flow of traffic north, the legislature reduced the size of the northeast corner of the Capitol lot so that Capitol Avenue would align with Piedmont Avenue where they join at Hunter Street (now Martin Luther King Jr. Drive). The arrival of the expressway and a parking deck constructed east of the statehouse in the late 1950s improved automotive access to the Capitol campus but also increased the volume of traffic and noise.[6]

As Capitol Hill began to take shape in the mid 1950s, Secretary of State Ben Fortson turned his attention to the statehouse.

Labor Building, 1955. The newly constructed Labor Building, viewed here from the corner of Trinity Avenue and Washington Street, extends up Washington and connects underground to the Judicial Building, which faces Capitol Square Avenue. The construction of these buildings and the extension of the Highway Department Building filled the two blocks south of the Capitol in the mid 1950s. (Courtesy of the Tracy O'Neal Collection, Special Collections Department, Georgia State University Library)

In 1955, the secretary of state became officially responsible for the Capitol, giving Fortson the authority he needed. He immediately commissioned a bottom-to-top condition assessment of the building, and the results were astounding. The survey identified a host of dangerous problems, such as ancient wiring and leaky sewer pipes, but the worst news came last: the structural support system for the dome was rotting.

Although it appeared to be made of stone, the dome was actually built of brick, wood, and metal, an economy measure taken over seventy years earlier to keep the construction costs within the original $1 million dollar budget. The dome's wooden supports, columns, ribbing, and balustrades had been covered with metal and painted to match the limestone of the rest of the exterior. For decades, the metal seams had been leaking, causing wood rot that now threatened the structural integrity of the dome itself. Fortson took the bad news to Griffin, who agreed to make the Capitol's renovation a legislative priority.

However, on the morning of January 10, 1956, when Governor Griffin stepped to the podium in the House of Representatives chamber to deliver his State of the State address, his oratorical focus was on another issue. Almost everyone in the joint session of the House and Senate (and a packed gallery) had come to cheer on their governor as he delivered what they

knew would be a stirring defense of racial segregation. Recent federal court decisions had undermined the foundations of Jim Crow by opening the Georgia Democratic primary to African American voters and ordering an end to racially separate schools, parks, playgrounds, and public transportation. With the *Brown v. Board of Education* decision of the U.S. Supreme Court two years earlier, it was only a matter of time before a federal court would order a public school or college in Georgia to admit a black student.[7]

Marvin Griffin had been elected governor two years earlier with, as he proudly proclaimed, segregation as the number one plank in his platform. He had also been elected with only 36 percent of the popular vote, thanks to the county-unit system. Griffin called the county-unit system and racial segregation Georgia's "two great traditions." These "traditions" were mutually sup-

Aerial view of the Capitol campus, 1958. By the late 1950s, the Capitol Complex had emerged, with the new Judicial/Labor Building and expanded Highway Department Building to the south (right in the photograph) of the Capitol and the new Agriculture Building to the north (left in the photograph). Above the Capitol and to the left, vestiges of the railroad age remain, while directly behind (east) the statehouse stands a new parking deck to serve the automobile era. The swath of open land visible in the upper right corner has been cleared for I-20's east-west right-of-way. (Courtesy of the Tracy O'Neal Collection, Special Collections Department, Georgia State University Library)

Association for the Advancement of Colored People (NAACP) against segregation at the University of Georgia and in the Atlanta Public Schools, Griffin rallied the cheering legislature and packed gallery, declaring, "[T]he time has come to gird ourselves for battle, steel ourselves for sacrifice, use every means at our command to prevent this devastating tragedy." To a whistling ovation, Griffin proclaimed: "All attempts to mix the races, whether they be in the classrooms, on the playgrounds, in public conveyances, or in any other area of close personal contact on terms of equality, peril the mores of the South."[10]

The 1956 legislative session was the climax mark of segregationist rhetoric in the Capitol. Governor Griffin staged his legislative addresses as pep rallies to bolster white majority support for his declarations of defiance and for his plan to subvert the federal court orders that challenged state-supported Jim Crow. In response to Griffin's "no surrender" program, the legislature authorized the governor to close the public schools rather than integrate them and permitted local school boards to lease public-school property for use as private schools.[11]

Georgia's 1956 legislative agenda also included the act of transforming the Georgia state flag into an emblem of the segregation cause. Answering Griffin's appeal to "play on the team or leave the field," the legislature overwhelmingly approved a bill to alter the state flag by adding the well-known Confederate battle emblem, the "stars and bars." Ever since the Dixiecrats had waved the battle flag at the 1948 Democratic National Convention, it had become a popular prop at segregationist rallies. Now, House floor leader Denmark Glover marshaled his colleagues by noting that the battle emblem

portive, for the county-unit system gave the power to decide who would hold statewide office to rural counties, where the black vote was tightly suppressed. At midcentury, almost forty rural counties in Georgia had black majorities, but none sent African American representatives to the Georgia Capitol.[8]

Governor Griffin came before the 1956 Georgia General Assembly to discuss what he called "the most vital question that has ever been before this legislative body." His opening declaration of defiance brought his audience to their feet: "[T]here will be no mixing of the races in the public schools and college classrooms of Georgia anywhere or anytime as long as I am governor." He exhorted his fellow white elected leaders to join him: "The time has come to stand up and be counted. We must either play on the team or leave the field. We must never surrender."[9]

In response to lawsuits being advanced by the National

would "replace the meaningless stripes with something having meaning in the hearts of all true Southerners." The redesigned flag with its Confederate battle emblem would fly over and inside county courthouses, colleges and schools, and other public buildings across the state for the next forty-five years.[12]

Amid the passion of the 1956 legislative session, the General Assembly did focus on more mundane matters, such as their leaking, creaking Capitol. The legislators authorized $150,000, what would be the first in a series of Capitol appropriations, for renovating the third-floor chambers and spaces emptied by the departure of the judicial branch. A. Thomas Bradbury was awarded the design contract for the renovations. The special committee appointed to address the issue of space voted to devote the entire third floor to the use of the legislature, opening up space for up to eighteen committee meeting rooms and additional offices for committee chairs and staff. The former State Supreme Court Room became a large committee and hearing room that ultimately served the House and Senate Appropriations Committees.[13]

The renovations in the House and Senate chambers focused on functionality and produced dramatic changes in the legislative halls. The windows that had provided light and ventilation now brought in traffic noise that drowned out voices during legislative debates. The renovation sealed the legislative halls from the outside by replacing the original clear glass with stained glass that was light blue with swirls of white. The result created a churchlike feel in the legislative halls, especially when the chambers were empty.

Speaking and voting were made easier with the introduction of new technology. Each desk had a microphone that could be activated when a legislator wanted to speak from the floor. Each desk was also equipped with green "yea" and red "nay" electrical switches, which connected to the new voting boards hung on the side walls of the chambers. The large electric boards listed each legislator's name with a green light and a red light, one of which would light up during roll-call votes. Decorative changes to the chambers were minimal, but the walls and ceilings received a fresh coat of paint, and new linoleum floors were installed.[14]

The changes in the chambers were only the beginning. The state library was subdivided to provide space for large committee meetings and the staff of the clerk of the House. Eventually, further subdivision of the library would lead to the total disappearance of this grand space. Three floors of legislative offices would be inserted into the two-story space.

State library moving out of the Capitol, c. 1956. With the departure of the judicial branch of government, many spaces on the third floor became available for new uses. The state library space was eventually divided both horizontally and vertically into three floors of small offices. (© 2006 The Atlanta Journal-Constitution; reprinted with permission from the *Atlanta Journal-Constitution*)

Columns and fireplaces would be covered by walls, and the decorative ceiling plaster would be hidden beneath acoustical tile. Today the reception room used by Governor John Gordon during the Capitol dedication is a warren of small pine-paneled offices and workrooms.

The renovations also included the offices of elected officials. The lieutenant governor had a conference room added next to his office, a change that would become common in the ensuing decades for many committee chairs. The departure of the attorney general and staff allowed the governor's suite to expand into the northwest quadrant of the second floor. The governor's new private office featured a floor-to-ceiling panel of black-and-white Georgia marble, carved with the state seal at its center, as its focal point. Danish-style modern furnishings included a desk, a credenza, a conference table, and chairs. A contemporary newspaper account called the offices "as swank as a movie set." The governor's reception room, located just off the lobby of the west Capitol entrance, was "furnished as colorfully and comfortably as the lobby of a resort hotel."[15]

The interior renovations did not overlook the rotunda. From 1955 to 1960, Fortson transformed the circular space into the Georgia Hall of Fame, a sculpture gallery. The old information center, whose visitor's desk had served as a temporary office for Ellis Arnall during the Three Governors Controversy, was cleared away for a ring of thirteen marble busts. Each honored a famous Georgian; each was funded by a patriotic society.

The topping off of the Capitol renovation came with the reconstruction of the dome, the addition of a new roof, and the replacement of wooden-framed clear glass windows in the atria clerestories with aluminum frames and frosted glass panes. Work on these projects began after the legislature appropriated $971,095 in the 1957 legislative session.

The following year, scaffolding rose atop the roof of the Capitol from the base of the dome drum to the top of the statue of Freedom. A freight elevator carried almost two million pounds of limestone to replace the sixteen wooden columns and the fifty-three-foot metal-covered-brick upper band of the drum that supported the dome. The dome itself was rebuilt by stripping off the exterior layers of paint and metal, exposing the original terra-cotta tile base, and recovering it with layers of asphalt and portland cement to create a smooth, waterproof surface. Overlapping eighteen-square-inch metal squares were attached in preparation for the application of gold leafing 1/500th of an inch thick. The gold that had been delivered to Governor Marvin Griffin by wagon train in August 1958 had been sent on to a Philadelphia firm that had produced the leaf. In January 1959, six steeplejacks hung from ropes around the dome, applying the gold leaf and a striking focal point to the statehouse. Soon the dome was a symbol of Georgia state politics, with "under the gold dome" entering the political lexicon.

As Governor Marvin Griffin spent his term in office spearheading the renovation of the Capitol, little did he expect that

Georgia Hall of Fame, Capitol rotunda. When Mrs. Forrest E. Kibler, a member of the United Daughters of the Confederacy, proposed the idea of a Hall of Fame for the Capitol rotunda, Secretary of State Ben Fortson supported the project enthusiastically and supervised its implementation. The first phase of the hall included thirteen busts of early state leaders, each sponsored by a patriotic organization. (Courtesy of Diane Kirkland and the Georgia Department of Economic Development)

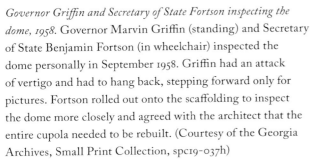

Governor Griffin and Secretary of State Fortson inspecting the dome, 1958. Governor Marvin Griffin (standing) and Secretary of State Benjamin Fortson (in wheelchair) inspected the dome personally in September 1958. Griffin had an attack of vertigo and had to hang back, stepping forward only for pictures. Fortson rolled out onto the scaffolding to inspect the dome more closely and agreed with the architect that the entire cupola needed to be rebuilt. (Courtesy of the Georgia Archives, Small Print Collection, spc19-037h)

Damage to dome balustrade and metal sheathing, 1956. The *Atlanta Constitution* sent a photographer to capture the deterioration of the Capitol dome in the mid-1950s. A close-up of the balustrade spindles shows the original, corroded, dented metal spindles as well as several wooden two-by-four makeshift replacements. In the second photograph, the metal sheathing, which had been painted to feign limestone, has pulled loose to expose the wooden underpinnings. (© 2006 The Atlanta Journal-Constitution; reprinted with permission from the *Atlanta Journal-Constitution*; BOTTOM *Atlanta Constitution*, June 24, 1956, E1)

Reconstruction of the Capitol Dome, 1958. A new stone balustrade and stone sheathing cover the lower half of the dome wall during its reconstruction. The exposed brick, which had been covered with metal, is being repointed in preparation for the addition of stone cladding. The hollow metal caps above the scaffolding have yet to be removed and replaced with stone. (© 2006 The Atlanta Journal-Constitution; reprinted with permission from the *Atlanta Journal-Constitution*)

the new gold dome would soon become a beacon attracting protestors to the political order he had worked so hard to maintain. Within a decade, statehouse politics would change dramatically.

With court-ordered school desegregation looming, some white Georgians sought ways to comply and to avoid violence. They were willing to see the system of segregation dismantled in order to protect such institutions as the public schools. A small number of white legislators, those who had voted against the school-closing law and the flag change, represented this growing segment of citizens. One such legislator, Representative James Mackay from DeKalb County, worked with white and black civic leaders to advance equality and to oppose the county-unit system, which maintained segregationists in power. However, in 1956 the voices of Mackay and other white urban progressives were drowned out by the shouts and cheers of the segregationists in the Capitol.[16]

As the General Assembly passed radical legislation to keep African Americans from attending white schools, black leaders were working quietly in Atlanta and other urban areas to assault the color line. For over a decade, civic leaders in Atlanta had been negotiating with some success to desegregate city

ABOVE TOP *Skeleton of the cupola, c. 1958.* The Capitol's cupola was so damaged that it required almost total replacement. (Courtesy of Mary B. Garner)

ABOVE BOTTOM *Steeplejacks applying gold to the dome, 1959.* In January 1959, steeplejacks gilded the Capitol dome in a multistep process. After cleaning the monel surface, they covered it with three coats of primer and a yellow sizing before using a brush to apply the thin sheets of gold leaf. (Courtesy of Mary B. Garner)

OPPOSITE PAGE *Scaffolding for the reconstruction of the Capitol dome, 1958.* To facilitate rebuilding the dome, scaffolding rose from the base of the drum to the top of the dome, extending over sixty feet away from the structure in some places. A construction elevator hauled up workers, equipment, and two million pounds of Indiana limestone. (Courtesy of the Georgia Archives, Small Print Collection, spc19/36c)

AN APPEAL
FOR HUMAN RIGHTS

We, the students of the six affiliated institutions forming the Atlanta University Center — Clark, Morehouse, Morris Brown, and Spelman Colleges, Atlanta University, and the Interdenominational Theological Center—have joined our hearts, minds, and bodies in the cause of gaining those rights which are inherently ours as members of the human race and as citizens of these United States.

We pledge our unqualified support to those students in this nation who have recently been engaged in the significant movement to secure certain long-awaited rights and privileges. This protest, like the bus boycott in Montgomery, has shocked many people throughout the world. Why? Because they had not quite realized the unanimity of spirit and purpose which motivates the thinking and action of the great majority of the Negro people. The students who instigate and participate in these sit-down protests are dissatisfied, not only with the existing conditions, but with the snail-like speed at which they are being ameliorated. Every normal human being wants to walk the earth with dignity and abhors any and all proscriptions placed upon him because of race or color. In essence, this is the meaning of the sit-down protests that are sweeping this nation today.

We do not intend to wait placidly for those rights which are already legally and morally ours to be meted out to us one at a time. Today's youth will not sit by submissively, while being denied all of the rights, privileges, and joys of life. We want to state clearly and unequivocally that we cannot tolerate, in a nation professing democracy and among people professing Christianity, the discriminatory conditions under which the Negro is living today in Atlanta, Georgia—supposedly one of the most progressive cities in the South.

Among the inequalities and injustices in Atlanta and in Georgia against which we protest, the following are outstanding examples:

(1) Education:
In the Public School System, facilities for Negroes and whites are separate and unequal. Double sessions continue in about half of the Negro Public Schools, and many Negro children travel ten miles a day in order to reach a school that will admit them.
On the university level, the state will pay a Negro to attend a school out of state rather than admit him to the University of Georgia, Georgia Tech, the Georgia Medical School, and other tax-supported public institutions.

According to a recent publication, in the fiscal year 1958 a total of $31,632,057.18 was spent in the State institutions of higher education for white only. In the Negro State Colleges only $2,001,177.06 was spent. The publicly supported institutions of higher education are inter-racial now, except that they deny admission to Negro Americans.

(2) Jobs:
Negroes are denied employment in the majority of city, state, and federal governmental jobs, except in the most menial capacities.

(3) Housing:
While Negroes constitute 32% of the population of Atlanta, they are forced to live within 16% of the area of the city.
Statistics also show that the bulk of the Negro population is still:
a. locked into the more undesirable and overcrowded areas of the city;
b. paying a proportionally higher percentage of income for rental and purchase of generally lower quality property;
c. blocked by political and direct or indirect racial restrictions in its efforts to secure better housing.

(4) Voting:
Contrary to statements made in Congress recently by several Southern Senators, we know that in many counties in Georgia and other southern states, Negro college graduates are declared unqualified to vote and are not permitted to register.

(5) Hospitals:
Compared with facilities for other people in Atlanta and Georgia, these for Negroes are unequal and totally inadequate.

Reports show that Atlanta's 14 general hospitals and 9 related institutions provide some 4,000 beds. Except for some 430 beds at Grady Hospital, Negroes are limited to the 250 beds in three private Negro hospitals. Some of the hospitals barring Negroes were built with federal funds.

(6) Movies, Concerts, Restaurants:
Negroes are barred from most downtown movies and segregated in the rest.
Negroes must even sit in a segregated section of the Municipal Auditorium.
If a Negro is hungry, his hunger must wait until he comes to a "colored" restaurant, and even his thirst must await its quenching at a "colored" water fountain.

(7) Law Enforcement:
There are grave inequalities in the area of law enforcement. Too often, Negroes are maltreated by officers of the law. An insufficient number of Negroes is employed in the law-enforcing agencies. They are seldom, if ever promoted. Of 830 policemen in Atlanta only 35 are Negroes.

We have briefly mentioned only a few situations in which we are discriminated against. We have understated rather than overstated the problems. These social evils are seriously plaguing Georgia, the South, the nation, and the world.

We hold that:
(1) The practice of racial segregation is not in keeping with the ideals of Democracy and Christianity.
(2) Racial segregation is robbing not only the segregated but the segregator of his human dignity. Furthermore, the propagation of racial prejudice is unfair to the generations yet unborn.
(3) In times of war, the Negro has fought and died for his country; yet he still has not been accorded first-class citizenship.
(4) In spite of the fact that the Negro pays his share of taxes, he does not enjoy participation in city, county and state government at the level where laws are enacted.
(5) The social, economic, and political progress of Georgia is retarded by segregation and prejudices.
(6) America is fast losing the respect of other nations by the poor example which she sets in the area of race relations.

It is unfortunate that the Negro is being forced to fight, in any way, for what is due him and is freely accorded other Americans. It is unfortunate that even today some people should hold to the erroneous idea of racial superiority, despite the fact that the world is fast moving toward an integrated humanity.

The time has come for the people of Atlanta and Georgia to take a good look at what is really happening in this country, and to stop believing those who tell us that everything is fine and equal, and that the Negro is happy and satisfied.

It is to be regretted that there are those who still refuse to recognize the over-riding supremacy of the Federal Law.

Our churches which are ordained by God and claim to be the houses of all people, foster segregation of the races to the point of making Sunday the most segregated day of the week.

We, the students of the Atlanta University Center, are driven by past and present events to assert our feelings to the citizens of Atlanta and to the world.

We, therefore, call upon all people in authority—State, County, and City officials; all leaders in civic life—ministers, teachers, and business men; and all people of good will to assert themselves and abolish these injustices. We must say in all candor that we plan to use every legal and non-violent means at our disposal to secure full citizenship rights as members of this great Democracy of ours.

Willie Mays
President of Dormitory Council For the Students of Atlanta University

James Felder
President of Student Government Association For the Students of Clark College

Marion D. Bennett
President of Student Association For the Students of Interdenominational Theological Center

Don Clarke
President of Student Body For the Students of Morehouse College

Mary Ann Smith
Secretary of Student Government Association For the Students of Morris Brown College

Roslyn Pope
President of Student Government Association For the Students of Spelman College

"An Appeal for Human Rights," 1960. Students from the Atlanta University Center colleges paid for a full-page advertisement appealing to white political leaders to take the steps necessary to give them the rights guaranteed by the U.S. Constitution. A week later students staged a sit-in in the Capitol cafeteria and at ten eating facilities in other government buildings after they were denied service. (© 2006 The Atlanta Journal-Constitution; reprinted with permission from the *Atlanta Journal-Constitution; Atlanta Constitution,* March 9, 1960, 13)

departments and facilities. Older black leaders preferred this low-key, behind-the-scenes approach in which they negotiated with white elected officials who needed their votes. For these leaders, public protests, such as a demonstration at the statehouse, would be ill advised. The entrenched climate of intimidation made the Capitol's great plaza off limits to their protests. However, a new generation of African Americans was coming into maturity with new ideas. Emboldened by victories in federal court, inspired by the Montgomery bus boycott, and frustrated by the slow pace of change, these younger leaders advocated public protests in the streets of Atlanta and even in the statehouse itself.

On March 9, 1960, student leaders from the Atlanta University Center colleges published a full-page advertisement in the *Atlanta Constitution* that carried the headline: AN APPEAL FOR HUMAN RIGHTS. The students proclaimed: "[We do] not intend to wait placidly for those rights which are already legally and morally ours to be meted out to us one at a time." They went on to declare that they could not "tolerate, in a nation professing democracy . . . the discriminatory conditions under which the Negro [was] living . . . in Atlanta, Georgia—supposedly one of the most progressive cities in the South." The proclamation served notice that an age of active African American protest had begun in Georgia's capital.[17]

One week later, the Atlanta students acted. Following the lead of students several months earlier in Greensboro, North Carolina, small groups of young, well-dressed African Americans walked into ten cafeterias and restaurants at government-operated or -regulated facilities and requested to be served lunch.

The cafeteria on the ground floor of the Capitol was one of the protesters' targets. Six African Americans, including the Reverend Otis Moss Jr. and five Atlanta University Center students, walked up to the tray table at the head of the serving line. Mrs. R. E. Lee, the white proprietor, halted service and ordered her black employees who were serving white customers to move back from their stations. She called upstairs to the governor's office and spoke to Peter Zack Greer, Governor Ernest Vandiver's executive secretary, who ordered state troopers and Georgia Bureau of Investigation agents to arrest the students. In a hearing the following day, the assistant manager of the cafeteria testified that her supervisor "refused service to the students and asked them to leave because they were Negroes," and that "the policy of that facility [was] not to serve Negroes."[18]

The modest demonstration of the six African American students who requested service in the Capitol cafeteria opened the statehouse doors to black political advocacy. After the students' arrest, the Capitol would become a focus for black protest. On May 17, 1960, the fundamental issue of school desegregation brought demonstrating students back. Hundreds of African American students gathered to march down Hunter Street (now Martin Luther King Jr. Drive) from their Atlanta University Center campuses to the state Capitol. The demonstration was to mark the sixth anniversary of *Brown v. Board of Education*, which had yet to result in a single African American admission to a white public school or college in Georgia.

When white University of Georgia students had demonstrated at the Capitol in the 1940s, they had been allowed to gather on the great west plaza, climb the statue of Tom Watson, and bring a petition to the governor's office. A different reception awaited the Atlanta University Center students.

Governor Ernest Vandiver did not want African Americans demonstrating on the Capitol grounds. To defend the statehouse, he ordered scores of Georgia state troopers, armed with clubs and guns, to surround the Capitol. Troopers connected water hoses to disperse the demonstrators if they attempted to march onto Capitol Square. A more conciliatory Herbert Jenkins, the Atlanta chief of police, met the students as they approached Washington Street and directed them to march around the statehouse rather than gather on the west plaza to

State troopers ringing the Capitol, 1960. When Atlanta University students announced a pro-integration march to the Capitol on May 17, 1960, Governor Vandiver responded with a show of force to keep the protestors off the statehouse grounds. He ringed the Capitol with more than eighty state troopers, who, armed with pistols, billy clubs, and tear gas, connected fire hoses to hydrants and turned on lawn sprinklers. (Courtesy of AP / Wide World Photos)

State trooper directing protestors away from the Capitol, 1960. Local police officers directed the first group of protesters away from the Capitol. The second wave of students encountered state troopers who pushed them away forcibly. (© 2006 The Atlanta Journal-Constitution; reprinted with permission from the *Atlanta Journal-Constitution*; *Atlanta Constitution*, May 18, 1960, 1)

African Americans sitting in the House gallery, 1952.
Until the General Assembly was integrated in
1963, African Americans who wanted to watch
the legislature at work had to sit in a small side
section of the balcony. (Courtesy of the Georgia
Archives, RG1-18-92, box 1-2, 4454)

air their grievances. Following his advice, the students circled
the Capitol and marched down to Auburn Avenue for protest
speeches. Despite the hostile reception from state officials, the
demonstration signaled a new day for African Americans in
Georgia. They had brought their pleas for justice to the streets
of the capital in the shadow of the statehouse.[19]

With African Americans demonstrating in the streets and
federal court decisions on desegregation on the way, white
civic and business leaders in Atlanta and other Georgia cities launched an immense public relations campaign "to keep
the public schools open." Future governor George Busbee, a
junior legislator, introduced legislation to create a commission
that would hold public hearings around the state and make
recommendations that might avoid the state-mandated school
closings. The 1960 legislative vote that created the Sibley Commission was the beginning of the end of segregation. Named
after its chair, John A. Sibley, the commission recommended
that the massive resistance laws be repealed and that each
school board be allowed to decide what to do when faced with
a federal court order to desegregate.[20]

The public turning point for statehouse politics came in January 1961. Just days before the opening session of the General
Assembly, a federal court ordered that Charlayne Hunter and
Hamilton Holmes be admitted to the University of Georgia for
the January term. Governor Vandiver, who had been elected on the pledge of
admitting "no not one," was legally obligated by the state to close the university.
Vandiver decided instead to follow the Sibley Commission's recommendation;
he would allow the university's integration while assuring rural white counties
that they retained the option of closing their schools to avoid desegregation.
To achieve this, the governor had to convince the General Assembly to modify
state law to allow limited integration in Georgia.[21]

When Governor Vandiver arrived in the hall of the House of Representatives
to deliver his State of the State address on January 9, he encountered a different
atmosphere than that which had greeted Marvin Griffin just five years earlier.
Grim-faced legislators sat quietly awaiting his speech of concession. Capitol
reporter Celestine Sibley noted numerous signs of change in the old political
order that day in the House chamber. "Gone was the ribald, carnival air of
the old political hustings. Gone were the jokes and the hearty, back slapping
reunions. No high school bands played, no care-free heaps of peanut shells
littered the aisles."[22]

Governor Vandiver began his address by ordering a one-week "holiday" for
the University of Georgia to give the legislature time to repeal the school-
closing law. His speech was greeted with only the most sparing applause,
despite the standing-room-only white audience in the gallery. A dozen African

American spectators sat in a roped-off section; according to Sibley, they "remained expressionless and impassive during Gov. Vandiver's address."[23]

The segregated African Americans in the House gallery, quietly observing Vandiver's capitulation, presaged the ultimate desegregation of the statehouse. Integration of the General Assembly came two years later, with the arrival of a black legislator. In the spring of 1962, the second of Marvin Griffin's "twin pillars" of white supremacy was felled. In April a federal court ruled that Georgia's county-unit system of elections was unconstitutional, and in May the court ordered in *Toombs v. Fortson* that the General Assembly must reapportion districts on the basis of population. A special session in the fall of 1962 reapportioned the Senate, resulting in the increase of Atlanta's Fulton County representatives from one to seven. The House reapportioned its seats three years later.

Even with the district boundaries being drawn to give advantage to white legislators, reapportionment dramatically increased the opportunities for African Americans to be elected to seats in the statehouse. Encouraged by the elimination of the white primary and the county-unit system and by voter registration drives, black voters elected Leroy Johnson to the Senate in the October 1962 Democratic primary. Johnson carried District 38 in Fulton County, the first African American to be elected to the legislature since William Rogers resigned in 1907 and the first elected to the Senate since 1874.[24]

On January 14, 1963, the *Atlanta Daily World* reported that the "integration of the legislature came quietly in the Senate" as the thirty-four-year-old Johnson sat down among his white colleagues for the opening session. About a dozen African Americans in the gallery witnessed the historic occasion. In a low-key statement to the press, Johnson acknowledged how profoundly his election had changed the political landscape for Georgia's black citizens: "Let me say very clearly that the mere fact that I am here in the legislature serves as an inspiration and hope for Negro girls and boys throughout the state and South. . . . As a boy I could not realistically dream of being a state senator."[25]

For more than fifty years prior to Johnson's election, the only African Americans who crossed the plaza and entered the statehouse daily were those who worked in the few service jobs available to them. Leroy Johnson knew that one of his first tasks as a senator would be to challenge the Jim Crow practices still in place in the statehouse. White senators now had to share their private lavatory with a black legislator. Despite the demonstration of the Atlanta University Center students three years earlier, the Capitol cafeteria still served only white patrons.

Senator Leroy Johnson conferring with Senator Harry Jackson in the Senate chamber, 1963. Elected in 1962, Senator Leroy Johnson (right) was the first African American to serve in the Georgia General Assembly in fifty-five years and the first black man elected senator in eighty-six years. He represented District 38 in Fulton County and Atlanta. His arrival in the Senate brought desegregation to the Capitol, evidenced here by the integrated gallery. (Courtesy of AP / Wide World Photos, January 15, 1963)

After the end of his first legislative session, Johnson and a colleague from Atlanta, Senator James Wesberry, teamed up for the desegregation mission. The two purchased lunches together in the cafeteria line and then sat at a table where six other white patrons were eating. The six immediately relocated to another table, and the two senators had a quiet, "integrated" lunch together. Undeterred by the rebuke, Johnson and Wesberry returned to the cafeteria regularly until the sight of whites and blacks eating together was considered common.[26]

Johnson recognized that his status as an elected politician would allow him to break other color lines. Racial separation was the norm in virtually every aspect of governmental action, from separate voting registration desks and lines in county courthouses to separate polling places in precincts. Senator Johnson challenged segregated driver's-license registration at the renewal table on the first floor of the Capitol. When he arrived at the front of the "white only" line, the examiner directed him to the "colored" table. Johnson refused, and after calling a supervisor for instructions, the clerk gave Johnson an application.[27]

Governor Carl Sanders, who took office in 1963, knew that

he had to respond to Johnson's presence in the Capitol. Considered a moderate progressive, the urban Sanders described himself while campaigning as a "segregationist but not a damn fool." Once in office, Governor Sanders ended Jim Crow in the statehouse when he issued an executive order that required the removal of the "white" and "colored" signs placed over water fountains and restrooms in state buildings.[28]

With Leroy Johnson in the Senate, African Americans had taken a significant first step toward political equality. The next step, the integration of the House of Representatives, would not occur for three more years. For their votes to have an effect, the House districts needed to be redrawn. This occurred in February 1964, when the hand of the Georgia General Assembly was forced again by its nemesis, the U.S. Supreme Court. Ruling in *Wesberry v. Georgia*, the court gave the Georgia House only four days to reapportion itself. Time ran short, and Representative Denmark Groover almost fell off the House chamber balcony trying to reach the clock that was stopped at 11:50 in order to prolong the session. The bill that was passed was actually a map with districts drawn in crayon; it was translated into a piece of legislation the next morning.

With legislative redistricting achieved, the opportunity for black representation in Georgia increased greatly. The Voting Rights Act of 1965 and subsequent registration drives increased the percentage of black registered voters, especially in Georgia cities. Thus the stage was set for a dramatic change in the Georgia General Assembly and in the Capitol.

When the reapportioned legislature convened on January 10, 1966, nine African Americans took seats in the House. All represented urban districts; seven came from Atlanta, and

Representative Denmark Groover leaning over the House gallery balustrade, 1964. In February 1964, the U.S. Supreme Court ruled that the Georgia General Assembly had to reapportion itself. With just four days remaining in the session, the House and the Senate struggled to craft a bill. Near midnight on February 21, when the session was required by law to end, Representative Denmark Groover leaned over the House chamber railing in an attempt to stop the chamber's official clock. Falling to the floor, the clock stopped at 11:50. The reapportionment bill passed shortly after midnight. (© 2006 The Atlanta Journal-Constitution; reprinted with permission from the *Atlanta Journal-Constitution*; *Atlanta Journal*, February 22, 1964, 1)

one each from Columbus and Augusta. In the Senate, Horace Ward from Atlanta joined Leroy Johnson. The presence of eleven African Americans in the Georgia General Assembly was significant, but their arrival did not assure a biracial government. Many of the external signs of Jim Crow had been eliminated in the Capitol, but the attitudes that had sustained segregation prevailed.[29]

Leroy Johnson had been sworn in as a senator in January 1963 without fanfare, but this would not be the case with the House. Among the freshman class was twenty-six-year old Julian Bond, a veteran of the 1960 student sit-in movement and spokesman for the Student Nonviolent Coordinating Committee (SNCC). Future congressman John Lewis and other SNCC leaders had spoken out against the war in Vietnam, arguing that its draft took

Julian Bond sitting during the swearing in of the members of the House of Representatives, 1966. Julian Bond and ten other African Americans were elected to the Georgia General Assembly in 1965. On the morning of January 10, 1966, Bond remained seated while the other new legislators took the oath of office. Bond had publicly denounced U.S. intervention in Vietnam, sparking protests from his fellow legislators, who voted to deny him his seat. (© 2006 The Atlanta Journal-Constitution; reprinted with permission from the *Atlanta Journal-Constitution*; *Atlanta Journal*, January 10, 1966, 1)

a disproportionately large number of blacks. Some SNCC leaders advocated that draft cards be burned in symbolic protest. Bond had maintained that, although he would not burn his own draft card, the SNCC had the right to advocate such a demonstration. Bond was in the minority in 1960, when the overwhelming sentiment of both black and white Georgians was patriotic support for the war. For white rural legislators angry over integration, Bond's political stance, coupled with his civil rights involvement, made him an opportune target. They decided to deny him his seat in the Georgia House of Representatives.

When Speaker George T. Smith gaveled the House to order for its opening session on January 10, 1966, it was a foregone conclusion that Bond would not be allowed to serve. The gallery was packed with Bond supporters, including his parents, John Lewis, and members of the SNCC. To avoid outbursts from the gallery, Speaker Smith devised an unprecedented mass swearing-in ceremony to replace the usual practice of administering the oath of office individually to new members. Just before the ceremony, by prearrangement, Clerk of the House Glenn W. Ellard received a petition that requested that Bond be denied his seat. Ellard sent the document to Bond's desk and asked the representative-elect to remain seated while Georgia Court of Appeals Judge Charles Pannell administered the oath of office to the other incoming legislators.

After the swearing-in ceremony, Speaker Smith appointed a twenty-eight-member committee that included two African Americans to consider whether Bond's statements on the war should disqualify him from serving in the General Assembly. The Speaker instructed the committee to make a recommendation that day, to avoid giving the SNCC time to organize a demonstration in or around the Capitol. The committee met that afternoon and voted 23 to 3 not to seat Bond. Both black committee members and one white legislator formed the minority. That evening the House reconvened and voted 184 to 12 not to seat Bond.

The patriotic legislators, bent on denying Bond his seat, seemed oblivious to the fact that only a decade earlier, the Georgia General Assembly had voted overwhelmingly to resist federal law. The irony was not wasted on *Atlanta Constitution* columnist Ralph McGill, however, who cited Tom Watson, whose statue dominates the Capitol entrance, to point out an earlier example of resistance to federal military policy. While the nation was engaged in World War I, McGill reported, "Tom Watson, in his bitter years of anger and fury, of anti-Semitism, anti-Catholicism, and anti-Negroism . . . did not merely urge opposition to the draft, he called upon American soldiers not to serve if drafted."[30]

The vote against Julian Bond did not pass without protest. On January 14, two coordinated marches—one from Ebenezer Baptist Church led by Atlanta University Dean Horace Mann Bond, the father of Julian Bond, and the other from the Atlanta University Center—converged on the Capitol. Governor Sanders did not allow the demonstrators to protest on the Capitol grounds, so they gathered on Washington Street, in front of the west plaza.

With the Capitol as his backdrop, Atlanta native Dr. Martin Luther King Jr. addressed the fifteen hundred protestors from the bed of a pickup truck. Behind King, a sea of blue-uniformed state troopers stood ready. King told the crowd: "It is ironic to hear the Georgia Legislature speak so reverently about protecting the U.S. Constitution. This same legislature allowed one of its governors to say there was not enough money in the U.S. Treasury to enforce integration in Georgia, and one of its members who talked most bitter about Bond cheered those [white students] who rioted in 1960 at the University of Georgia [when Charlayne Hunter and Hamilton Holmes arrived on campus]."[31]

King left the demonstration after his speech, and the protestors remained to march with their placards outside the Capitol. After circling the statehouse three times, some dared to move onto the Capitol grounds and attempt to enter the building itself. As they pushed past the outer ring of troopers, a scuffle ensued outside the Capitol's south entrance. Public Safety Director Lowell Conner, emerging from the melee, complained: "I thought that we could treat these people like decent, law-abiding human beings. But it looks like that won't work." Connor ordered his troopers to break out their helmets and nightsticks in anticipation of further assaults. The Capitol grounds remained off limits to black protest.[32]

Bond's constituents supported him, reelecting him twice while he pursued his case in the federal courts. Bond's col-

Protestors at the Capitol, 1966. Julian Bond's supporters protested his exclusion from the General Assembly with a speech by Martin Luther King Jr. on the street in front of the west entrance to the Capitol on January 14, 1966. After the speech, a small group circled the Capitol. When they attempted to take their protest into the Capitol at the south entrance, they were forcibly rebuffed by state troopers (in center of photograph). (Courtesy of AP / Wide World Photos)

leagues continued to deny him his seat until ultimately, the U.S. Supreme Court ordered that Bond be seated.[33]

Despite the controversy over Julian Bond, members of the 1966 General Assembly had to adjust to a biracial legislature. Four days after the confrontation on the steps to the south doorway, twelve-year-old Ronald Bickers became the first African American to serve as a legislative page. The eleven black representatives all served on committees and voted on House bills, and their presence brought more integration to the Capitol. As the work of the General Assembly proceeded through its first month, the *Atlanta Constitution* reported that "veteran House members said they were a little surprised at the ease with which the lower chamber, still strongly rural-flavored, ha[d] accepted the Negroes."[34]

Among the other members of the freshman class of 1966 was Grace Towns Hamilton, the first black woman elected to serve in the Capitol. Reapportionment had not only improved electoral opportunities for African Americans, but also opened the door for Georgia women.

From their initial foray into Capitol politics in 1923, when Bessie Kempton and Viola Ross Napier entered the Georgia House of Representatives, women had played limited roles in state politics. Very few were elected; only eleven women served in the House and seven in the Senate in the first fifty years after the passage of the Nineteenth Amendment. In addition, those elected before 1966 had relatively short tenures in office. The average term for the seven women elected to the Senate was 2.3 years, and 4.5 years for the eleven in the House. Of the longer serving women in the House, Bessie Kempton was reelected three times and Helen Douglas Mankin four times. Mankin, who served from 1937 to 1946, when she resigned to run for Congress, was the only woman to build on her Georgia statehouse experience to run successfully for national office.

When Grace Hamilton and two other newly elected female legislators arrived at the Capitol in early 1966, only one woman was serving in the House and the Senate was all male. Hamilton was the first of a new generation of women whose long tenures would win them leadership roles in the General Assembly. Hamilton would serve eighteen years and be appointed to influential committees. A new era of democracy was dawning for women as well as African Americans. The Civil Rights era in Georgia had laid the groundwork; the modern women's movement built on it. A sign of the maturation of women's role in Capitol politics came in 1970, in the General Assembly's be-

Representative Helen Douglas Mankin with her husband, Hamilton Douglas, 1946. Helen Mankin served in the Georgia General Assembly and was the first woman elected to the U.S. Congress from Georgia, a victory she won in a special election on February 12, 1946. This picture was taken the following day. (Courtesy of the Lane Brothers Collection, Special Collections Department, Georgia State University Library)

lated, but symbolically important, vote to ratify the Nineteenth Amendment, fifty-one years after its adoption.

During these years of political change, the interior of the Capitol was becoming more crowded with displays. Secretary of State Fortson installed two eye-catching exhibits when he hung flags from the fourth-floor balustrade in each atrium. The north end, the Hall of Flags, featured all the flags that had flown over Georgia. The south atrium, where a flag from each of the forty-eight states was hung, became the Hall of States. At the same time, museum acquisitions were on the rise, thanks to a change in its mission. Museum staff members were charged with collecting and displaying samples of all of Georgia's flora and fauna, and soon new mounted displays of animals and fish appeared on walls and in the corridors. Visitors to the Capitol could learn more about their state, but the exhibits also distracted them from the architectural grandeur of the building.

The transformation of the Georgia Capitol from a bastion of segregation to a temple of democracy was not achieved by the mere presence of African American legislators. The process had its setbacks, but gradual progress continued. In January 1967,

Representative Grace Towns Hamilton and eight other members of the black legislative class of 1966. Grace Towns Hamilton, one of only four women serving in the General Assembly in 1966, would serve eighteen years in the House, eventually winning positions on influential committees. (Courtesy of Herman "Skip" Mason Jr.)

avowed segregationist Lester Maddox became governor, but during his tenure, the legislature continued quietly to change its old ways. On February 21, 1967, Bishop R. Randolph Shy of the Christian Methodist Episcopal Church was the first African American to serve as House chaplain and to lead the representatives in their daily morning prayer. Such modest changes were accompanied by substantial progress as well, as some black representatives advanced into positions of legislative leadership. Senator Leroy Johnson was gaining seniority, and because he was known to work well with his colleagues, was appointed chair of the Senate Committee on Scientific Research. In the House, Representative Albert Thompson from Columbus was named vice chair of the House Committee on Temperance.

The General Assembly was learning to live with integration, and Maddox's views were beginning to be considered out of the mainstream of Georgia politics. Veteran black legislators, reelected to a third term in 1970, were now in their fifth session. Reflecting on his five years of legislative experience, Representative William Alexander spoke for his colleagues, saying: "We've learned the rules, learned how to get things done and we've gained more confidence." Representative Grace Towns Hamilton offered the observation that her white legislative colleagues in the House were showing "some signs of maturity." Her example was the vote on a measure to excise from the budget the salary of Dean Rusk, a former secretary of state and a professor at the University of Georgia, because his daughter had married an African American. She noted that only thirteen yeas supported the resolution.[35]

The gubernatorial contest to succeed Lester Maddox produced a result that would ultimately reconcile the democratic rhetoric of Georgia's political leaders with the democratic symbolism of the Capitol architecture. However, the election campaign of Jimmy Carter in the summer and fall of 1970 did not suggest the seismic shift in Georgia state politics that lay ahead.

Before his election as governor, Carter had served in the Georgia Senate representing the southwest Georgia seat centered around Americus. Although this district contained a majority black population, Carter gained his Senate seat with a platform that would appeal to white voters. Carter used this same strategy in his gubernatorial campaign, speaking in support of segregationist George Wallace. He declared that Wallace should be able to speak to a legislative assembly in the Georgia Capitol and promised to facilitate such a session if he was elected governor. Consequently, Carter won the election with the white majority, but with only 5 percent of the black vote.

RIGHT *Fourth-floor Capitol Museum displays, c. 1995.* Secretary of State Ben Fortson's vision for the interior of the Capitol was to create a living monument to the state, its history, and its resources. Colorful state flags hung from the balustrades of the north and south atria. Seen here is a collection of Georgia's marine life in display cases and on the walls of the fourth floor. (Courtesy of Diane Kirkland and the Georgia Department of Economic Development)

BELOW *Replacing the torch held by Miss Freedom, 1966.* The Capitol's maintenance improved after the expensive renovations of the 1950s. When a windstorm blew Miss Freedom's glass flame off its torch, an aerial repair was planned and executed. Here a technician leans out from a hovering helicopter after fitting the new flame into place. (© 2006 The Atlanta Journal-Constitution; reprinted with permission from the *Atlanta Journal-Constitution*; *Atlanta Constitution*, August 29, 1966, 1)

Plantings on the Capitol grounds. Ben Fortson's vision included the floral enhancements to the exterior setting of the statehouse. During the 1960s, extensive flower beds were added to the Capitol grounds, supplied with colorful annuals from a newly purchased greenhouse. (Courtesy of Diane Kirkland and the Georgia Department of Economic Development)

On January 12, 1971, Jimmy Carter was sworn in as Georgia's seventy-sixth governor on a specially constructed stage that extended over the steps at the west entrance to the Capitol and enveloped the statue of Tom Watson. When Governor Carter stepped to the podium for his inaugural address, the state's segregationist tradition appeared secure. Lester Maddox joined him on the stage, not only as the outgoing governor but also as the newly elected lieutenant governor. Few suspected that Carter was about to break the segregationist traditions of the state's highest elected leaders. As he began his eight-minute address, the sun began to break through the clouds on the cold, wintry day. Carter's brevity accentuated a message that challenged his white supporters and signaled a new age for democracy in Georgia statehouse.

After his introductory remarks, Carter issued a clear, un-equivocal declaration to his fellow Georgians: "I say to you quite frankly the time for racial discrimination is over. Our people have already made this major and difficult decision." Then, accompanied by stunned gasps from many whites in attendance, the governor went on to say: "No poor man, rural, weak or black person should have to bear the additional burden of being deprived of the opportunity of an education, a job, or simple justice." While his remarks gave hope to the one-third of the state's citizens who were African American, Carter's assertion that the days of Jim Crow were over was addressed to his fellow white citizens and to the legislators who saw them-selves as representing their white constituents. Carter articulated the nature and difficulty of the task that lay ahead during his term by saying that "we cannot underestimate the challenge of the hundreds of minor decisions yet to be made."

For the first time in its eighty-two-year history, the Georgia Capitol was the stage for a governor to declare that justice and education could no longer be denied to black Georgians. Carter's words flew past the statue of Tom Watson in front of him, out into the grand plaza, and across the Capitol grounds. His message was intended for the world beyond the statehouse, but his call had a cleansing effect on the Capitol. Above the newly sworn-in governor, the statue of Freedom stood with torch raised atop the gold dome, now serving as a beacon to all citizens of the state.[36]

Inauguration of Governor Jimmy Carter on the Capitol steps, 1971. Governor Jimmy Carter surprised many Georgians with his inaugural speech, delivered from the Capitol's west steps on January 12, 1971. Reversing a century of segregationist rhetoric by Georgia's highest elected leaders, Carter declared that "the time for racial discrimination [was] over." (© 2006 The Atlanta Journal-Constitution; reprinted with permission from the *Atlanta Journal-Constitution; Atlanta Journal,* January 12, 1971, 1)

A RESTORED
CAPITOL

On February 17, 1974, Governor Jimmy Carter joined with Coretta Scott King and a large integrated audience of politicians, civil rights activists, and civic leaders to preside over a solemn and emotional ceremony on the second floor of the statehouse. The unveiling of the portrait of the Reverend Martin Luther King Jr. would be the first of many public events in the last quarter of the twentieth century that would help to transform the image of the Georgia State Capitol. A new song sounded inside the statehouse when those gathered clasped hands and lent their voices in the civil rights anthem "We Shall Overcome." While black and white political and civic leaders gathered together inside, about fifteen robed Ku Klux Klan members circled the Capitol in a marginalized display of protest. The seismic shift in state politics could not have been made any clearer.[1]

Unveiling of the portrait of Martin Luther King Jr., 1974. In 1973, Governor Jimmy Carter announced that three African Americans would be honored in the Georgia Capitol with portraits. The first portrait, of Martin Luther King Jr., was unveiled on February 17, 1974, in a solemn but emotional ceremony in which an integrated audience held hands while singing "We Shall Overcome." (Courtesy of the AP / Wide World Photos)

Three years earlier, incoming governor Jimmy Carter had declared an end to segregation in Georgia. Among the "hundreds of minor decisions yet to be made" to end racial discrimination in the state was how to deal with the one-hundred-year accumulation of memorials and portraits in and around the statehouse. On the grounds stood monuments to the creators and protectors of the old political order: John B. Gordon, Joseph E. Brown, Tom Watson, and Eugene Talmadge. Inside the corridors were lined with portraits of governors who had supported Jim Crow. Above the west entrance and in front of both the House and the Senate chamber flew the state flag with its Confederate battle emblem.

Two and a half years into his term of office, Governor Jimmy Carter took steps to introduce symbols of the new political order into the Capitol. In October 1973, Carter asked Secretary of State Ben Fortson to help him "rectify" the absence of African American portraits in the statehouse and appointed him to an eight-member, biracial committee to help select the first three honorees.

Carter was acutely aware that "black children and other blacks who visit the state capitol ought to be able to see something they are proud to identify with." He instructed the panel to recommend a short list of African Americans who had toiled to advance equality and justice for all of Georgia's citizens. Native Atlantan and recipient of the 1964 Nobel Peace Prize Martin Luther King Jr. was an obvious choice, but he was not

Portrait of Lucy Craft Laney, third floor. The other two African Americans whose portraits were unveiled during Carter's administration were Henry McNeal Turner (page 37), one of the expelled black legislators of 1868, and Lucy Craft Laney, an educator from Augusta. Both portraits can be found on the third floor of the Capitol. (Courtesy of Diane Kirkland and the Georgia Department of Economic Development)

without his detractors among whites who were slow to adjust to the new racial realities. When the committee began its deliberations, Secretary of State Ben Fortson took the lead, saying, "[T]here's one name we don't need to debate over, if we debate we're just wasting time, and that name is Martin Luther King, Jr." Fortson's advocacy carried the entire panel, an indication of the emerging consensus that the civil rights movement should be considered a significant part of the state's political history. Of the five names that the panel recommended, Governor Carter chose Martin Luther King Jr., Henry McNeal Turner, and Lucy Laney.[2]

Six months after the King portrait unveiling, the other two African American leaders were similarly honored. On August 11, 1974, portraits of Bishop Henry McNeal Turner (1834–1915), who had been among the legislators who were expelled from the Capitol in 1868, and Lucy Craft Laney (1854–1933), an educator in Augusta, were unveiled in the Capitol.

Between the two events, Governor Carter announced a plan to rearrange the past governors' portraits into chronological order with the "historic" governors being placed on the second floor and more "modern" ones on the third. The Carter plan relocated the portrait of Lester Maddox, the most recent of the modern governors and the reigning lieutenant governor, from its spot outside the governor's office. Treating this as a personal slight, Maddox had his portrait removed from the third-floor corridor and hung in his office. After further negotiations, the collection was rearranged so that all the gubernatorial portraits were hung on the second floor and the Maddox portrait returned to public view.

The actions of Georgia's white elected leaders to join with black political and civic leaders to bring new symbols to the statehouse were augmented by the efforts of the growing numbers of African Americans in the General Assembly. The Legislative Black Caucus, established as a support group for African American legislators, voted to erect a monument on the Capitol grounds that would commemorate the struggles of their nineteenth-century predecessors to exercise their rights as elected representatives. They chose to commission a statue depicting an event that had taken place in the Atlanta City Hall / Fulton County Courthouse Capitol (the predecessor building to the current Capitol): the expulsion of the black members of the House and the Senate during the 1868 legislative session. They undertook a fund-raising campaign and commissioned Atlanta sculptor John Riddle to create the memorial. On February 16, 1978, black politicians from across Georgia gathered for the dedication of "Expelled Because of Their Color," the first statue honoring African Americans on the Capitol grounds.

"Expelled Because of Their Color" monument. Intended as a tribute to the black representatives who were turned out of the General Assembly in 1868, this statue depicts African Americans' struggle for equality in Georgia. It also represents the emergence of black political power in the state; the piece was erected by the Legislative Black Caucus of the Georgia General Assembly in 1978. (Courtesy of Diane Kirkland and the Georgia Department of Economic Development)

"Expelled" memorialized the struggle of blacks to participate in government in the immediate aftermath of the Civil War, but it also celebrated the reemergence of black political participation in the late twentieth century. The 1868 expulsion of thirty-two duly elected representatives signified the lengths to which the white majority would go to exclude African Americans from public office. After a century of exclusion, the 1978 monument also recognized black achievement: twenty-two African American representatives served in the General Assembly, and they were influential enough to have a monument to their struggle erected on the Capitol grounds. As the number of African American legislators grew, so did their influence in the General Assembly.

Grace Towns Hamilton, elected in 1966, gained a reputation for evenhandedness that led to her appointments on committees charged with local and state apportionment issues. In 1974, Hamilton helped to shape a new Atlanta City Charter that established black representation in a number commensurate with their proportion of the population. Hamilton worked to create legislative and congressional districts at the state level that would increase opportunities to elect African American representatives in Washington. She also participated in the critical reapportionment battles that occurred after the censuses of 1970 and 1980.

The Capitol campus underwent significant changes in the 1970s, the most striking of which was the completion of Georgia Plaza Park, on the block directly west of the Capitol, which had been key to the 1920s "City Beautiful" plans for a governmental district. In 1965, the City of Atlanta and Fulton County government joined with the state to develop a plan for the plaza, which

Georgia Plaza Park, c. 1980. The design for Georgia Plaza Park was intended to create a rugged and natural oasis adjacent to City Hall, the Fulton County Courthouse, and the State Capitol. Originally the park was an open plaza with three reflecting ponds with fountains and a pergola covered with wisteria vines. Later alterations seen in this photograph included tables for outdoor eating. (Courtesy of Sasaki Associates, Inc.)

would also be adjacent to City Hall and the Fulton County Courthouse. The three governments authorized the State Office Building Authority (now the Georgia Building Authority) to begin development of the park with an initial outlay of $350,000. An underground parking structure was planned to generate fees to pay back the authority, and federal funds were anticipated to help pay capital construction costs. The park was designed by Sasaki, Dawson, DeMay Associated, with the local architectural firm of A. Thomas Bradbury designing the substructure and parking facility. Ground was broken in March 1969; the project took three years and $6.1 million to complete.

While the plaza was under construction, the state initiated a new master plan for the continued development of the Capitol campus. Unveiled in February 1975, the plan called for a new generation of high-rise state office buildings to the north and northeast of the Capitol, structures that were conceived as a radical departure from the existing campus. Bradbury's classically detailed marble buildings, massed at the height of the body of the Capitol, were intended to complement the statehouse and to allow its gold dome to serve as the area's focal point. The new master plan envisioned three buildings, all taller

Statue of Richard B. Russell Jr. The oversized likeness of Richard B. Russell Jr., twentieth-century Georgia governor and U.S. Senator, was designed to stand across the street from the Capitol in Georgia Plaza Park. Instead, the statue of the renowned national defense advocate and opponent of civil rights legislation was placed on the Capitol grounds, where it dwarfs nearby figures of Georgia's past. (Courtesy of Diane Kirkland and the Georgia Department of Economic Development)

RIGHT *Capitol Master Plan.* In February 1975, the Capitol Hill Master Plan Overview Committee unveiled their twenty-five-year plan to double office space in the district around the statehouse. Their design proposed tall, slender towers to the northeast and southeast of the Capitol that abandoned the low-scale, neoclassical style of the older buildings ringing the statehouse. (© 2006 The Atlanta Journal-Constitution; reprinted with permission from the *Atlanta Journal-Constitution*)

BELOW *Aerial view of Capitol complex, 1999.* The completion of the James H. "Sloppy" Floyd Veterans Memorial Building (right foreground) in 1980 provided a great deal of office space for government workers, but the building's height and mass obscures public view of the Capitol from the northeast. (Courtesy of Georgia Aerial Surveys, Inc., www.georgiaaerialsurveys.com)

than the dome, immediately adjacent to the Capitol. A second group of skyscrapers, even taller, would be built further to the northeast. More state office buildings would be built over the expressways.

Eventually, only one of the buildings in the 1975 plan was constructed. Originally called the Twin Towers State Office Building, it is now known as the James H. "Sloppy" Floyd Veterans Memorial Building. Erected between 1975 and 1980, this structure was built in tandem with MARTA's Georgia State Station, which gave Capitol workers access to Atlanta's growing rapid-rail transit system.

As state government continued to expand into new offices, the Capitol retained its role as the functional, as well as the symbolic, center of state government. Inside, the structure was divided by function with separate blocks of offices being controlled by the governor, the secretary of state (who was also responsible for the museum displays), the Speaker of the House, and the lieutenant governor (on behalf of the Senate).

BELOW *Capitol corridor, 1990s.* The Capitol's interior looked shabby by the early 1990s. Inappropriate orb lighting fixtures and institutional paint colors gave the public spaces a drab appearance. In the chambers, clutter, outdated systems, and glaring overhead lights made for an unpleasant work environment. (Courtesy of Diane Kirkland and the Georgia Department of Economic Development)

The remaining public spaces, the exterior, and the grounds were the responsibility of the Georgia Building Authority. The divided authority led to piecemeal renovation projects, each undertaken by one of these entities in the 1970s and 1980s.

By the early 1990s, several state leaders were concerned about the Capitol's condition and began to call for an investment in its renovation. Major capitol restoration projects were underway in Texas and South Carolina, further piquing the interest of several Georgia legislators in such an undertaking. In 1993, the General Assembly established the Commission on the Preservation of the Georgia Capitol to develop a consensus plan for restoration of the statehouse. The first Capitol Commission in 1883 had been given a mandate and a budget: to oversee the design and construction of a new Capitol building whose cost should not exceed one million dollars. The second commission, 110 years later, was given a mandate but no budget: to advise the governor and the General Assembly on how to restore the Capitol as a working center of state government. Funding was not addressed.

The commission membership reflected the mid- to late twentieth-century democratization of Georgia state government. The original commission members had all been white males, while the second commission counted six women and one African American among its thirteen members. Among the ap-

pointees were W. W. Law, an African American leader of the NAACP in Savannah who had led the fight against segregation from 1950 to 1976, and James Mackay, the former legislator and United States Congressman who had spoken out against Georgia's color line during the 1950s.

Before developing a restoration plan, the commission needed to determine the restoration needs of the Capitol by documenting the building thoroughly, from its original construction to its current condition. A federal program, the Historic American Building Survey (HABS), provided a methodology, expert advice, and most of the necessary funds. The Georgia Building Authority contracted with the Atlanta firm of Lord, Aeck & Sargent (LAS) to oversee the documentation and prepare preliminary restoration plans.

Commission on the Preservation of the Georgia Capitol, c. 1996. The Commission on the Preservation of the Georgia Capitol was established by the General Assembly in 1993 to initiate a Capitol restoration plan. Although formed without a budget, the commission was able to convince state leaders to fund a multiyear, multimillion-dollar rehabilitation project. The commission appears here in the Capitol atrium before its restoration. Front Row: W. W. Law, Elizabeth Lyon, Linda King, Helen Catron, Marguerite Williams, James Mackay. Back Row: Caroline Ballard Leake, Smith Wilson, Luther Lewis, Tim Crimmins (chair), Dorothy Olson. (Courtesy of the Georgia Capitol Museum)

As the data was collected and analyzed, the commission struggled with a plan to fund the actual restoration work, a multiyear project that would require many millions of dollars. Such a project had little chance of capturing legislative interest without a compelling need. In mid-1995, the compelling need appeared dramatically in the form of a huge, heavy chunk of falling plaster crashing to the floor of the southwest third-floor corridor. No one was hurt, but the danger was obvious, especially when a subsequent investigation revealed substantial plaster failure in all the second- and third-floor ceilings. Luther Lewis, the GBA director and ex officio member of the commission, had all the plaster removed from the corridor ceilings and roped off the rotunda as a precaution. Bare corridor ceilings and "Danger" signs barring access to the rotunda served as distress signals to everyone who worked in or visited the building.

Recognizing an opportunity in the perilous incident, the commission asked LAS to develop a plan that would restore the public spaces to their original 1889 appearance. The commission recommended a $6.2 million plan that addressed the basics: repair the plaster; reproduce the original paint colors; remove almost a century of grime covering the wooden doors and trim; clean and polish the marble floors and wainscoting; and introduce less intrusive modern lighting into the corridors and rotunda.

Expecting lukewarm legislative support, the commission phased the request over three years and convinced Governor Zell Miller to recommend $2 million for phase one. However, the legislators who had supported the establishment of the

Plaster hole in a corridor ceiling, 1995. The first phase of the Capitol's rehabilitation, which focused on the public spaces, began with a fallen patch of plaster. Legislators returned to the statehouse in early 1996 to find shabby-looking public spaces, a roped-off rotunda, and a $6.2 million dollar request for the restoration of the atria and rotunda. Faced with a significant safety issue and the fast-approaching 1996 Centennial Olympics, the legislature authorized the project. (Courtesy of Lord, Aeck & Sargent Architecture)

commission wanted the project done more quickly and worked to get full funding. Led by Senator George Hooks, chair of the Senate Appropriations Committee, the 1996 General Assembly authorized the entire $6.2 million restoration, to begin immediately after the legislative session.

Orchestrating a major construction project in a working statehouse was a challenge. Plaster repair and replacement required an elaborate web of scaffolding along the corridors, in the three-story atria, and in the four-story rotunda. Construction materials had to be carried in and moved about. Wood needed to be chemically stripped and refinished; marble cleaned and polished. All of this noisy, dirty, disruptive work had to be timed carefully so that it did not interfere with the daily functioning of the Capitol or with the legislative session, which ran each year from January to April.

With work scheduled to begin in the early spring and the 1996 Centennial Olympics arriving in July, the commission opted to stage a demonstration project. The northeast corner of the first-floor atrium became a test lab where different preservation alternatives were "mocked up" and a small exhibit explained the project. The demonstration project sought to build consensus for

Helicopter hovering by the Capitol dome, c. 1995. The first step the commission authorized was a thorough documentation of the building. Historic building specialists used a special photogrammetric camera to take photographs that produced measured drawings of the Capitol exterior. Here a helicopter hovers by the dome while it is photographed. Teams of architects and students worked their way through the entire Capitol, measuring and drawing, while a historian researched the history of building and its site. (© 2006 The Atlanta Journal-Constitution; reprinted with permission from the *Atlanta Journal-Constitution*, August 6, 1994, C14)

OPPOSITE PAGE *Scaffolding in the rotunda,*
1996. Elaborate scaffolding became
a common sight in the Capitol, as
construction progressed through the
atria, the rotunda, and the House and
Senate chambers. (Courtesy of Lord,
Aeck & Sargent Architecture)

the public space plan and, with the bulk of the project still to be funded, to generate support for a future, more extensive restoration program. The demonstration project also allowed the architects and commission members to preview different design solutions and choose the best approach before construction began.

Seeing things in context was critical. Expecting to find an elaborately decorated and stenciled paint scheme typical of late nineteenth-century public buildings, LAS hired a historic paint expert to analyze paint chips and determine the original wall colors and patterns in the Capitol corridors. The results were underwhelming, a two-tone paint scheme that on sample cards, appeared to be beige and taupe. Once the colors were applied to the walls in the demonstration project, their true hues, a peachy beige and a soft green, emerged. Both shades reflect light and change their tint in different lighting conditions. Restoration brought back the beauty of original finishes as well. With a simple cleaning and a light polish, the pink marble wainscoting became more vibrant, and

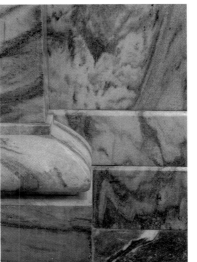

Demonstration project in the north atrium,
1996. The public space repairs grew into a more comprehensive approach that returned the atria and the rotunda to their original appearance, but with both reproduction and modern light fixtures. A corner of the north atrium became a demonstration project where original finishes were unveiled and different lighting schemes were tested. (Courtesy of Lord, Aeck & Sargent Architecture)

the light gray floor tiles lost their dull look. The graining patterns on the light-oak office doors and surrounds emerged as they lost their dark, dirty layers of lacquer.

The demonstration project was most helpful in dealing with elements that needed

Marble wainscot. Most of the Capitol's "Etowah Pink" marble wainscot required only a light cleaning. The marble flooring was dirtier and in poor condition. It had to be removed and reset before its final cleaning and polish. (Courtesy of Diane Kirkland and the Georgia Department of Economic Development)

more than simple restoration. The transoms above each corridor door were easily restored or, in some cases, reconstructed, but the glass panes proved tricky. Restoring the original clear glass would reveal lowered ceilings and mechanical systems, so the commission decided to paint the back of the glass. The paint analyst discovered that many of the offices had been painted in varying shades of green, so after many mockups, the commission selected a soft green shade that resembled the surrounding trim color.

As they considered different restoration possibilities in the demonstration project, the commission members adopted a mission statement to serve as a guiding principle for their decisions:

> To preserve and rehabilitate the Georgia State Capitol and its site, retaining original building fabric and functions while accommodating contemporary needs.

Restoring the original fabric—paint, marble, and wood finishes—in the demonstration project had been straightforward, but "accommodating contemporary needs" in the corridors was more complicated.

The walls of the hallways were filled with portraits, and the atria's natural lighting from the clerestory windows above did not provide sufficient illumination. Modern visitors expected to be able to see the paintings clearly, so some form of supplemental lighting was needed. The commission first considered electric reproductions of the original gas wall sconces, but learned that they would add little more than ambience. After several mockups and long discussions, the commission chose small modern ceiling fixtures that illuminated the portraits but were as unobtrusive as possible.

Another lighting challenge for the public spaces was underfoot. Edbrooke and Burnham used glass-block flooring as a trim in the atria and as a centerpiece in the rotunda. The glass had been covered with carpeting for many years, and the space below was no longer open basement space. Once the block

ABOVE *North atrium before restoration*. Before restoration, the two atria were decorated with flags and cluttered exhibits, painted in hues of blue and gold, and lighted with 1960s fixtures. (Courtesy of Diane Kirkland and the Georgia Department of Economic Development)

OPPOSITE PAGE *North atrium after restoration*. The north atrium, now shorn of its flags, has been finished in its original colors and fitted with replicas of its original lighting fixtures. (Courtesy of Diane Kirkland and the Georgia Department of Economic Development)

LEFT *Wooden door after restoration*. The original wood doorways in the public areas were stripped and refinished, then hand polished with pumice and wax to match the "fine furniture finish" specified in 1889. The glass transoms over the doors were back painted in a soft green to match the surrounding paint scheme. (Courtesy of Diane Kirkland and the Georgia Department of Economic Development)

Rotunda. New lighting was added to the rotunda to improve the visibility of the paintings and to emphasize the architectural features of the room. (Courtesy of Diane Kirkland and the Georgia Department of Economic Development)

was revealed and cleaned, soft lighting was placed beneath it to emulate its original appearance when the basement below was lit by gas lamps.

The mission statement would be tested intensely in the complex task of restoring the legislative chambers. When the General Assembly returned to the Capitol in early 1997, the restoration of the public spaces was well underway, and the legislators were presented with a second, more ambitious funding request. The centerpiece of the $30 million, two-year plan was the rehabilitation of the House and Senate chambers. Both

halls had been marred by the additions of cumbersome light and sound systems. Windows that had been designed to let in natural light had been sealed with insulation and sheetrock for soundproofing, then covered over with heavy drapes. The original coved ceiling and chandeliers had been removed and replaced with cheap acoustical tiles and harsh sodium-vapor lights.

Late twentieth-century technological advances offered legislators the opportunity to restore the chambers to their original luster while upgrading their systems, but achieving the dual goals of the mission statement was often a delicate balance. The first task of the architects was to discover the historic appearance of the legislative halls. Both chambers were essentially two-story boxes whose initial visual character had long been covered, modified, or destroyed. Research using historic photographs and other documents revealed the original features of the chambers: decorative stenciling on the walls and ceiling; wooden windows, shutters, and surrounds; carpets with flowered patterns; and fireplaces decorated with tiles and topped with mirrored mantles.

The second task of the architects was to design a restoration that would allow these spaces to function well as places of work. Late twentieth-century legislators had modern expectations: bright, even lighting, good sound quality, temperature and humidity control, and sophisticated electronic communications.

As the planning proceeded for the transformation of the House and Senate chambers, another team explored options to rehabilitate the Capitol's artwork and exhibits. The corridors were cluttered with paintings, sculpture, and museum exhibits of varying quality and relevance. Heavy drapes blocked the third- and fourth-floor rotunda openings. Nylon flags hung from the fourth-floor balustrade over each atrium, and irreplaceable historic flags were displayed in glass cases, where they were deteriorating from unfiltered sunlight and variations in temperature and humidity. The team designed new exhibits that would complement the architecture, protect the historic artifacts, and relate more to the history of the Capitol and the state. The historic flag collection moved into a newly created state-of-the-art storage and display facility on the first floor.

As the legislative chambers neared completion, the architects and the commission turned to the only vestige of the judicial branch's tenure in the statehouse, the former supreme court

BELOW *House of Representatives before restoration, 1997.* Before restoration, both chambers were closed off to natural light for forty years. Behind the heavy curtains, foam insulation covered replacement windows. The decorative wall stenciling had been painted over many times, and all the original lighting fixtures had been removed. The coved plaster ceiling had been replaced by acoustical tiles and glaring overhead lights. (Courtesy of Lord, Aeck & Sargent Architecture)

LEFT *House of Representatives, 1895.* This 1895 photograph provided the best visual record of the House chamber's original appearance. It provided evidence for the restoration of the carpet pattern, the fireplace treatments, the chandelier, and the ceiling. A similar photograph of the Senate chamber does not exist. (Courtesy of the Kenan Research Center at the Atlanta History Center)

Flag Room, first floor. Georgia's irreplaceable flags were the most endangered artifacts in the Capitol, so conservation was the top priority in the design of the flag room. A few flags are displayed on a rotating schedule, and a touch-screen kiosk provides additional information about the collection. Behind the display room, a storage room contains archival cases for flag storage. (Courtesy of Diane Kirkland and the Georgia Department of Economic Development)

Museum exhibit. The Capitol Museum was entirely redone, its content refined to focus more on the building's history and function while displaying the best of the existing collections. Historic museum cases were modified to control lighting and humidity levels; a few new cases were designed to match. (Courtesy of Diane Kirkland and the Georgia Department of Economic Development)

Museum tour group. Large groups of youngsters are a common sight in the Capitol, as hundreds of school groups visit the statehouse each year. Here Secretary of State Cathy Cox speaks to students about Georgia's natives, assisted by museum director Dorothy Olsen. (Courtesy of Diane Kirkland and the Georgia Department of Economic Development)

chamber. Since the court had moved to the Judicial Building in 1956, the space had been converted to a large committee meeting room and was known as the "Appropriations Room" after the powerful joint committee that used it. As in the legislative chambers, the windows had been sealed and draped, the ceiling modified, the electric chandelier and sconces removed, and sodium-vapor lights installed. Unlike the legislative chambers, the supreme court chamber no longer had its original furniture, and there was little photographic evidence of the room's original appearance. Early twentieth-century historic photographs

Plasterer working on a ceiling, 1996; worker, 1997; House of Representatives under restoration, 1999. Work on the chambers occurred only when the legislature was out of session, and then it went on around the clock. (Courtesy of Lord, Aeck & Sargent Architecture)

of the judges sitting at the bench provided only glimpses of the chamber, so restoration decisions were often based on historic treatments in other parts of the building.

Although the rehabilitation project was carefully phased, at times it seemed that the Capitol was under siege. Huge scaffolding structures appeared in the rotunda for a few months and then were taken down, only to reappear, reconfigured, in one of the atria. Crews worked hours when political activity at the Capitol was at low ebb. During the atria restoration, workers labored at night, arriving in the early evening and departing before the sun rose. Cleaning crews would then tidy up before the Capitol opened for business. This schedule ran for the nine months the General Assembly was not in session. For the restoration of the House and the Senate, people worked around the clock. As soon as the last legislator departed in March 1998, workers removed the desks and chairs for refurbishment and storage. Then they erected scaffolding for the plaster, electrical, and heating and air conditioning work in the walls and ceilings.

When the legislators returned in January 1999, they found a work in progress. The replastered white walls around them and the recoved ceiling above awaited their decorative finishes. A stripe of stenciling that ran from the tiny dome overhead, across the ceiling, and down the wall provided a hint of the lively decoration to come. Less obtrusive overhead lighting supplemented the natural light coming through the clear glass windows before them, which offered views of the grounds outside for the first time in over forty years. The legislators sat at new, temporary desks; the refurbished original desks would be installed after the restoration was completed. When the General Assembly adjourned in March 1999, the scaffolding returned, and the second and final phase of the restoration began.

Meanwhile, hundreds of miles away, a historic lighting specialist was working on one of the final, but most visible, elements of the project. Virtually all the original lighting fixtures in the Capitol had been removed by 1960. With only fuzzy historic photographs and some vague furnishing specifications, the expert identified the original manufacturer and reconstructed the two- and three-globe wall sconces that appeared throughout the statehouse. Historic photographs of the grand stairway lampposts were also blurry, so their overall form was recreated and their ornamental details created. The focal points of each chamber, the magnificent chandeliers, took two and a half years to reconstruct and were installed just in time for the dedication of the refurbished legislative halls.

At 10:00 a.m. on January 10, 2000, trumpets sounded above the din in the Capitol rotunda as the members of the Georgia General Assembly milled about, exchanging stories and creating a cacophony that reverberated throughout the halls and atria. They had assembled there to reenact a historic march and to celebrate a historic restoration. Their predecessors had gathered 111 years earlier

Workers welding at night, 1997. Restoring a public building while it remains in use requires careful scheduling. Most of the work in the public spaces was done at night. (Courtesy of Lord, Aeck & Sargent Architecture)

to process through the streets of downtown Atlanta to a new statehouse. Now, after two years of construction, members of the House and the Senate were preparing to march into their newly restored halls, which had been returned as closely as possible to their 1889 appearance.

Now with a second trumpet call, officials, legislators, staff members, and visitors gathered to listen to Governor Roy Barnes, Lieutenant Governor Mark Taylor, House Speaker Tom Murphy, and Capitol Commission Chair Tim Crimmins. When the brief speeches were over, the time arrived to process to the newly appointed chambers. In 1889, the press had described that procession as a "kind of go-as-you-please" affair, and the same could be said of the legislative march in 2000. Led by Speaker Murphy, the members of the House turned and moved en masse up the stairs of the south atrium and ambled in no particular order down the west third-floor corridor to their chamber. The Senate formed a more stately procession behind Lieutenant Governor Mark

Lobbyist at work by historic light fixture; torchieres, atrium stairway; chandelier, Senate chamber. Virtually all the original lighting fixtures in the Capitol had been removed by 1960. With only a few historic photographs and some vague furnishing specifications, a historic lighting expert identified the original manufacturer and reconstructed the wall sconces and atria's torchieres. The focal point of each chamber, its magnificent chandelier, took two and a half years to reconstruct. (Courtesy of Diane Kirkland and the Georgia Department of Economic Development)

Taylor and marched two-by-two up the steps of the north atrium and down the east corridor to their chamber.

With the legislators working inside their restored chambers, attention turned to the Capitol's exterior. A gentle washing returned the limestone exterior to its original creamy hue. Only a few stones were damaged enough to require patching, but the mortar was completely repointed. The windows were repaired and refinished, their frames painted a deep brown to suggest the original stained finish. Finally, Miss Freedom was removed from her perch and repaired inside and out.

When the presiding officers in each hall gaveled the 2000 legislative session to order, natural light shone in from shuttered windows, ornate chandeliers glistened overhead, and a riot of Victorian colors cascaded from ceiling to carpet. At each of the restored desks, where there had originally been inkwells, legislators found electronic voting switches, microphones and micro speakers, and receptacles to link their laptop computers. All these electronics were connected to miles of wiring beneath the floor that was funneled into conduits hidden in the fireplace chimneys.

While the restoration brought back the original look of the House and the Senate, there were profound differences in the 1889 and 2000 opening events that went far

House of Representatives and Senate chamber after restoration. Although restored as closely to their original appearance as possible, the rehabilitated House and Senate chambers have also been redesigned to function as modern work spaces. (Courtesy of Diane Kirkland and the Georgia Department of Economic Development)

Miss Freedom being removed for repair, in transit, and under repair. The century-old statue of Freedom atop the Capitol was showing her age. Lifted by helicopter from the top of the dome (top left), the two-ton statue (right) was lowered and trucked to a workshop. There its internal support system was replaced, and its thick copper skin was stripped and repainted (bottom left). A second flight returned Miss Freedom to her perch above the cupola. (TOP LEFT and RIGHT Courtesy of Diane Kirkland and the Georgia Department of Economic Development; BOTTOM LEFT Courtesy of Heather Little Limited, September 2004)

beyond the building's appearance or function. With the exception of one marginalized African American, only white men had taken their seats to conduct the affairs of government in July 1889. For many years to follow, the Georgia Capitol was a place of government by and for the few. However, decades of cumulative changes eventually broke through the web of restraints, and now, at the very beginning of the twenty-first century, women and men, black and white, gathered in the legislative halls to represent all Georgians.

Other profound political changes took place as the Capitol was undergoing its restoration. Where once factions of the Democratic Party struggled for dominance in the statehouse, Republicans vied with Democrats for political control. On January 13, 2002, there was another first on the Capitol steps. After a swearing-in ceremony in Atlanta's World Congress Center, Governor Sonny Perdue became the first Republican elected governor since Reconstruction, and the first to ascend the steps of the 1889 Capitol. In advance of the 2002 legislative

Fireplace, House of Representatives. Most of the original fireplaces in each chamber had been removed or covered over. Original tile fragments found behind the removed panels allowed restorers to reproduce the original colors and pattern of the tile hearth and facing in the House chamber. (Courtesy of Diane Kirkland and the Georgia Department of Economic Development)

Legislative desks and chairs. Both chambers still had their original furniture, although the desks and chairs had been repaired, modified, and rebuilt several times. The desks were reworked during the restoration to accommodate laptop computers and new sound and voting systems. (Courtesy of Diane Kirkland and the Georgia Department of Economic Development)

Martin Luther King Jr. funeral procession, 1968, and Coretta Scott King funeral, 2006. The evolution of Georgia's democracy can be seen clearly in these two photographs. At the top, Martin Luther King Jr.'s 1968 funeral procession passes the Capitol, which was locked that day by order of Governor Lester Maddox. Below, Coretta Scott King's coffin is carried into the Capitol, as the King family, Atlanta Mayor Shirley Franklin, and Mary and Governor Sonny Perdue watch. Thousands flocked to the rotunda on February 4, 2006, to pay their respects to Mrs. King, the first African American and first woman to lie in state in the Capitol. (TOP Courtesy of Jo Freeman, www.jofreeman.com; BOTTOM Courtesy of AP / Wide World Photos)

session, Governor Perdue used his influence to help Republicans gain control of the Senate. Two years later, when Republicans gained a majority of House seats, Glenn Richardson became the first Republican Speaker of the House to serve in the 1889 Capitol.

In the three decades since Carter's inaugural, the issues that have divided Georgians for over a century have not all been resolved. One of the "hundreds of minor decisions still to be made" in the twenty-first century was what to do with the 1956 flag, which had been adopted as a symbol of resistance to integration. This issue occupied two governors and two sessions of the General Assembly during the first four years of the twenty-first century. African American legislators were instrumental in keeping the issue alive through a long process involving both legislative and public votes. Eventually, the General Assembly adopted a design that features the state seal. Some Georgians still argue passionately that the removal of the Confederate battle flag emblem was either an affront to their heritage or an indemnification long overdue.

Capitol Symbols, 2005. A refurbished Miss Freedom with torch of liberty raised and sword ready in its defense stands atop a renovated and renewed Capitol. (Courtesy of Diane Kirkland and the Georgia Department of Economic Development)

Like any American statehouse, the Georgia State Capitol is an architectural symbol meant to represent democratic ideals. As a working capitol, the building has acquired layers of meaning with the numerous events that have occurred within its walls and on its grounds. Throughout its history, the Georgia Capitol has served as a stage for those who fought for and those who resisted equal rights. The gap between the ideals and the practice of democracy within its walls and on its grounds is not unique to Georgia, but the story of overcoming this gap is Georgia's own. Today the Georgia Capitol proudly represents this struggle and the imperfect, but far more equitable, form of democracy that has resulted from it.

NOTES

Preface

1. Henry-Russell Hitchcock and William Seale, *Temples of Democracy: The State Capitols of the U.S.A.* (New York: Harcourt Brace Jovanovich, 1976), 3–26.

2. Gary B. Nash, *First City: Philadelphia and the Forging of Historical Memory* (Philadelphia: University of Pennsylvania Press, 2002), 2–3, 6–7.

Chapter One. A Dedicated Capitol

1. *Atlanta Constitution, Macon Telegraph*, July 4, 1889.

2. Charles T. Goodsell, *The American Statehouse: Interpreting Democracy's Temples* (Lawrence: University of Kansas Press, 2001), 15.

3. Goodsell, *American Statehouse*, 16–17.

4. Ibid., 26–27.

5. *Atlanta Constitution*, February 10, July 5, 1889.

6. Ibid., July 4, 5, 10, 11, 15, 20, August 10, 1889.

7. Ibid., July 4, 1889

8. Ibid., July 5, 1889.

9. Ibid.

10. Ibid.

11. *Savannah Morning News*, July 5, 1889.

12. *Atlanta Constitution, Augusta Chronicle, Savannah Morning News*, July 5, 1889.

13. *Savannah Morning News*, July 5, 1889.

14. *Atlanta Constitution*, February 10, 1889.

Chapter Two. A Rented Capitol

1. *Daily New Era*, January 14, 1868; *Atlanta Constitution*, January 13, 1889; Unmarked clipping from the Joseph Emerson Brown and Elizabeth Grisham Brown Collection, Richard B. Russell Library for Political Research and Studies, University of Georgia Libraries, Athens, Georgia.

2. *Atlanta Constitution*, January 13, 1869. City directories show no evidence of the fifth floor being rented as lodgings; the state may have used these apartments for legislators. Half of the first floor was leased through the mid-1870s; tenants included a billiard hall and oyster house, a homeopathic physician, and several insurance companies.

3. Anne H. Farrisee, "History of the Georgia State Capitol," located at the HABS/HAER "Built in America" Web site (http://memory.loc.gov/ammem/collections/habs_haer/), 14–30. (Type "Georgia State Capitol Atlanta" in the search box.)

4. Joseph Waring, *Cerveau's Savannah* (Savannah: Georgia Historical Society, 1973), 13; personal conversations and correspondence with Ed Cashin of Augusta State University and Don Rhodes of the *Augusta Chronicle*, July 2002.

5. William Harden, *A History of Savannah and South Georgia* (Chicago: Lewis Publishing, 1913), 240.

6. Yulssus Lynn Holmes, *Those Glorious Days: A History of Louisville as Georgia's Capital, 1796–1807* (Macon, Ga.: Mercer University Press, 1996), 29–30; Charles T. Goodsell, *The American Statehouse: Interpreting Democracy's Temples* (Lawrence: University of Kansas Press, 2001), 27, 42–45.

7. Leola Selman Beeson, "The Old State Capitol in Milledgeville and Its Cost," *Georgia Historical Quarterly*, September 1950, 197–200; "GMC-3 Old Capitol Building Renovation," Office of Public Relations, Georgia Military College, n.d., 1–3.

8. James C. Bonner, *Milledgeville, Georgia's Antebellum Capital* (Athens: University of Georgia Press, 1978), 43–46.

9. William Irvine, "Diary and Letters of Dr. William N. White, a Citizen of Atlanta—Written 1847, 90 Years Ago," *Atlanta Historical Bulletin*, July 1937, 48.

10. George White, *Statistics of the State of Georgia* (Savannah: W. Thorne Williams, 1849), 205; *Historical Collections of Georgia* (New York: Pudney & Russell, 1855), 412; *Journal of the Senate of the State of Georgia (1853–54)*, 39.

11. Kenneth Coleman, ed., *A History of Georgia* (Athens: University of Georgia Press, 1977), 208–12.

12. *Daily New Era*, February 28, 1868; S. P. Richards Diary, February 1868, Atlanta History Center manuscript file, box 1, folder 6, p. 157.

13. Royce Shingleton, *Richard Peters: Champion of the New South* (Macon, Ga.: Mercer University Press, 1985), 163; *Daily New Era*, June 17, 1868.

14. Numan V. Bartley, *The Creation of Modern Georgia*, 2nd ed. (Athens: University of Georgia Press, 1990), 50–54; Russell Duncan, *Freedom's Shore: Tunis Campbell and the Georgia Freedmen* (Athens: University of Georgia Press, 1986), 46–52.

15. *Atlanta Constitution*, July 5, 1868; Coleman, *History of Georgia*, 212–14.

16. Russell Duncan, *Entrepreneur for Equality: Governor Rufus Bullock, Commerce, and Race in Post–Civil War Georgia* (Athens: University of Georgia Press, 1994), 64–65.

17. This thirty-thousand-dollar outlay compared favorably with the estimated forty-thousand-dollar City Hall / County Courthouse expansion.

18. Coleman, *History of Georgia*, 214.

19. *Atlanta Constitution*, Atlanta *Daily Intelligencer*, January 11, 1870.

20. Bartley, *Creation of Modern Georgia*, 70; Edward King, *The Great South* (Baton Rouge: Louisiana State University Press, 1972), 354; Edmund L. Drago, *Black Politicians and Reconstruction in Georgia: A Splendid Failure* (Baton Rouge: Louisiana University Press, 1982), 83, 146.

21. http://www.sos.state.ga.us/archives/rs/aghr.htm, accessed June 1, 2004.

22. Bonner, *Milledgeville, Georgia's Antebellum Capital*, 227. Certainly the estimated value seems suspiciously high; when the state sold the Opera House Capitol in 1890, it received less than $134,300. Kimball's profit is hard to calculate exactly, but it was substantial, probably around $225,000.

23. Coleman, *History of Georgia*, 295; Laughlin McDonald, *A Voting Rights Odyssey: Black Enfranchisement in Georgia* (Cambridge: Cambridge University Press, 2003), 80–84.

24. *Atlanta Constitution*, July 19, 1877.

25. Ibid., December 21, 1877; Bonner, *Milledgeville, Georgia's Antebellum Capital*, 227.

26. *Savannah Morning News*, December 6 and 7, 1877; *Columbus Daily Enquirer Sun*, December 7, 1877; *Macon Telegraph & Messenger*, December 7, 1877.

27. *Atlanta Constitution*, February 10, 1889.

28. *Acts and Resolutions of the General Assembly of the State of Georgia*, 1882–83, Public Laws, 18.

Chapter Three. A Budget Capitol

1. Anne H. Farrisee, "History of the Georgia State Capitol," located at the HABS/HAER "Built in America" Web site (http://lcweb2.loc.gov/ammem/hhhtml/hhhome.html), 32–114; *Atlanta Journal*, September 2, 1885; *Atlanta Constitution*, September 3, 1885.

2. Richard N. Current, ed., *Encyclopedia of the Confederacy* (New York: Simon & Schuster, 1993), 909–10; Numan V. Bartley, *Creation of Modern Georgia*, 2nd ed. (Athens: University of Georgia Press, 1990), 246n28.

3. *Atlanta Journal*, September 2, 1885

4. Ibid.

5. *Atlanta Constitution*, January 18, 1884.

6. Ibid., January 17 and 18, 1884.

7. Minutes, February 11, 1884, Board of Capitol Commissioners Records.

8. "First Annual Report," Board of Capitol Commissioners Records, 19.

9. "Quarrying Notes," *Manufacturer and Builder* 16, no. 12 (December 1884): 275.

10. Marcus A. Bell, "Georgia's Capitol, an Appeal to the Members of the General Assembly" (Atlanta, Georgia), November 10, 1884, Georgia Archives.

11. *Atlanta Constitution*, April 13, 1885.

12. Ibid., June 29, 1890.

13. Taking Atlanta's payment of $55,625 into account, the maximum amount for the Capitol that could have come out of the state surplus was $170,303.59.

14. *Atlanta Constitution*, February 5, 1888.

15. "The Report of the Committee appointed under and by virtue of the Joint Resolution, approved September 20, 1887, for the purpose of estimating the probable cost of furnishing and equipping the New State Capitol," November 23, 1888, Board of Capitol Commissioners Records.

16. *Atlanta Constitution*, February 27, 1889.

17. Ibid., March 1, 1889; Henry-Russell Hitchcock and William Seale, *Temples of Democracy: The State Capitols of the U.S.A.* (New York: Harcourt Brace Jovanovich, 1976), 150–92.

18. Minutes, March 20, 1889, Board of Capitol Commissioners Records.

Chapter Four. A New South Capitol

1. Edward Frantz, "A March of Triumph? Benjamin Harrison's Southern Tour and the Limits of Racial and Regional Reconciliation," *Indiana Magazine of History*, December 2004, 293–320.

2. George Leonard Chaney, "The New South: Atlanta," *New England Magazine*, November 1891, 377–94; "Recent Architecture in Atlanta," *Harper's Weekly*, August 3, 1889, 623.

3. Chaney, "New South," 386.

4. *Atlanta Constitution*, April 16, 1891.

5. Frantz, "March of Triumph," 293–320.

6. August Meier and Elliott Rudwick, "The Boycott Movement against Jim Crow in the South, 1900–1906," *Journal of American History* 55 (March 1969): 768; John Dittmer, *Black Georgia in the Reconstruction Era* (Urbana: University of Illinois Press, 1977), 16–17.

7. *Atlanta Journal*, October 9–10, 1891; *Atlanta Constitution*, October 10, 1891; *Acts and Resolutions of the General Assembly of the State of Georgia*, 1890–91, Public Laws, 157–58.

8. In the 1921 case heard by the Georgia Court of Appeals, the court upheld the provision that permitted conductors to expel a passenger for failure to obey their orders, but went on to limit their police power by ruling that conductors could only order arrests in cases where passengers were disorderly. Russell Duncan, *Entrepreneur for Equality: Governor Rufus Bullock, Commerce, and Race in Post–Civil War Georgia* (Athens: University of Georgia Press, 1994), 123; Meier and Rudwick, "Boycott Movement against Jim Crow in the South," 768; Dittmer, *Black Georgia in the Reconstruction Era*, 16–17.

9. *Atlanta Constitution*, May 30, 1893.

10. Ibid.

11. Ibid.

12. "The City of Atlanta," *Harper's New Monthly Magazine*, December 1879, 42.

13. Norman C. Delaney, "John McIntosh Kell: A Confederate Veteran in Politics," *Georgia Historical Quarterly*, Fall 1973, 379.

14. *Acts and Resolutions of the General Assembly of the State of Georgia*, 1890–91, Resolutions, 559; *Atlanta Constitution*, Septem-

ber 26, 1891; *Report of the Keeper of Public Buildings and Grounds*, 1909–10, Georgia Archives.

15. *Atlanta Constitution*, February 18, 1894; Ida Husted Harper, *The History of Woman Suffrage: 1883–1900*, vol. 4 (Indianapolis: Hollenbeck Press, 1902), 583–85.

16. *Atlanta Constitution*, February 5, 1895.

17. Ibid., February 18, 1895.

18. Harper, *History of Woman Suffrage: 1883–1900*, 4:583–85.

19. *Atlanta Constitution*, December 15, 1898.

20. Ibid. The Republican President McKinley tended to his African American political base after his visit to the Georgia statehouse by traveling with his cabinet officers to Alabama, where he met with Booker T. Washington and the faculty and students of the Tuskegee Institute. Booker T. Washington, *Up from Slavery: An Autobiography* (New York: Doubleday, 1901), 303–10.

21. *Atlanta Constitution*, January 14–15, 1904; Anne H. Farrisee, "History of the Georgia State Capitol," located at the HABS/HAER "Built in America" Web site (http://lcweb2.loc.gov/ammem/hhhtml/hhhome.html), 151–52.

22. *Atlanta Constitution*, May 28, 1907.

Chapter Five. A Memorialized Capitol

1. *Atlanta Constitution*, May 28, 1907.

2. Ibid.

3. Ibid. The history of the commission was written by W. Lowndes Calhoun, who chaired the Monument Association. At the dedication ceremony, Calhoun's history was delivered by Capitol Commission secretary William "Tip" Harrison, who was also a member of the Gordon Monument Commission.

4. J. J. Ansley, *History of the Georgia Woman's Christian Temperance Union: From Its Organization, 1883 to 1907* (Columbus, Ga.: Gilbert Printing, 1914), 216–20.

5. *Atlanta Constitution*, July 25, 1907.

6. Ibid.

7. Ibid.

8. Ibid., July 31, 1907.

9. Ibid., July 28, 1907.

10. Laughlin McDonald, *A Voting Rights Odyssey: Black Enfranchisement in Georgia* (Cambridge: Cambridge University Press, 2003), 41.

11. *Atlanta Journal*, August 15, 1907; *Savannah Tribune*, August 17, 1907.

12. *Atlanta Constitution*, August 13 and 15, 1907; Michael Perman, *Struggle for Mastery: Disfranchisement in the South, 1888–*

1908 (Chapel Hill: University of North Carolina Press, 2001), 292–93.

13. *Atlanta Constitution*, August 15, 1907.

14. Ibid., August 13 and 15, 1907; *Atlanta Journal*, August 15, 1907.

15. J. Morgan Kousser, *The Shaping of Southern Politics: Suffrage Restriction and the Establishment of the One-Party South, 1880–1910* (New Haven, Conn.: Yale University Press, 1974), 218–23.

16. *Acts and Resolutions of the General Assembly of the State of Georgia*, 1902, Resolutions, 726; *Report of the Keeper of Public Buildings and Grounds*, 1909–10, Georgia Archives.

17. Steve Oney, *And the Dead Shall Rise: The Murder of Mary Phagan and the Lynching of Leo Frank* (New York : Pantheon, 2003), 353–65, 368–70, 385, 480–87, 489–511.

18. Ibid., 510–11; Nathaniel E. Harris, *Autobiography: The Story of an Old Man's Life with Reminiscences of Seventy-five Years* (Macon, Ga.: J. W. Burke, 1925), 357.

19. Josephine R. Floyd, "Rebecca Latimer Felton: Champion of Women's Rights," *Georgia Historical Quarterly*, June 1946, 87; A. Elizabeth Taylor, "Women Suffrage Activities in Atlanta," *Atlanta Historical Journal*, Winter, 1978–79, 49–54.

20. *Atlanta Constitution*, July 20 and 25, 1919.

21. *Acts and Resolutions of the General Assembly of the State of Georgia*, 1921, Public Laws, 106; *Atlanta Constitution*, July 23, 1921; Ida Husted Harper, *The History of Woman Suffrage: 1900–1920*, vol. 6 (1922; repr., New York:, Arno Press, 1969), 142.

22. *Atlanta Constitution*, January 17, 1931; January 19, 1933.

23. Ibid., July 30, 1919.

24. *Atlanta Journal*, January 28, 1923; *Acts and Resolutions of the General Assembly of the State of Georgia*, 1923, Resolutions, 891.

25. *Atlanta Constitution*, February 17, 1929.

26. "Governor's Message," *Journal of the House* (1929), 216, 413–14; *Acts and Resolutions of the General Assembly of the State of Georgia*, 1929, Resolutions, 1516; *Atlanta Constitution*, September 10, 1929.

27. *Atlanta Journal Magazine*, September 8, 1929; *Atlanta Journal*, April 14, 1935.

28. *Acts and Resolutions of the General Assembly of the State of Georgia*, 1925, Resolutions, 1608; *Atlanta Journal*, October 17, 1928.

Chapter Six. A Civic Capitol

1. *Atlanta Constitution*, August 28, 1932.

2. Robert Sherrill, *Gothic Politics in the Deep South: Stars of the New Confederacy* (New York: Grossman, 1968), 37–48.

3. *Atlanta Journal*, December 4, 1932.

4. William Anderson, *The Wild Man from Sugar Creek: The Political Career of Eugene Talmadge* (Baton Rouge: Louisiana State University Press, 1975), 85–89; *Atlanta Constitution*, June 20, 1933.

5. *Atlanta Constitution*, February 25, 1936; *Atlanta Journal*, February 25, 1936; Anderson, *Wild Man from Sugar Creek*, 143–45; *Atlanta Journal-Constitution*, December 30, 1956.

6. *Atlanta Journal-Constitution*, December 30, 1956.

7. Sherrill, *Gothic Politics in the Deep South*, 37.

8. *Acts and Resolutions of the State of Georgia*, 1937–38, Appropriations, 63; *Atlanta Journal Magazine*, 1949 (undated article in University of Georgia Special Collections file); *Atlanta Constitution* May 19, August 5, September 11, and November 16, 1938; January 2 and 8, 1939.

9. *Atlanta Constitution*, October 16, 1941.

10. James F. Cook, *Carl Sanders: Spokesman of the New South* (Macon, Ga.: Macon University Press, 1993), 248, 255–57.

11. *Atlanta Constitution*, March 7, 1946; Laughlin McDonald, *A Voting Rights Odyssey: Black Enfranchisement in Georgia* (Cambridge: Cambridge University Press, 2003), 49.

12. McDonald, *Voting Rights Odyssey*, 52–53; Calvin Kytle and James A. Mackay, *Who Runs Georgia?* (Athens: University of Georgia Press, 1998), 72.

13. Kytle and Mackay, *Who Runs Georgia?* 11.

14. Harold Paulk Henderson, *The Politics of Change in Georgia* (Athens: University of Georgia Press, 1991), 175.

15. Ellis Gibbs Arnall, *What the People Want* (Philadelphia: J. B. Lippincott, 1947), 14; Herman Talmadge, interviews by Harold Paulk Henderson, June 26 and July 17, 1987, Georgia Government Documentation Project, Georgia State University Special Collections, Atlanta, Georgia; Herman E. Talmadge and Mark Royden Winchell, *Talmadge: A Political Legacy, a Politician's Life* (Atlanta: Peachtree Publishers, 1987), 84–87; *Atlanta Constitution*, January 15, 1947.

16. *Atlanta Constitution*, January 15, 1947.

17. Henderson, *Politics of Change in Georgia*, 179; Arnall, *What the People Want*, 11–12.

18. Charles Myer Elson, "The Georgia Three-Governor Controversy of 1947," *Atlanta Historical Bulletin*, Fall 1976, 80–81; Sherrill, *Gothic Politics in the Deep South*, 40–41; Talmadge and Royden, *Talmadge*, 89, 91; *Atlanta Constitution*, January 17 and 18, 1947.

19. Harold P. Henderson, "M. E. Thompson and the Politics of Succession," in *Georgia Governors in an Age of Change*, ed. Harold P. Henderson and Gary L. Roberts (Athens: University of Georgia Press, 1988), 58–59; Sherrill, *Gothic Politics in the Deep South*, 41.

20. Henderson, "M. E. Thompson and the Politics of Succession," 61.

21. Herman Talmadge, interviews by Harold Paulk Henderson.

Chapter Seven. A Contested Capitol

1. *Atlanta Constitution*, August 5, 1958.

2. *Atlanta Journal-Constitution*, August 27, 1950.

3. *Atlanta Journal-Constitution*, January 12, 1964.

4. Letter from John P. Bondurant, Athens Lumber Company, to Secretary of State Ben Fortson, April 8, 1954, Georgia Capitol Museum files.

5. Minutes of the State Office Building Authority, July 23, 1951, July 31, 1953.

6. *Atlanta Journal*, March 11, 1954; *Atlanta Constitution*, May 23, 1954.

7. *Atlanta Journal*, January 6, 1956.

8. Kenneth Coleman, ed., *A History of Georgia* (Athens: University of Georgia Press, 1977), 392; Calvin Kytle and James A. Mackay, *Who Runs Georgia?* (Athens: University of Georgia Press, 1998), xi; Gary L. Roberts, "Tradition and Consensus: An Introduction to Gubernatorial Leadership in Georgia, 1943–1983," in *Georgia Governors in an Age of Change*, ed. Harold P. Henderson and Gary L. Roberts (Athens: University of Georgia Press, 1988), 9.

9. *Atlanta Journal*, January 10, 1956; *Atlanta Constitution*, January 11, 1956.

10. *Atlanta Journal*, January 10, 1956; *Atlanta Constitution*, January 11, 1956.

11. Laughlin McDonald, *A Voting Rights Odyssey: Black Enfranchisement in Georgia* (Cambridge: Cambridge University Press, 2003), 54–57, 65–67.

12. http://www.netstate.com/states/symb/flags/ga_flag.htm, accessed June 16, 2004.

13. *Acts and Resolutions of the General Assembly of the State of Georgia*, 1956, Resolutions, 671–72, 816–17.

14. *Atlanta Journal-Constitution Magazine*, January 8, 1956.

15. Ibid., January 27, 1957.

16. *Atlanta Journal*, January 10, 1956; Coleman, *A History of Georgia*, 364–65; Kytle and Mackay, *Who Runs Georgia?* xxiv–xxvii.

17. *Atlanta Constitution*, March 9, 1960.

18. *Atlanta Constitution*, March 16 and 17, 1960.

19. *Atlanta Daily World*, May 18, 1960.

20. Coleman, *History of Georgia*, 369–70.

21. *Atlanta Journal*, January 9, 1961.

22. *Atlanta Constitution*, January 10, 1961.

23. Ibid.

24. McDonald, *Voting Rights Odyssey*, 88.

25. *Atlanta Daily World*, January 15, 1963; *Atlanta Constitution*, May 10, 1965.

26. James F. Cook, *Carl Sanders: Spokesman of the New South* (Macon, Ga.: Macon University Press, 1993), 239.

27. Ibid., 240.

28. Ibid., 241; *Atlanta Inquirer*, January 15, 1966.

29. *Atlanta Daily World*, January 12, 1965; *Atlanta Inquirer*, February 21, 1970; Coleman, *History of Georgia*, 401; Laughlin McDonald, Michael Binford, and Ken Johnson, "Georgia," in *Quiet Revolution in the South*, ed. Chandler Davidson and Bernard Grofman (Princeton, N.J.: Princeton University Press, 1994), 75, 102.

30. *Atlanta Constitution*, January 11, 1966.

31. *Atlanta Daily World*, January 15, 1966.

32. Ibid.; *Atlanta Constitution*, January 16, 1966.

33. *Atlanta Daily World*, January 15, 1966; *Atlanta Constitution*, January 14, 1966; McDonald, *Voting Rights Odyssey*, 136–38.

34. *Atlanta Constitution*, January 18 and 28, 1966.

35. *Atlanta Inquirer*, February 21, 1970.

36. Coleman, *History of Georgia*, 403–5; Peter G. Bourne, *Jimmy Carter: A Comprehensive Biography from Plains to Post Presidency* (New York: Scribner, 1997), 1–5.

Chapter Eight. A Restored Capitol

1. *Atlanta Constitution*, January 4, 1974; February 18, 1974.

2. *Atlanta Daily World*, October 12, 1973; *Atlanta Constitution*, October 11, 1973.

BIBLIOGRAPHIC ESSAY

This history of the Georgia Capitol began with a documentation project initiated in 1994 by Timothy Crimmins, chair of the Commission on the Preservation of the Georgia Capitol, and Anne Farrisee, who served as project historian. A collaboration between the National Park Service and Lord, Aeck & Sargent Architecture produced a complete set of architectural drawings, a set of documentary photographs, and a narrative history of the Capitol. The documents from this project can be found at the HABS/HAER "Built in America" Web site of the Library of Congress (http://memory.loc.gov/ammem/collections/habs_haer/) To see the documents, type "Georgia State Capitol Atlanta" in the search box.

The documents available at "Built in America" capture the Georgia statehouse as it appeared in the mid-1990s through 52 measured drawings of the Capitol produced by Lord, Aeck & Sargent Architecture (for an example, see pages 6–7); 267 black-and-white photographs (for an example, see page 6); 13 color transparencies taken in 1994 by John "Jet" Lowe; and the "Historical Context" written by Anne Farrisee.

Farrisee's "Historical Context" was the starting point for this narrative history. It describes the earlier capitols in Georgia, the move to Atlanta, and the push in the late 1870s for a new statehouse, which led to the passage of the Capitol Act in 1883. The report details the construction history of the building and its 1889 dedication. From there, it accounts for changes to the building, additions of new state office buildings, and some of the important events in Georgia history that transpired in the statehouse. Its bibliography contains a more complete list of documentary sources for the Capitol history than this short bibliographic essay.

Two studies of American state capitols create a context for this history. The first, Henry-Russell Hitchcock and William Seale, *Temples of Democracy: The State Capitols of the U.S.A.* (New York: Harcourt Brace Jovanovich, 1976), focuses on the architectural styles of statehouses. More recently, Charles T. Goodsell, *The American Statehouse: Interpreting Democracy's Temples* (Lawrence: University of Kansas Press, 2001), looks at the building type and its setting within the landscape of capital cities. Both studies show that the use of classical architectural detail was a conscious attempt of nineteenth-century Americans to adorn monumental governmental buildings so that they could be perceived as democratic temples. These studies inspired us to compare the democratic symbolism of the Georgia Capitol with the governmental practice within.

Governmental edifices are constructed to make lasting impressions. Capitol commissions choose architectural features such as Miss Freedom atop the Georgia Capitol to add symbolic meanings to their buildings. However, the finished look of the statehouse is only the beginning of its symbolic layering. The additions of art and statuary and their dedicatory ceremonies are conscious efforts to bring additional meanings to governmental buildings. Gary B. Nash's *First City: Philadelphia and the Forging of Historical Memory* (Philadelphia: University of Pennsylvania Press, 2002) recounts how local and national historical memories were shaped in Philadelphia through the collections and exhibitions of the city's past. For relevance to this study, he explains how the 1826 visit of the Marquis de Lafayette helped to transform the Pennsylvania State House in Philadelphia into the national icon now known as Independence Hall.

The architectural context of the Capitol in Atlanta is established by Elizabeth Mack Lyon's "Business Buildings in Atlanta: A Study in Urban Growth and Form" (Ph.D. dissertation, Emory University, 1971) and *Atlanta Architecture, The Victorian Heritage: 1837–1918* (Atlanta: Atlanta Historical Society, 1976). Contemporary accounts of the architects of the Capitol can be found in "The Architect of the Georgia Capitol," *Southern Architect and Building News*, October 1891, 85–88.

For an overview of the capitals that preceded Atlanta, see Edwin L. Jackson, "The Story of Georgia's Capitol and Capitals," available online at http://www.cviog.uga.edu/Projects/gainfo/capital.htm.

What little documentation that exists of Georgia's first capitol in Savannah can be found in Joseph Waring, *Cerveau's Savannah* (Savannah: Georgia Historical Society, 1973), and William Harden, *A History of Savannah and South Georgia* (Chicago: Lewis Publishing, 1913). Louisville's brief history as the first planned capital city in Georgia is recounted in Yulssus Lynn Holmes, *Those Glorious Days: A History of Louisville as Georgia's Capital, 1796–1807* (Macon: Mercer University Press, 1996). The Milledgeville capitol is better documented in James C. Bonner, *Milledgeville, Georgia's Antebellum Capital* (Athens: University of Georgia Press, 1978), and in an earlier article by Leola Selman Beeson, "The Old State Capitol in Milledgeville and Its Cost," *Georgia Historical Quarterly*, September 1950, 197–200.

The push by Atlantans to become the capital city is recounted in Harold Davis, *Henry Grady's New South: Atlanta, a Brave and Beautiful City* (Tuscaloosa: University of Alabama Press, 1990). Franklin Garrett, *Atlanta and Environs: A Chronicle of Its People and Events* (1954; repr., Athens: University of Georgia Press, 1969), gives the details of the city's three Capitols: the City Hall / County Courthouse, the Kimball Opera House, and the current 1889 structure. Biographical accounts of those who played critical roles in Atlanta's capitols can be found in Royce Shingleton, *Richard Peters: Champion of the New South* (Macon: Mercer University Press, 1985); Alice Reagan, *H. I. Kimball, Entrepreneur* (Atlanta: Cherokee Publishing, 1983); and Janet V. Lundgren, "Frank P. Rice and the Political Culture of Late Nineteenth-Century Atlanta," *Atlanta Historical Bulletin* 29, no. 3 (Fall 1985): 27–34.

Documentary sources for the construction of the Capitol can be found in Anne Farrisee's bibliography in her "Historical Context" at the American Memory Web site of the Library of Congress: http://memory.loc.gov/ammem/collections/habs_haer/. Edbrooke and Burnham's original drawings on linen are located at the Georgia Archives. They are dated 1897 (eight years after completion) and signed by the members of the Board of Capitol Commissioners. Images of the original four elevations are available online in the Georgia Secretary of State's Virtual Vault at http://www.sos.state.ga.us/archives/Vault/ArcVirtualVault/ (see the front endsheet for the west elevation). The Georgia Archives has records of the boards and agencies that oversee the Capitol, including the Board of Capitol Commissioners records, the annually published *Report of the Keeper of Public Buildings and Grounds*, and the Minutes of the State Office Building Authority (now the Georgia Building Authority).

The acts creating the Capitol and authorizing funding for its renovations can be found online on the Galileo Web site of the University System of Georgia—http://www.galileo.usg.edu—under Georgia, Laws and Legislation, Georgia Legislative Documents. This Web site also contains the Constitutions of 1877, 1945, 1976, and 1983; the 1921 Women's Suffrage Act; and Governor Ernest Vandiver's Public Education Address (January 18, 1961).

The *Atlanta Constitution* and the *Atlanta Journal* published accounts of the meetings of the Capitol Commission, the cornerstone and dedication ceremonies, and the appearance of the building when it was completed, and news of the wear and tear as the building began to age. When we began this study, the newspapers were available on microfilm and required hours of searching for relevant details of Capitol construction. As we concluded our work, online availability of *Atlanta Constitution* issues through NewspaperArchive.com permitted word searches and allowed us to add such detail as information about George Crouch, the sculptor who executed all the ornamental work on the Capitol.

When it was completed in 1889, the Georgia Capitol immediately became a symbol of a reconstructed Georgia and a beacon for the growing importance of Atlanta. Illustrations of the exterior and interior of the new statehouse appeared in contemporary accounts by George Leonard Chaney, "The New South: Atlanta," *New England Magazine*, November 1891, 377-95; and anonymous pieces, "Recent Architecture in Atlanta," *Harper's Weekly*, August 3, 1889, 623; and "The Industrial Region of Northern Alabama, Tennessee, and Georgia," *Harper's New Monthly Magazine*, March 1895, 617–26.

The historical events in the Capitol that we have selected to help shape this account make use of the standard works in Georgia history. Governor Jimmy Carter, who is credited in this book for making the integration of state government the first priority of his gubernatorial term, should also be credited for making possible the publication of the first broadly inclusive history of the state. What is now the standard history of Georgia, *A History of Georgia*, edited by Kenneth Coleman (Athens: University of Georgia Press, 1977), was commissioned by Governor Carter and published in 1977, soon after Carter became the thirty-ninth U.S. president.

The exclusion of African Americans from the political life of Georgia is detailed in Laughlin McDonald's *Voting Rights Odyssey: Black Enfranchisement in Georgia* (Cambridge: Cambridge University Press, 2003). McDonald explains the legal, extralegal, and illegal methods that white Georgians used to keep African Americans from the polls, and he explains the ups and downs of the struggle of black Georgians to win back this basic civil right. Three other studies are critical to understanding how white majority rule was established during Reconstruction in Georgia: Russell Duncan, *Freedom's Shore: Tunis Campbell and the Georgia Freedmen* (Athens: University of Georgia Press, 1986); Edmund L. Drago, *Black Politicians and Reconstruction in Georgia: A Splendid Failure* (Baton Rouge: Louisiana University Press, 1982); and John Dittmer, *Black Georgia in the Reconstruction Era* (Urbana: University of Illinois Press, 1977).

The larger southern context for the political events in Georgia can be found in C. Vann Woodward, *Origins of the New South 1877–1913* (Baton Rouge: Louisiana State University Press, 1951); Michael Perman, *Struggle for Mastery: Disfranchisement in the South 1888–1908* (Chapel Hill: University of North Carolina Press, 2001); J. Morgan Kousser, *The Shaping of Southern Politics: Suffrage Restriction and the Establishment of the One-Party South, 1880–1910* (New Haven, Conn.: Yale University Press, 1974); and a contemporary account, Edward King, *The Great South* (Baton Rouge: Louisiana State University Press, 1972).

A national framework for the temperance debates and the political role afforded to women can be found in J. J. Ansley, *History of the Georgia Woman's Christian Temperance Union: From Its Organization, 1883 to 1907* (Columbus, Ga.: Gilbert Printing, 1914). Another contemporary account is S. Mays Ball, "Prohibition in Georgia: Its Failure to Prevent Drinking in Atlanta and Other Cities," *Putnam's Magazine*, March 1909, 694–99.

The struggle for women's suffrage in Georgia is detailed in Ida Husted Harper, *The History of Woman Suffrage*, vols. 4 and 6 (Indianapolis: Hollenbeck Press, 1902, 1922; repr., Arno Press, 1969). This history, which focuses on the state-by-state struggle as reported by local suffragists, provides accounts of the legislative agenda of women's rights leaders in Georgia and their treatment by the male legislators in the General Assembly. Two articles highlight biographical detail of the suffrage leaders in Georgia and Atlanta: Josephine R. Floyd, "Rebecca Latimer Felton: Champion of Women's Rights," *Georgia Historical Quarterly*, June 1946, 81–104; and A. Elizabeth Taylor, "Women Suffrage Activities in Atlanta," *Atlanta Historical Journal*, Winter 1978–79, 49–54.

The details of the Leo Frank case that played out in the Capitol can be found in Steve Oney, *And the Dead Shall Rise: The Murder of Mary Phagan and the Lynching of Leo Frank* (New York: Pantheon, 2003). C. Vann Woodward's *Tom Watson, Agrarian Rebel* (New York: Oxford University Press, 1963) details Watson's descent into demagoguery. Nathaniel E. Harris's *Autobiography: The Story of an Old Man's Life with Reminiscences of Seventy-five Years* (Macon: J. W. Burke, 1925) gives an account of the hostility Governor Harris found in the Capitol after his predecessor commuted the death sentence of Leo Frank.

Numan V. Bartley's *Creation of Modern Georgia* (Athens: University of Georgia Press, 1990) sets the political, economic, and social contexts for the transformation of Georgia in the twentieth century as does Harold Paulk Henderson, *The Politics of Change in Georgia* (Athens: University of Georgia Press, 1991). Robert Sherrill's *Gothic Politics in the Deep South: Stars of the New Confederacy* (New York: Grossman, 1968) does not slight Georgia's political leaders in his description of the machinations to combat the struggle by African Americans to gain their basic civil rights. Calvin Kytle and James A. Mackay capture the white rural domination of Georgia politics in the mid-twentieth century in *Who Runs Georgia?* (Athens: University of Georgia Press, 1998).

Out of the Three Governors Controversy came firsthand accounts by the two major participants. Within a year of leaving office, Ellis Arnall published his story in *What the People Want* (Philadelphia: J. B. Lippincott, 1947). Herman E. Talmadge (with Mark Royden Winchell) waited forty years to bring out his political autobiography, *Talmadge: A Political Legacy, A Politician's Life* (Atlanta: Peachtree Publishers, 1987). Talmadge also provided a candid oral interview for the Georgia Government Documentation Project in the Special Collections Department at the Georgia State University Library. The controversy has been recounted in other academic studies, including Charles Myer Elson, "The Georgia Three-Governor Controversy of 1947," *Atlanta Historical Bulletin*, Fall 1976, 72–93; and Harold P. Henderson and Gary L. Roberts, eds., *Georgia Governors in an Age of Change* (Athens: University of Georgia Press, 1988).

We consulted a number of gubernatorial biographies to write our political accounts of the Capitol. The standard biography of Eugene Talmadge is William Anderson, *The Wild Man from Sugar Creek: The Political Career of Eugene Talmadge* (Baton Rouge: Louisiana State University Press, 1975). Other gubernatorial sketches can be found in Harold P. Henderson and Gary L. Roberts, eds., *Georgia Governors in an Age of Change* (Athens: University of Georgia Press, 1988); James F. Cook, *Carl Sanders: Spokesman of the New South* (Macon, Ga.: Macon University Press, 1993); Bruce Galphin, *The Riddle of Lester Maddox* (Atlanta: Camelot, 1968); and Peter G. Bourne, *Jimmy Carter: A Comprehensive Biography from Plains to Post Presidency* (New York: Scribner, 1997).

The New Georgia Encyclopedia—located at http://www.georgiaencyclopedia.org—is an excellent online source that became available as we were completing our study. It has been invaluable for its inclusive entries about the events that are critical to the history of the Capitol, from suffrage to civil rights, Eugene Talmadge to Jimmy Carter.

Our story of the Capitol includes both narrative and visual accounts, and many of the images found in this study can now be found online. The Georgia Archives online collections include the Vanishing Georgia Collection of the Georgia Archives, located at http://dbs.galib.uga.edu/vanga/html/vanga_basic_search_default.html, and the Virtual Vault at http://www.sos.state.ga.us/archives/Vault/ArcVirtualVault. Georgia State University's online Library Photographic Collections include the Lane Brothers Collection at http://www.library.gsu.edu/spcoll/collections/AV/lane/, and the Tracy O'Neal Collection at http://www.library.gsu.edu/spcoll/Collections/AV/oneal/.

The Visual Works Section of the Digital Library of Georgia—http://dlg.galileo.usg.edu/MediaTypes/Visualworks.html—also contains images we used. For the Capitol in particular, a number of the historic photographs in this volume can be found at the Web site of the Georgia Secretary of State at http://www.sos.state.ga.us/state%5Fcapitol/capitolguide.

Not every image found in this volume was found online, however. Besides the contemporary shots taken by Diane Kirkland of the Georgia Department of Economic Development, we consulted the archived collections at the Atlanta History Center and the *Atlanta Journal-Constitution*.

INDEX

Italicized page numbers refer to images and their captions.